Political Wings

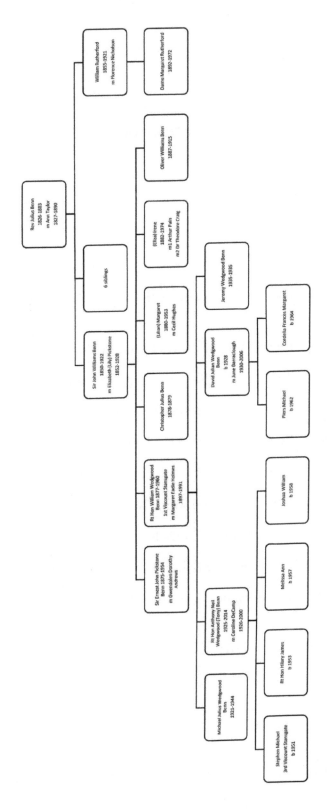

Benn family tree.

Contents

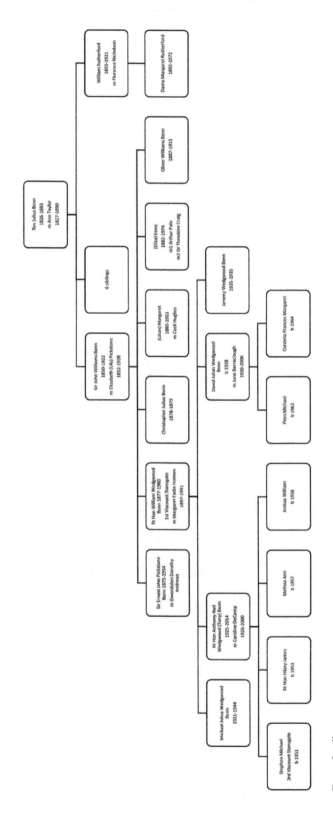

Benn family tree.

Contents

First published in Great Britain in 2015 by
Pen & Sword Aviation
an imprint of
Pen & Sword Books Ltd
47 Church Street
Barnsley
South Yorkshire
S70 2AS

Copyright © Alun Wyburn-Powell 2015

ISBN 978 1 47384 814 6

Typeset in Ehrhardt by
Mac Style Ltd, Bridlington, East Yorkshire
Printed and bound in the UK by CPI Group (UK) Ltd,
Croydon, CRO 4YY

Pen & Sword Books Ltd incorporates the imprints of Pen & Sword
Archaeology, Atlas, Aviation, Battleground, Discovery, Family
History, History, Maritime, Military, Naval, Politics, Railways, Select,
Transport, True Crime, and Fiction, Frontline Books, Leo Cooper,
Praetorian Press, Seaforth Publishing and Wharncliffe.

For a complete list of Pen & Sword titles please contact
PEN & SWORD BOOKS LIMITED
47 Church Street, Barnsley, South Yorkshire, S70 2AS, England
E-mail: enquiries@pen-and-sword.co.uk
Website: www.pen-and-sword.co.uk

Political Wings

William Wedgwood Benn, first Viscount Stansgate

Alun Wyburn-Powell

Pen & Sword
AVIATION

Acknowledgements

I have thoroughly enjoyed researching and writing this book. This has been due to a fortunate combination of an intriguing subject, enthusiastic surviving family members, an extensive range of archives, a dynamic publisher, generous reviewers, an award from the Society of Authors and my own supportive family.

The Benn family has been outstandingly kind and encouraging. I initially interviewed Tony Benn and his brother David about their father. Subsequently, Tony's children Stephen, Hilary, Melissa and Joshua invited me to Stansgate and provided me with photographs from the voluminous family collection. Hilary's son, James has researched the military careers of some of his ancestors and has been very helpful in piecing together some of the wartime events. David, as now the only surviving member of his generation of the family, has written the foreword. Ruth Winstone, editor of Tony Benn's diaries, has been a valuable source of information and advice.

William Wedgwood Benn was a witty and courageous person, but he was also by his own admission a 'file-merchant'. He collected and preserved records of most aspects of his life, from sorties in the RAF to charts of how much sleep he had each night. Some of his papers were lost in a fire and others in a flood, but many survive. The Stansgate Papers are now mainly to be found at the Parliamentary Archives, where the staff are exceedingly helpful and friendly and the surroundings literally palatial.

I would especially like to thank Steve Richards, Michael Crick, Vernon Bogdanor, Norman Franks, Richard Doherty and Martin Bowman for reading drafts of the book and for their encouraging comments.

The research for the project was supported by the Society of Authors who selected the biography for an Authors' Foundation Award. I am very grateful to the assessors, Helen Simpson, Simon Brett, Sameer Rahim, Fiona Sampson and Frances Wilson and also to Paula Johnson at the Society.

The Labour History Group and the Liberal Democrat History Group provide a mine of useful information for a project like this, as well as organising meetings and discussions. William Wedgwood Benn, in common with other political defectors, belongs in the history of both parties. From studying these sometimes-neglected figures it is clear that there is more in common between the parties than current tribal politics sometimes admits.

Frank Meeres, archivist at the Norfolk Record Office in my adoptive home city of Norwich, kindly provided photographs of the Boulton and Paul catalogue, from which the Benns' 'ancestral home' at Stansgate was chosen.

My publishers, Pen & Sword, have been very efficient, decisive and helpful. Laura Hirst, Lisa Hooson, Matthew Blurton and the team have been a pleasure to work with. Karyn Burnham has edited the book with judgement and diligence and Jon Wilkinson has certainly brought the jacket to life.

I can truly say that without my dear wife Diana and son Chris, this book would never have been written. While we were on a walk in Hampstead, we saw a piece of paper tied to a gate, advertising a talk by Tony Benn, which triggered the idea, which started a chain of events, which led to this biography of Tony's father.

I would like to dedicate the book to the memory of Tony Benn (1925–2014).

Alun Wyburn-Powell
Norwich 2015

Foreword

by David Wedgwood Benn, son of William Wedgwood Benn
and younger brother of Tony Benn

As the last surviving member of my generation, I write as the only one who knew my father well. I remember him as a vibrant, vivid personality which is difficult to convey to anyone who did not actually meet him. Besides that, his life had many different facets. He married somewhat late in life – when he was forty-three - and was already fifty-one when I was born. As a result, his life before marriage was something of a closed book, shrouded in family legend which was sometimes difficult to separate from fact.

Alun Wyburn-Powell has, in this book, carried out a hugely ambitious exercise in family history backed up by a wealth of documentation – including Census details from the Nineteenth century and diaries - most of which were new to me. All this has given our family an entirely new insight into our Victorian roots.

William Wedgwood Benn, the first Viscount Stansgate, was one of a large group of Liberal MPs who changed parties and joined Labour in the 1920s. However, as this book points out, he was never a key player. This was partly because he was not pushy and partly because he was never involved in economic cabinet decisions. During his first term in government (1929–31) he was dealing with India and during his second term (1945-46) he was dealing with the negotiation of a new Anglo-Egyptian treaty.

My father was born into a family of Congregationalist Victorian radicals whose religious beliefs were closely linked with a belief in justice. In 1903 he suffered a shock which affected the rest of his life, on discovering that his much-loved uncle William Rutherford Benn (the father of Margaret Rutherford) had murdered his own father, the Reverend Julius Benn. He fell into a deep depression, being unable to reconcile this tragedy with Divine goodness. To help him recover, his father sent him on a holiday to Egypt and South Africa. On his return home he felt worse than ever. Only when he plunged into work in the family publishing firm did he begin to recover – and this convinced him that overwork was the cure for depression and that holidays were depressing. It also led him to adopt the principle of 'Job first' and the job somehow stood above him. This set a pattern for the rest of his life: an alternation of overwork followed by exhaustion, accompanied by constant (and largely groundless) worries about money. This was partly due to his puritanical upbringing and partly due to the experience of seeing bailiffs move into the family home to enforce a judgment which was overturned on appeal.

My uncle, Sir Ernest Benn, differed from my father both in style and character. Although, like my father, he championed free speech, he ruled his family autocratically, was against the dole and advocated policies which were indistinguishable from Thatcherism – except that he would not have approved of a woman prime minister. One family legend was about childhood poverty. However, by the beginning of the last century, thanks to the business talents of Ernest Benn, the Benns had come into considerable wealth – as shown by the purchase of the Old Knoll in Blackheath, London – a huge house with an enormous garden recently sold for £5,000,000, although it had long since passed out of the Benn family.

My father's life did follow a consistent pattern. As a child he had a reputation for mischievousness, but this reflected a desire to deflate what he saw as sanctimonious Victorian hypocrisy, particularly in relation to money or religiosity. Ridicule was his main weapon. He prided himself on his filing system and pointed to the absurdity of filing alcoholism under A, drunkenness under D and temperance under T. He made a point every day of reading, marking and cutting the then authoritative *Times* and tried to create a pre-electronic binary system where for example the figures 1006 represented Foreign Affairs, 10065 represented Russia and 100651 represented the Ukraine. By 1940 this project had become unsustainable but these volumes, now held in the Parliamentary Archives in the Victoria Tower, represented a unique chronicle of the 1920s and 30s. My father did continue to read and mark the *Times* until the end of his life because he was convinced that in order to make an impact it was essential to get one's facts right.

My father was a fighter, but only in what he regarded as a just cause. He was always afraid that as a member of the House of Lords, whose debates he used to describe as 'old gentlemen's political croquet', he would be rendered harmless. As a student at University College, London, he had denounced the Boer War. But in both World Wars he joined the Forces believing that an issue of moral principal was at stake. His wartime service took him to Gallipoli in 1915, and his war record earned him both the DSO and the DFC.

Needless to say all his worries took their toll on the family. When my father was in a buoyant mood he cast a ray of sunshine and when depressed he cast a pall of gloom.

Dr. Wyburn-Powell rightly points out my father's distrust of his former friend Lloyd George over the sale of honours. My father's own sense of honour led him to resign his seat when he changed from Liberal to Labour in 1927. By no means all today's politicians follow this example.

Both my parents, as this book points out, strongly championed the ministry of women. And in the 1930s my parents' religious convictions gave rise to a lifelong friendship with Reinhold Niebuhr, the American theologian and political scientist.

My father's removal from the Attlee government in 1946 came as a very severe blow. It was not, as he thought, a slur on his expertise but simply reflected the need of a Prime Minister to appoint a younger generation of leaders. However his election in 1947 as World President of the Interparliamentary Union earned him a fresh lease of life.

Like many other people, my father had been bitterly disappointed by the onset of the Cold War after 1945 and was unhappy about the conduct of the Labour Foreign Secretary Ernest Bevin which he felt had aggravated the conflict. He therefore resolved to convert the IPU from a mere tourist agency for parliamentarians into a surrogate United Nations. His policy took him to Eastern Europe in 1948 and in 1955 to Russia (where I accompanied him in both cases) and subsequently to China. The IPU headquarters in Geneva, heavily dependent on American money, did not welcome this and my father was deeply wounded when told by an American delegate that if he admitted 'Red China' to the organization the Americans would walk out. His policy did, however, bear some fruit. When he resigned in 1957 he was elected President of Honour on the initiative of the American delegate seconded by the delegate of the Soviet Union. The messages of condolence on his death included a letter from the Chinese ambassador, a message from the chairman of the Soviet Interparliamentary group and a telegram from the Queen.

As a son, I naturally cannot pretend to be neutral. I will therefore quote from tribute to him by the Conservative Lord Chancellor, Lord Hailsham who highlighted his chivalrousness and said he wondered whether my father ever paused to consider the affection he aroused among those who had little agreement either with his causes or with his ways of pursuing them. A *Times* obituary on the day after his death emphasised that his integrity of purpose was manifest, that his physical bravery was matched by high moral courage, that he stood in awe of nobody and that the spell of his charm could vanquish the most acute exasperation that he might provoke so that even his victims soon forgave him.

Today, at a time when voter confidence in politicians is lower than ever and when the belief is widespread that politicians are 'in it for themselves', my father stands as a striking counter-example. That was his life's main achievement.

David Wedgwood Benn
London, 2015

Introduction

In December 1916 a 39-year-old second lieutenant serving at a seaplane base in the Middle East received a telegram from the new prime minister, Lloyd George, inviting him to join the cabinet. The unmarried officer consulted his father and one friend, before turning down the post. He was probably the one person who could have held the warring factions of the Liberal Party together. The officer survived the war unscathed. The Liberal Party nearly died. The officer was William Wedgwood Benn, now most widely-remembered as the father of Tony Benn.

The best-known things about William Wedgwood Benn are that he was born in the East End of London and that he was an hereditary peer – a viscount. These true, but seemingly contradictory, facts explain very little about his life. Labelling him as an 'East Ender' is little more revealing than describing Gladstone as a 'Scouser'; two of the four seats which Benn represented as an MP were actually in Scotland. Later in life, William Wedgwood Benn became Viscount Stansgate, which sounds as though he was elevated along an established family path into the aristocracy; it *was* an hereditary peerage, but he was the first of the line. The Stansgate name comes from a place which is sometimes now referred to as his ancestral home. When he was in his twenties, this pre-fabricated 'ancestral home' was chosen out of a catalogue, delivered on a barge, and built on land which his father had recently bought in Essex. However, only four years later, the house was sold.

At different stages of his life, William Wedgwood Benn was known by many different names – as William, Will or Willy (by his family and his wife), Billy, Bill or 'Billy Dawdle' (by his childhood friends), Wedgwood or 'Wedgie' (by his political friends and associates), Captain Benn (by the press and Hansard between 1918 and 1942), as Viscount Stansgate (from 1942 to his death), as 'Dear Old Pa' to his children and as 'Tappa' to his grandchildren. He will remain simply Benn throughout this book, as there was much more consistency about him than all the renaming would suggest.

Chapter One

A Fledgling Dynasty with a Flat-Pack Ancestral Home 1877–1906

Looking back, the life of William Wedgwood Benn (1877 to 1960) clearly spanned what we can now see as the early stages of one of Britain's greatest political dynasties, launched on the back of profits from publishing a trade magazine. But when William Wedgwood Benn was born, the publishing business was not even a twinkle in his father's bank account, the family was not involved in politics and the pieces of their 'ancestral home' had not even left the factory in Norwich. The Wedgwood name seems to hint at a connection with the pottery business, but Benn's parents were not actually sure if there was a family connection. So, what was the family's ancestry and did it really matter?

No-one escapes the genetic legacy of their forebears, but for some, their inheritance is crucial to the course of their lives. Ancestors, known or unknown, will have passed on their DNA, influencing longevity and appearance. Others may hand down money, a family home, a famous name or even a title. Some may be the subject of family stories, which – true or not – influence how later generations see themselves. What someone wrongly thinks happened to their ancestors could have as much bearing as what actually did. William Wedgwood Benn's life is defined more than most by his inheritance and his legacy.

Benn's DNA was a good inheritance. His ancestors tended to outlive their contemporaries. Even a vague awareness of this can have an effect on someone's life: an old man in a hurry, a slow starter, a léger dilettante, someone who grew up too fast – all could be the result of suspicion of one's likely longevity. Tony Benn wrote confidently, while his father was still alive, that he would live to the age of eighty-two (he nearly reached eighty-nine).[1] Benn's ancestry meant that he could reasonably expect a generous lifespan (although he made decisions at several stages which put this in jeopardy, and he was always eager to use every day to the maximum, as though it was to be his last). Benn inherited a terrier-like make-up – short, solid, brave, lively, eager and highly intelligent. In appearance he was attractive in a neat, friendly, youthful and open-looking way, quite the opposite of the formulaic tall, dark and handsome.

Benn's ancestors before his parents' generation passed on no money, title, land or property. The name Wedgwood was indeed connected to the eponymous potters. It was Benn's middle name, given to him (but not to his siblings) because his mother was fairly sure that she had a distant family connection to the Wedgwoods. She was correct in her belief – both in the connection and the distance. The connection, in fact, pre-dated the founding of the pottery business. The common ancestors were Gilbert Wedgwood (1588–1678) and his wife Margaret Burslem (1594–1655), four generations *before* Josiah Wedgwood (1730–1795), founder of the pottery business. The Wedgwood name was an asset and a liability at different times, but it was just a middle name, not a share in a valuable business.

The connection to Josiah Wedgwood the potter meant that Benn also had a very distant family link to Charles Darwin and composer Ralph Vaughan-Williams. Darwin was the grandson of Josiah Wedgwood and Vaughan-Williams was his great-great grandson. Other famous relatives included Margaret Rutherford, who was his cousin and his much more distant relative, but his contemporary in politics, Josiah Wedgwood MP.

Benn was certainly influenced by stories about his forebears. The most striking was about his paternal grandfather, Julius – a semi-literate, religious, melancholic and unlucky man. The family story was that Julius ran away from home in 1842, aged fifteen, contemplating suicide by jumping in the Mersey. He had fallen out with his step-mother, who had brought money from a brick-making business to the impoverished family, who had been living in a damp and smelly cellar in Ardwick, a mile east of the centre of Manchester. Julius's father was, according to the family legend, either a master quilt-maker, or possibly a licenced victualler (a profession very much at odds with the views of later teetotal generations). Rescued by a rich philanthropic Quaker, Julius was taken in, fed, taught and set up as a linen-draper's assistant in Limerick, Ireland. Here he was converted to Congregationalism by the Rev. John De Kewer Williams, author of the rather dour-sounding *Words of truth and soberness, earnestly addressed to the Independents of England*. At the age of twenty-two, according to the family legend, Julius uprooted himself again. He left his job and home in Ireland in disgust after finding that his employer had tried to trick a customer by mis-describing goods. Benn was thus fed a story which hinged on his grandfather's uprooting his entire life on a matter of principle, because of some dodgy linen.

The gist of the story turns out to be true, but some rather important details were missing. The 1841 census does indeed show Julius, prior to his departure for Ireland, living in Chapel Street, Ardwick with his widowed father, William, listed as a weaver (not a purveyor of alcohol – although many people did also use their homes as public houses at the time), an older sister and two younger brothers. Later censuses show that Julius's father remarried and that he moved back to Leeds, the city where he was born. Here, he had four more children with his second wife, Ann. In Leeds he worked as a shoemaker, later rising slightly in status to cordwainer – a maker of shoes from fine new leather, as opposed to re-using old leather, the method employed by most shoemakers. Julius's father remained in Leeds until his death at the relatively advanced age of seventy-eight. Julius's brothers do not seem to have shared the aversion to their step-mother, as they remained in the same household into their twenties, while they both worked as boilermakers. Evidence for the family's increased wealth from the brick-making business brought by William's second wife is scanty and speculative. One of William Benn's neighbours listed in the 1841 Census was a 33-year-old woman called Ann Dean, a member of whose family was listed as 'brickmaker'. She was then lodging with a family called Clegg. Circumstantially, her details fit with the family legend and she may have been the Ann who became William Benn's second wife. William, a poor, widowed, single father working as a weaver, would have been likely to have found his new wife in the immediate neighbourhood. The family's circumstances do appear to have improved marginally in the years after their move to Leeds, as would have been the case for most families in Britain as the country industrialised and imported cheaper foreign food. However, they remained working class and poor.

One of the most important details missing from the story was that Julius actually left Ireland during the potato famine. It had ravaged the country over the previous three years, slashing the yield of the island's main food crop by seventy per cent between 1845 and 1848 – the year Julius departed. A million starved and a million more emigrated. Julius cannot have been unaffected, at least emotionally and intellectually, if not nutritionally, by the famine. He left the island amongst the million others, with the western side of the country (including Limerick) being the area worst affected by the exodus. It is also extremely likely that he was acutely aware of the part played in this Irish tragedy by the wealthy English Tory landlords and by the British government's policy of tariffs, which kept imported wheat and bread prohibitively expensive. Another factor, not totally unconnected to the potato famine, was the departure of John de Kewer Williams from Limerick in 1846 and the near-collapse of the Congregational church in Ireland – the dissolution of Julius's spiritual home. On his return to England Julius went to Hyde, seven miles to the east of Manchester, to look for a job as a school master's assistant. Drawn both by the religious creed and the companionship he had enjoyed through the church in Limerick, he visited the Congregational chapel. Here he met his future wife (Benn's paternal grandmother), the 19-year-old daughter of a shuttle-maker. Unfortunately for Julius, she shared the first name of Ann with his detested step-mother, but this does not seem to have dampened the attraction. Julius and Ann set up, and both worked in, a school at the chapel.

Benn's father was the first born child of Julius and Ann. His parents had been married on 13 February 1850 and he was born on 13 November 1850 – exactly nine months later to the day. He was given the names John Williams Benn – the Williams being in honour of the Reverend John de Kewer Williams. So, like the 'Welsh Wizard' Lloyd George, John Benn, a future leader of London politics, was actually born in Manchester.

Having been unlucky in timing his arrival in Ireland just before the start of the potato famine, Julius and family were more fortunate in leaving Lancashire before the cotton famine, caused by the American civil war, in the 1860s. The family decamped to the East End of London, which was to be a focus of the working life of three successive generations of the family. They initially settled in an 'awful little alley' called Commercial Place.[2] In the East End, Julius was involved in social work, including setting up a home for destitute boys. His work here led to his being offered the charge of the country's first reformatory and industrial school, which was to be set up at Tiffield in Northamptonshire. The family moved there and took up lodgings. Their landlord was Julius's deputy – making it a rather convoluted hierarchy. John Benn therefore also spent five years of his childhood in rural Northamptonshire.

The family returned to the East End of London for a combination of reasons. The principle cause was that Julius could not practise his Congregational faith in Tiffield and had to worship at the local Anglican church, whose doctrines he could not fully accept. However, as with the combination of principle and practicality which had led to his departure from Ireland, there was also another, more prosaic, reason for the move. Julius had got into financial difficulties, after a failed investment in an agricultural patent. He lost his savings and ended up in debt. He had to leave his job and also the lodgings. Julius's wife was by then in poor health and unable to walk without difficulty. One version of the family story has Julius pushing Ann in a bath chair, another in a wheelbarrow. Whatever the means of transport, the eventual destination was Stepney. Here Julius set up a toyshop and newsagent – a business which did not thrive, but which taught his son a good deal about commerce. The premises were also used as a depot for the British and Foreign Bible Society.[3] The toyshop premises were redeveloped and the family moved again and set up a different business, this time a recruitment agency for domestic staff.[4] Julius eventually returned to missionary work and became the minister of the Gravel Lane chapel. There was some controversy over whether he was entitled to the designation of 'Reverend' or not.[5]

So, on his father's side of the family, Benn's grandparents were Congregationalists, poor and from a working class background associated with the textile industry around Manchester. When Benn was born both his paternal and maternal grandparents were still alive. His maternal grandparents also came from Hyde and were non-conformists, but they were wealthier. Benn's maternal grandfather, John Pickstone, had been a manufacturing chemist and had bought some land and property. He retired to Altrincham, the town of his birth. Benn never got to know his maternal grandfather Pickstone particularly well, but did not feel that he had lost out as a consequence. Even to the teetotal Benn, who had a strong set of morals and could be rather puritanical, his grandfather was 'uncompromising', 'narrow' and 'unbending'.[6] His four sons (Benn's uncles) were named Benjamin Franklin Pickstone, Louis Kossuth Pickstone, John Bright Pickstone and Alfred Tennyson Pickstone. Benn wryly commented that he was 'never able to detect very much trace of the paternal influence in their behaviour', nor presumably did they live up to their names as a founding father of America, a Hungarian freedom-fighter, a Corn Law abolitionist, or a poet laureate. Benn later realised that his opinions of his grandfather were to some extent coloured by his father's 'kindly malicious recollections'. Pickstone's eldest daughter became a member of the Plymouth Brethren. As well as drink and frivolity, another object of Pickstone's disapproval was the proposed marriage of his younger daughter, Elizabeth, to Benn's father – 'this boy from London'.

Fortunately for the family, 'whatever was lacking' in Benn's maternal grandfather was 'made up' in his grandmother and Benn believed that his mother's sweetness and devotion could be traced to her mother. His maternal grandmother was born in 1817 in Nottinghamshire to a father born in Holland and a mother from Burslem in the Potteries, which supported her belief that she probably had a connection with the Wedgwood family.

Benn's mother, Elizabeth Pickstone (known in the family as Lily) met Benn's father in 1870, aged nineteen when he came to her parents' house in Hyde to perform a ghost play involving skulls and crocodiles.[7] How this play accorded with the alleged serious narrow-mindedness of her father is not clear. According to her future husband, Lily was a 'bounding', 'round', 'compact' figure (not terms usually applied in searching for a potential spouse). She described her own education as having concluded at a 'finishing school' in Stockport.[8] Her outlook on life was domestic – there was 'family' and 'the outside world'.[9]

So, Benn's father, 'this boy from London' as his prospective father-in-law, Pickstone, referred to him, had actually been born in Manchester in 1850, but had moved to St. George's in the East End of London the following year. In 1856 his family had moved to Northamptonshire, and he had arrived back in the East End again when he was nine. Leaving school at the age of eleven, he was sacked from his first job as an office boy. He then worked for a furniture wholesaler, attending art school at night. In 1868 he was promoted to junior draughtsman, then chief designer and, in 1873, junior partner. An entrepreneurial, hard-working and ambitious young man, Benn's father had to make up for what Pickstone considered to be his lack of substance in terms of wealth, education and contacts.

Benn's parents were married on 1 July 1874, after an official engagement lasting a year, to satisfy Pickstone. They went on to have six children. The eldest, Ernest, was born on 25 June 1875. William Wedgwood followed on 10 May 1877. Their third child, Christopher, was born on 27 November 1878, but died just over a year later on 29 December 1879. There followed two daughters, (Lilian) Margaret in December 1880 and (Eliza) Irene in February 1882, and finally a son, Oliver, born in July 1887. The death of one child out of six was unfortunately a fairly typical occurrence at the time.[10] Benn was two and a half years old when his younger brother, Christopher, died. He would have been unlikely to have carried any direct memories of his lost sibling or of his death because at that age children typically do not understand death and regard it as a temporary state. However, Benn is likely to have been influenced indirectly by the effect which it had on the family and by later discussion of their loss. Benn's sister, Margaret, was born around a year after Christopher's death. The changed family dynamics after Christopher's death would have been altered again by this new arrival. Typical effects of the death of a sibling tend to be guilt, anxiety, susceptibility to stress, but in some cases a feeling of invulnerability, greater emotional strength, ability to empathise with the bereaved and greater independence.[11] All of these were, in fact, characteristics displayed in abundance by the adult Benn.

It is widely recorded that Benn's origins were in the East End of London. However, there is no official definition of the East End, so it is quite hard to determine categorically if this is true. There is general agreement that it is bounded by the City of London to the West and by the River Thames to the south. The eastern boundary is usually taken to be the River Lea. However, the northern boundary is less well defined. The widest definitions include the 'southern part' of Hackney.[12] Benn was born at Ferncliff Road, almost exactly in the centre of the London Borough of Hackney.[13] So, by the most generous of definitions, Benn's birthplace just squeaked into the East End.

The East End was well-known for its significant concentrations of poverty. The house where Benn was born has since been demolished and the area was redeveloped by the GLC as the Mountford Estate, although the name Ferncliff Road survives. Records also survive of the relative affluence or poverty of the surrounding area towards the end of the Victorian era, thanks to the work of a future next door neighbour of Benn's, Beatrice Webb, and her cousin-by-marriage, Charles Booth, who produced the famous 1889 poverty maps of London. They concluded that thirty-five per cent of the East End population lived in abject poverty.[14] Conversely though, this meant that two-thirds of the population was living in better circumstances and Ferncliff Road was classed as being a mixture of 'well-to-do middle class' and 'fairly comfortable [with] good, ordinary earnings'. The poorest residents (unflatteringly described by Booth and Potter as 'lowest class, vicious and semi-criminal') and those just ahead of them ('very poor, casual' and in 'chronic want') were huddled in the small back streets and alleys, mainly concentrated nearer to the Thames, while the main arterial roads throughout the area were generally lined with better quality houses. Ferncliff Road was a short residential road running parallel to the main (and more prosperous) Amhurst Road.

The growing Benn family moved to 241 Dalston Lane, shortly before the birth of Benn's sister Margaret in May 1880.[15] The new home was about ten minutes' walk east of their old house, once again on the fringe of the East End. Dalston Lane was a busier and slightly more prosperous road – 'well to do middle class' according to Potter and Booth. This house, too, has since been demolished, but the original four-storey Victorian villas with steps up to the front doors survive on the opposite side of the road.

That same year, Benn's father launched the *Cabinet Maker*, a journal which was eventually to become the foundation of a thriving publishing business, Benn Brothers. In the early years though, Benn's father had to subsidise his earnings from the journal with performances at clubs and halls where he gave illustrated lectures. By nature, he was more of a showman than a businessman, but he was a good salesman. Once the business began to grow, it provided the money which enabled the family to become involved in politics, and in the process to begin a political dynasty. However, the first generation cannot know that they have started a dynasty, as a cricketer cannot know if the first run of an innings is going to be the foundation of a century. Benn's uncles, Henry, Julius and Robert, all joined the staff of the *Cabinet Maker*. On the back of an insecure income, never much above £1,000 per year, Benn's father turned his attention to politics.

In 1889, Benn's father was elected for East Finsbury as a Progressive on the newly-established London County Council, where he was to retain his seat for the rest of his life. He was elected on a platform of municipal control of gas and water supply, of liquor licences, and markets. He supported council housing, the abolition of the privileges of the City corporation and a fairer local taxation system. He assured his electorate that 'if elected, I shall be found among the party of progress'. He went on to be chairman of the LCC in 1904–5 and leader of the Progressives on the council from 1907 to 1918. In his last years, as the only remaining original member, Benn was widely known as the 'father' of the council.

Benn Senior's political ambitions were not confined to municipal administration and at the 1892 general election he fought and won the parliamentary constituency of Tower Hamlets, St. George for the Liberals. He claimed that he wanted to be 'the member for the back streets'.[16] This was to be the first of eight parliamentary contests, in five different constituencies, which he was to fight. His first term in Parliament spanned Gladstone's last premiership and the brief and ill-fated tenure of Rosebery – a colleague of his on the LCC, where both were to serve terms as chairman.[17] The 1895 election spelt the end of Rosebery's premiership after just over one year and the end of Benn Senior's representation of Tower Hamlets, St. George – by a margin of just four votes, adjusted to eleven after a recount. A bitter dispute erupted over the St. George's contest, in which Benn Senior demonstrated that 'restraint and calculation were never strong points in his vivacious character'.[18]

John Benn launched a legal challenge to the election of his Conservative opponent. In a retaliatory action, the Conservative victor, Harry Marks, claimed that Benn Senior had, among other irregularities, illegally paid for the printing and publication of a derogatory song about him. The court hearings over these 'futilities' stretched out for an 'unprecedented' forty days over this 'squalid dispute' as the *Times* referred to it, with most of the allegations being dismissed. Benn's counsel went to extraordinary lengths to try and obtain Marks's disqualification, alleging 352 instances of corrupt or illegal practices, all of which were struck out, withdrawn or failed. However, two counter-charges against John Benn were upheld – namely irregularities over paying for banners to be produced and in making returns about the funding of a club house. As the *Times* pointed out, the offences involved 'no grave moral guilt', but they did involve the expenditure of a vast amount of time, energy and legal fees.[19] But, these were not the only losses incurred by John Benn. He was disqualified from standing again in the same constituency for seven years.

However, this did not mark the end of the fledgling political dynasty. John Benn stood unsuccessfully for Deptford in 1897 and Bermondsey in 1900. At a by-election in 1904 he won Devonport, which he retained in 1906 and held until his defeat in January 1910. In December 1910 he unsuccessfully contested Clapham, in what was to be his last parliamentary contest. His parliamentary career thus spanned a total of eight and a half years – three years at Tower Hamlets, St. George from July 1892 to July 1895 and five and a half years at Devonport from June 1904 to January 1910, separated by a gap of nearly nine years and 240 miles.

Families are supposed to have a skeleton in the closet, and the Benn family is no exception. When Benn was born all four of his grandparents were still alive, but this was to change abruptly with the murder of his paternal grandfather, Julius, when Benn was just short of his sixth birthday. At the time Benn was not aware of the circumstances. Julius was murdered by his own son, William Rutherford Benn (Benn's uncle) on 4 March 1883. William Rutherford Benn had recently returned from honeymoon in Paris, where he had suffered a breakdown. He had had no prior history of mental illness. His wife of just eleven weeks, Florence, had brought him back to be cared for by his parents, but his condition continued to deteriorate and he had to be admitted to Bethnal House Asylum. After six weeks, William Rutherford appeared to be much recovered and he was released and collected by his father, Julius, who took him to Matlock Bridge in Derbyshire to recuperate. There, tragedy struck. William Rutherford smashed his father over the head with a chamber-pot (a Spode, not a Wedgwood) while he slept, and then slashed his own throat. The lodging house keeper called the police and a doctor, who was able to stitch William Rutherford's throat wound and save his life, but he was unable to resuscitate his father. William Rutherford Benn was then detained in Broadmoor.

The aftermath of the murder, apart from the distress of the events and the need to keep the details secret from the younger family members, caused an upheaval in family living arrangements. A new home was established at 37 Kyverdale Road, Stoke Newington – a Victorian terraced house, one of those which deceives potential occupants by being larger than it appears from the outside. This house is still standing. Here moved in Julius's invalid widow (able to move around with difficulty, but without the wheelbarrow) and her five unmarried children, Benn's father and mother and their three (soon to be four) children. So the 6-year-old Benn was then living with his grandmother, three uncles, two aunts, his parents, his older brother Ernest and his younger sister Margaret, soon to be joined by another sister, Irene. Julius left an estate valued at £118 7s 6d[20] – roughly equivalent to £12,000 in today's terms – not destitute, but certainly not a family fortune.

In 1885, improving family finances from the publishing business enabled a move to 17 Finsbury Square, an area now comprehensively redeveloped for offices. However, in 1890, a former employee set up a cheaper rival to the *Cabinet Maker*. This led Benn's father to resort to a drastic, but decisive, measure to solve the resulting financial crisis. The children were sent to live with their nanny in Southend, while their parents moved to a smaller home across the street in Finsbury Square, in a flat at the top of number fifty. From here Benn's father launched a new cheap rival paper, *The Furnisher and Decorator*. The new title undercut the rival's paper and drove it out of business. Benn's father then closed his cheap paper and the fortunes of the *Cabinet Maker* revived. During this same, difficult year, Benn's father underwent an abdominal operation without anaesthetic (fearing that his heart would not stand the sedation) and also Benn's paternal grandmother died.

Constantly on the move, in 1891 Benn's father rented *Hoppea Hall*[21] at Upminster, then a rural Essex village with a population of 1,400. This was a large, rather austere, three-storey brick-built house with small windows, dating back to at least the seventeenth century. It was demolished in January 1939 to make way for a post office, sorting office, petrol station and car park.[22]

William Wedgwood Benn shared the trait of many successful people – of not being fearful of making mistakes, but of making them (and many), admitting them, learning from them and refusing to be embarrassed by them. From the unfinished draft fragments of his autobiography, we get many insights into Benn's thinking about key stages in his life, but by no means the full story.[23] Tellingly, Benn started with an explanation that 'This is not a self-serving' autobiography nor the 'story of my inward struggles'.[24] For many, their major struggles are with the outside world. Benn publicly was successful and happy, but clearly he was hinting at some inner turmoil. He comes across as ahead of his age, in terms of his writing style, informality and self-disclosure. These were also traits that were recognisable to his family, friends and colleagues. On the other hand, the content of some of his writing does make him sound rather obsessive. He was a pioneer in the drive to achieve a work/life balance and was much influenced in his timekeeping regime by Arnold Bennett's book *How to Live on 24 Hours a Day*. Bennett warned his readers against becoming a slave to the system, but Benn seems to have skipped over this section![25] Benn explained that for him there were 'two purposes in life, one is repose and the other is work' – although in reality he placed the latter ahead of the former.[26] To keep track of how he used his time, Benn divided the day into half hour units. He kept a record for nearly fifty years of how he spent each day and even drew up daily graphs of his activities. Benn commented that Walter Citrine and Herbert Samuel used a similar system. Perhaps the greatest recorder of personal activity though was Gladstone, who went as far as recording every one of the 20,000 books that he read and noted with a whip symbol when he felt he was deserving of punishment (which was often). Benn did not seem to feel that he had strayed as badly as Gladstone, but he did get cross with himself for frittering time away or allowing others to do it for him. 'It makes one very much irritated with kind friends who come and waste time when you know that you have had a bad day and your chart is going to give … a shock at bedtime.'[27] Benn was self-aware enough to realise that his method of operation would not suit everyone. He described himself as a 'file merchant' and acknowledged that 'this may not interest everybody but for me is the most interesting thing of all'. Citrine, Samuel and Gladstone were all rather austere characters and their obsessive monitoring of time cannot have helped to alleviate this. Benn, however, had a lighter side and was witty and self-deprecating and keen on practical jokes.

So, who did the maturing Benn think he was? Or, perhaps first, did he think at all about who he was and where he fitted into the world? Late Victorian Britain was not consumed with introspection and self-analysis. (Freud published his major work, *Psychopathology of Everyday Life* in 1901, the year of Queen Victoria's death.) In late Victorian times some aspects of life carried labels, so no-one could escape all the markers of social position. On top of this, Benn was thoughtful, intelligent and self-aware. More than most, he had a realistic idea of himself. In many respects Benn was in the middle; having attended a 'Middle Class School', he was pigeonholed socially. He was clearly not a member of the aristocracy, nor from the working class. He was perched, slightly precariously, in the middle – literally within sight of both Parliament and extreme poverty; within touching distance of both ends of the social spectrum. His mother's side of the family were established middle class, while his father's newly-moneyed side, were well-aware of the risks to their financial security. Like most of the population, they believed that economic growth and technological developments had benefits for society as a whole and that most people could expect a rising standard of living.

In terms of religion, being a Congregationalist meant that Benn was not part of the established Church of England, but nor was he part of a very distinctive, and to some extent still repressed, minority, such as the Catholics or the Jews. Non-conformists had gained full political rights in 1828, one year ahead of the Catholics. Jews achieved the same position in 1858, but atheists were only granted equal status in 1888. Although Benn always identified himself as a non-conformist, he was not very religious. The church's teachings played a bigger part in his life than any form of religious practice.

In terms of place, Benn was first and foremost British, and generally proud of it, although he was not proud of Britain's record in Ireland and was in favour of self-determination for all peoples within the Empire. He was English, with little early connection to Scotland or Wales. He later developed strong links with Scotland and his grandfather, Julius, had lived in Ireland. Despite being urban, he grew to love a more rural life and took up sailing.

Within his family he was also in the middle – not the eldest, nor the youngest, sibling. Emotionally, Benn was secure. He was well-loved and well-treated by his family. He was intellectually well-nourished at home and to a fair extent at school. Physically, Benn was healthy and well-fed. He was not tall, and so he could not expect to dominate by his physical stature. But he was male, in a society which was male-dominated. However, he was a feminist and had positive female role-models within his family. Benn was born left-handed, but, in contradistinction to his political direction of travel, became right-handed, except when he was setting cutlery for a meal. This may have added to his sense of being internally conflicted and his constant fight against aspects of his own nature. The natural rate of left-handedness in the population has been estimated to be around ten per cent, but in Victorian England the rate was supressed to about three per cent.[28] Benn was polite, but not unduly deferential. According to his more business-like elder brother, Benn possessed 'more cheek and less tact than his father', who was in turn quite cheeky and sometimes tactless.

Throughout his life Benn almost certainly gave more pleasure to others than he ever allowed himself. He was a 'pitiless driver of himself', while being wonderful company to others.[29] Benn had a feeling of competence and adequacy, but not of privilege. He was not on this Earth to consume by right, nor was he there to be pushed around and down-trodden. He took little for granted, and felt that it was his place to care for others, both within his family and within society. For him, the rest of the world was not a foreign place. He felt obliged. He felt that he could pull some of the levers of power, but that he would have to work hard to get his hands on them. Temperamentally, Benn was a leader, but usually not *the* leader. He was a natural deputy managing director, an adjutant, the second in command. He was more of a doer than a thinker, exemplary in the execution of a complex task, but not necessarily the person to set the strategy. Politically, Benn knew that he was liberal, Liberal, radical and Gladstonian. He also continued to label himself as 'Victorian', even well after the death of Queen Victoria.

Benn had a clear idea of what he wanted to spend his working life doing, but he was also modest and aware of his place in the world. 'I myself planned to be a politician ... in general people are too ambitious in their objectives and ... wisdom comes with narrowing and deepening the objective'.[30] There were times when Benn 'realised at once that there was nothing that an individual like me could do to sway the great forces involved even if I had wished to do so, or knew what I wanted'.[31] Benn was ambitious, but realistic and not self-important.

With his father's mixed political fortunes, Benn was able to learn some valuable lessons, without having to experience it all himself. This is perhaps one of the underestimated, but enduring, values of a political dynasty – the cascading of knowledge and experience. Tony was later to remark that he felt that he had the benefit of the political memory of someone much older than himself, because of his father's and grandfather's experiences.

Benn's early education was at a school in Jenner Street in Stoke Newington and then, after the family moved to Finsbury Square, he went to Cowper Street Middle Class School, also attended by his brother Ernest. But, in 1889 the boys were au-paired with two French girls, Alice and Jeanne Bodson, whose parents kept a small hotel at 29 rue Caumartin in Paris. At the hotel, the Benn brothers were not allowed to speak English. The boys went to school at the Lyceé Condorcet on the rue Amsterdam. The 12-year-old Benn felt that the school history books did not agree with what he had learned in England and that perhaps he and Ernest were, 'rather too patriotic'. This might have been a reference to the fact that the boys had hung a Union Jack from their bedroom window, afterwards commenting bemusedly that British people did not seem 'popular' in Paris! Neither was their popularity enhanced by a little foray into industrial espionage. The boys had been encouraged by their father to sketch whenever they got the chance. Benn was a competent, but not particularly gifted, sketch-artist. He put his skills into practice by standing in front of the shop window of Maison Jansen, a high-class Parisian furniture and interior design shop. Pressing his notepad up against the window, he started to sketch all the items of furniture on display. The staff, unsure how to react, began moving all the display items out of the window. The sketches later appeared in the *Cabinet Maker*.[32]

M. Bodson was instructed to remove the boys to another school – a small private institution run by a man who had seen active service in the Siege of Paris, which had then taken place less than twenty years earlier. But their stay here did not last long either, coming to an end over a principled stand by the Benn brothers on some stolen aggregate and the cruelty shown to a girl called Henriette. The boys decided to address the whole class on their discovery that the school garden had been created with gravel stolen from a local park and on their objections to the treatment of Henriette. Fetched home by their father to return to Cowper Street School, Benn felt more British than ever, but that he had made the acquaintance of foreigners whom he really liked. He retained a life-long fondness for France, the French and the French language.

In 1892 when Benn's father was MP for Tower Hamlets, St. George, Benn moved into a house on Cable Street (which his father renamed Gladstone House). The property had been taken on to provide Benn's father with an address in his constituency, but as Ernest later admitted, it was 'only a blind and the resident candidate really lived in the luxury' of the Westminster Palace Hotel.

At Gladstone House, Benn adopted an unusual pattern of work. He would come home from school, have a meal and go straight to bed. He would then get up at midnight to do his homework, when the area was at its quietest. He lived mainly on a diet of oatmeal, bought in quantities of a hundredweight (45 kg) and made into porridge. Benn noticed that he shared his working habits with a local Jewish tailor and eastern European refugees. He had a great admiration for the Jewish people, particularly their idealism and generosity. He detected no anti-Semitism at that stage, even though Cable Street was later to become notorious for the battle with Oswald Mosley's blackshirts.

After matriculation, Benn wanted to go to Cambridge, but the family could not afford it. Instead, he got a Rothschild scholarship to cover the fees at University College London (UCL). Here he became president of the debating society, where he enjoyed the rough and tumble of political controversy. He moved a resolution in favour of Boer independence, but was 'put out of the (ground floor) window' by a group of medical students.[33] He graduated with first class honours in French [34] in 1898, and later UCL made him a fellow.[35] After graduating he went to work for the family firm of Benn Brothers Publishing, at a salary of £7 per week. The firm was to continue to pay him, even after he ceased to work for it. Initially, Benn lived with his brother Ernest in Thorburn Square, Bermondsey, in the house which his father took for his (ultimately unsuccessful) campaign to become the MP for Bermondsey in the 1900 election.[36] The brothers worked long days, leaving home on the 08.40 train and not returning until after 21.00.

The 23-year-old Benn was keen to follow in his father's political footsteps, but he was rejected as the prospective Liberal candidate for Tower Hamlets, St. George for the 1900 election, which was won by the Conservative Tommy Dewar. Dewar was a member of the eponymous whisky distilling family. At that time the Conservative Party was closely associated with the drinks trade, while the Liberals were regarded as the party of temperance. Dewar was only to serve one term in Parliament before he retired, but during that time he developed a reputation as a right-wing opponent of 'pauper immigration' and was seen as anti-Semitic. Such views were not a barrier to parliamentary service at the time; nor was the nature of the business conducted by his defeated Liberal opponent, Bertram Straus, who imported ivory, drugs, ostrich feathers and isinglass – a product obtained from the swim bladders of fish.[37]

However, in 1901 Benn put his name forward again and was this time selected as the prospective Liberal candidate for the constituency, where his father was still banned from standing, although he remained keen to find another seat. Benn started an energetic, self-funded campaign, using his father's local knowledge and deploying his own zeal for filing systems. He built up a profile of his prospective constituents. He had a printed card for each voter including the man's name (general election voters were all male), marital status, place of work, political leanings and even his religion. Benn estimated that about one sixth of the electors were Roman Catholics of Irish origin and that there were 'a few hundred Jews' among his declining electorate of barely more than 3,000.[38] The records were used for circulating petitions and invitations to meetings, where attendance was recorded. It was normal practice to display election posters, so most voters' political inclinations were visible for all to see.

A major source of employment for the constituents was in the London Docks – an area of thirty acres which included the Eastern, Western and Tobacco Dock, linked to the Thames by Shadwell and Wapping Basins. The main cargoes handled were luxury items such as wine, ivory, spices and coffee. These docks were not connected to the rail network, unlike the docks of Glasgow, Leith and others in the capital. Although there was a road transport revolution under way with motorised vehicles replacing horse-drawn at a rapid pace in the Edwardian years, most deliveries were still by horse. Horses ate, drank, urinated, defecated and frequently died in the street. They, along with coal fires, industrial effluent, tobacco smoke, cooking and unwashed human life, contributed to the smell of the city. The Great Stink of the 1850s had largely been flushed away thanks to the work of Bazalgette and others, but buildings were still blackened by air pollution. The Houses of Parliament were not seen in their current warm umber, but clothed in black soot.

In preparation for his hoped-for parliamentary career, Benn sought an internship with a Liberal MP – one with modest pay attached. He wrote what he considered to be the 'most seductive' application he could produce.[39] It generated three responses. Oswald Partington seemed interested at first, but nothing came of this. Charles Hobhouse also replied, but Benn had good reason to doubt his grasp of the proposed arrangement, as the reply was addressed 'Dear Mr Dyer', which, as Benn helpfully pointed out in his draft autobiography, was not his name. The third response though was to lead to a life-long friendship, advancement in his career and almost to marriage. This response came from Reginald McKenna.

In 1903 Benn's preparations for a parliamentary career were interrupted when he was sent on a sea voyage. According to his own account, it was necessitated as a 'result of overstrain'. The real reason seems to be that Benn found out that his uncle Rutherford had murdered his grandfather, Julius, back in 1883. After his release from Broadmoor, Rutherford had been reunited with his wife, Florence. They had a daughter together in 1892, Margaret Rutherford, the Oscar-winning actress. When Margaret was three, her pregnant mother, Florence, committed suicide by hanging herself from a tree. Margaret was sent to live with relatives. After Florence's death, Rutherford had decided to remarry, to an Englishwoman in India. As Rutherford's elder brother and guarantor of his conduct, Benn's father felt compelled to make sure that Rutherford's intended knew about his past mental illness and his father's murder. The marriage was called off. Greatly agitated, Rutherford returned to England, whereupon Benn's father had him committed again to an asylum. Benn was witness to Rutherford's unhappy return. The distress of finding out only at this stage that his uncle had murdered his grandfather and that his family had hidden the truth from him for twenty years sent Benn into a breakdown and seemed to be the origin of recurrent bouts of depression, which lasted for the rest of his life.[40] From then onwards, Benn's moods seemed to polarise. He was either 'tremendously buoyant' or the polar opposite – gripped by a grim and depressive seriousness.[41] The depression seemed to arise mainly when he was not working. Holidays and the break from pressure and routine seemed to send him into a bleak mood. Memories of the 1903 sea voyage probably contributed to this; as Benn reflected: 'You just carry about with you the very thing you are travelling to escape'.

The voyage gave Benn time to dwell on, and to some extent come to terms with, the family tragedy, but also to develop some skills of independence and self-reliance. He certainly needed these. The 25-year-old Benn set sail on 14 March 1903. Shortly after his arrival in Durban, his luggage was stolen. The response from the police was to search the Indian encampment. Benn was unimpressed, to say the least, with the Boers and their treatment of other races. Short of money, Benn stayed in a cheap boarding house, five to a dormitory, where he learned much about the lives of working class European expatriates. Instead of heading for the Canaries as originally planned, Benn cashed in the return half of his ticket, got Ernest to send him some more money and then returned to the UK via the East African coast, the Suez Canal, Port Said, Naples and Lisbon. As if to emphasise his need for escape, Benn avoided the other British passengers and pretended to be French.

Improving fortunes meant that the family moved yet again, this time to Blackheath in southeast London, where they took up residence at the *Old Knoll*. This was in fact half of a very large house, which had been subdivided. John Benn could not resist remodelling houses, particularly taking out walls and creating spaces which could be used for performing plays. However, this house was not enough to satisfy all his interests.

Of all the family's many homes, the one which has since come to be described as their 'ancestral home',[42] was in fact a pre-fabricated house, chosen from a catalogue, delivered on a barge and constructed in Essex, at Stansgate on the banks of the Blackwater Estuary, opposite Osea Island.[43] The family had previously spent all their holidays at Southend and for several years had a small house there, but when the town started to get 'a bit crowded' they looked around the area for something quieter.[44] In 1898, while he was at university, Benn's parents went off on a property hunt. They took their penny-farthing bicycles on the train to Southminster and cycled along the banks of the Blackwater, until they found a place which they fell for immediately. It was just a grassy field looking out over the estuary. They negotiated successfully with the owner of the land and on 26 February 1899, on the occasion of her seventeenth birthday, Benn's younger sister Irene laid the foundation stone for a new holiday home. There was little stone available locally, so the rest of the house was to be built of wood. The design for a pre-fabricated house was picked out from the catalogue of Boulton and Paul, at a cost of £600.[45] It was landed in sections by boat. Many such buildings were shipped around the empire, where they provided a reminder of vernacular Victorian taste to British colonial officials serving far from home. The house originally had no bathroom, no mains water, no electricity and no gas. The interior had bare boards for walls, with no wallpaper. It had ornate Victorian wood detailing on the outside walls and it was topped off by a thatched roof.

Once they had established themselves at Stansgate, the family always had at least two boats. Benn became a proficient sailor, often taking his boat, the *Montrose*, across to France. Of all the forms of transport which Benn eventually mastered, some with difficulty, sailing was probably the one at which he was most proficient. Irene also had her own dinghy. Most of the family loved being at Stansgate, especially Benn who spent the happiest times of his life there. However, his father found that 'the air was too strong' and it made him ill: he suffered from migraines. He sold the house to a merchant banker[46] and instead bought a pair of cottages at Crowborough in Sussex, which were knocked together to form a 'golfing weekend residence', known as *Twitten Corner*.[47]

So, only four years after the Stansgate 'ancestral home' kit had been assembled in Essex, it no longer even belonged to the family.

Chapter Two

Liberal MP for the Backstreets 1906–14

The Tower Hamlets, St. George constituency existed from 1885 to 1918. It was a compact, poor inner-London borough, which returned one MP. (Over twenty constituencies still returned two MPs.) It sat on the north bank of the Thames and comprised the parishes of St. George in the East and Wapping.[1] In 1906 the main features of the constituency were the London Docks and densely-packed squalid housing. Since then the area has been transformed almost beyond recognition by wartime bombing, the decline of the docks and regeneration under the London Docklands Development Corporation. The area contains the scenes of Oswald Mosley's Battle of Cable Street and the dispute at Rupert Murdoch's Wapping printing plant.

Tower Hamlets, St. George had a small electorate and was marginal. In 1885, against the general trend, the Conservatives had won the seat, but in each election since 1886 the seat had gone to the party which formed the government. The Conservatives won the seat in 1886, 1895 and 1900. Benn's father had won it for the Liberals in 1892, by a margin of 398 votes (13.6 per cent), but had lost it at the following election in 1895, by just eleven votes. The 1900 election with a different Tory candidate had produced a Conservative majority of 296 (11.4 per cent). The scope of the franchise remained constant from 1885 to 1918. No women had the vote in parliamentary elections and nationally fewer than sixty per cent of men were enfranchised. Among men over 21, the excluded were generally the poor. They were not included on the register if they had moved home within the last year, or if the rental value of their lodgings was too low.[2] While many of the poorest were excluded, some voters qualified for more than one vote if they were university graduates or had business premises. In Tower Hamlets, St. George in the early 20th century the electorate was only slightly more than 3,000 and declining. Today by comparison, an MP represents around

70,000 voters. St. George contained London's highest concentration of people of Irish origin.

After five years of nursing the constituency, Benn won the seat in the Liberals' landslide election victory of 1906. It was called after the Conservatives had left office in disarray over tariffs, allowing Sir Henry Campbell-Bannerman (C-B to his followers) to form a Liberal government at the end of 1905.

1906 general election Tower Hamlets, St. George:

W.W. Benn	Liberal	1,685
H.H. Wells	Conservative	1,064
	Lib majority	621 (22.6 per cent)

The *Evening News* reporting Benn's election, pointed out (presciently) that his father's publication of the *Cabinet Maker* could be a happy omen for him. It made a point of mentioning that Benn was the 'baby of the House' and commented that with his 'clean-cut features, light hair, and eyes sparkling [he did] not look a day more than twenty-two'.[3] From photographs, the estimate of 'twenty-two' was on the high side. When Benn met Prime Minister Campbell-Bannerman's wife, Charlotte, for the first and only time at No 10 (she died in August 1906), she commented to her husband 'But Henry this boy can't possibly be a member of Parliament'.[4] Despite the backhanded compliment, Benn remained very fond of the 'kind, genuine, spontaneous' C-B.

Benn's father was returned as Liberal MP for Devonport at the 1906 election. The Benn political dynasty had emerged, with father and son together in the Commons. Until 1911 MPs were unpaid, hence the disproportionate number of members who were independently wealthy or who followed professions such as the law, which could involve attendance in court in the morning and at the Commons in the afternoon and evening. Benn could afford to undertake his unpaid parliamentary work, as he continued to receive his full salary of £207 per year from the family business.[5] His father was knighted in 1906; his parents becoming Sir John and Lady Benn. After the 1906 election seven fathers and sons sat together in the Commons – Joseph and Austen Chamberlain, Russell and Walter

Rea, Sir John and John Brunner, Sir Charles and Henry McLaren, Sir Charles and Duncan Schwann (who anglicised themselves to Swann in 1913), Sir George and Frank Newnes and Sir John and William Wedgwood Benn. Sir George Newnes gave a party at his house in Carlton Gardens for the inter-generational group of parliamentarians. All attended except the Chamberlains: Joseph Chamberlain was ill. He had played a major role in the Conservative divisions over tariffs before the 1906 election, but had a stroke later the same year.

The Commons chamber which greeted Benn was recognisably the same building as today, apart from its having wooden columns supporting the galleries, which made the chamber appear smaller. The dress was very different – all members wore top hats and Benn went to work in the standard attire of a frock coat. Snuff was dispensed at the door by a member of staff. This was Britain at the height of empire – the most industrialised nation with the largest navy in the world, a country that was able to host the 1908 Olympics at only two years' notice, after Italy had to withdraw in the wake of the Vesuvius eruption. The host nation topped the medal table, winning more than three times the number of medals of the second-placed United States. This was also the high water mark of Liberal politics. Subsequent historians have argued that the Liberal Party was already in decline by the Edwardian years. But the main proponent of this point of view, George Dangerfield, although admired for the elegance of his prose, has trouble sustaining his argument in the face of the scale of the 1906 Liberal election victory (400 seats of the 670 in the Commons) and the evidence that there were more defectors into the party than away from it in that period.[6] The Liberal Party had an abundance of talent and was carving out a new political role under the banner of New Liberalism – state intervention in welfare, with Lloyd George as a leading advocate.

Benn made his maiden speech in the House of Commons on 6 March 1906, the day after Ramsay MacDonald's. His first speech was to raise the case of constituents who had been imprisoned for the non-payment of rates, when in fact the tenants had paid rates to their landlord along with their rent, but the landlord had failed to pass this on to the council. The answer from John Burns, President of the Local Government Board, was that the tenants were liable for the rates, not the landlord, and the tenants should not have been paying the rates to the landlord in the first place. Benn no longer had a high regard for Burns. During the docks strike of 1889 Burns, together with Tom Mann and Clement Edwards, had held meetings at Benn's father's house in Cable Street after they had been addressing the crowds of dock workers. The strike had ultimately been successful, catalysing the growth of union membership among lower-skilled and poorly paid workers and drawing attention to the precarious existence of the casual workforce. But, Benn felt that once in government Burns had even become afraid of his under-secretary and 'tremblingly determined' to follow 'the right line'. Benn joked that when Burns rose to speak in the House of Commons, there was time for a 'cup of tea before he would reach his first finite verb'.[7]

This was to be the first of Benn's thousands of interventions in Parliament and he waited only ten days before making his next. Over the course of the 1906 Parliament, Benn raised a variety of local issues including the discontinuation of the rail link between the City and Wapping, the religious education of children in the local workhouse, old age pensions for widows of foreigners, safeguarding the livelihoods of costermongers and regulations to do with the Port of London Authority. Benn recognised the importance of London's position in international trade. In a debate, with arguments on globalisation which still resonate, the Commons resolved 'that this House is of the opinion that the conditions of the Port and docks of London urgently demands attention, with a view to the management thereof being forthwith placed in the hands of a public authority'. Benn argued that London was falling behind its international competitors and that 'the interest of labour in the question of the improvement of the port was very great' with the livelihoods of 5,600 bargemen and lightermen and 19,710 dock and wharf labourers at stake.[8] Lloyd George agreed to investigate. It led to the passage of the Port of London Act 1908, with very little opposition, establishing the Port of London Authority, which is still in existence, supervising navigation from the tidal limit on the Thames at Teddington downstream to a point opposite Margate. Once it was established, Benn continued to take a keen interest in Parliament in the Authority's activities, including asking if it would establish a 'receiving house for immigrants detained under the Aliens Act'. The 1905 Aliens Act for the first time had introduced immigration controls and registration, and gave the home secretary overall responsibility for immigration and nationality matters. It was designed to prevent paupers or criminals from entering the country and set up a mechanism to deport those who slipped through. One of its main objectives was to control Jewish immigration from Eastern Europe.

On 3 April 1908 Campbell-Bannerman became terminally ill. He relinquished the premiership to Asquith and, nineteen days later, became the only premier to die at 10 Downing Street. Benn's view of Asquith was reverential. He was 'an Olympian, massive of thought, and massive in integrity … we were all afraid of him'. Nothing was ever to shake Benn's opinion of Asquith. However, his views on Lloyd George, who took Asquith's former role at the Treasury, underwent a significant decline over the following twenty years. Aside from his unerring loyalty to Asquith, the politician to whom Benn was most devoted was Reginald McKenna. McKenna had been Liberal MP for Monmouthshire North since 1895 and had been appointed to his first ministerial office as Financial Secretary to the Treasury (Asquith's deputy) on 12 December 1905, when the Liberals had taken over the government from the Conservatives. After the 1906 election McKenna appointed Benn his unpaid parliamentary private secretary. Benn was to keep this role and follow McKenna in his two subsequent posts as President of the Board of Education from 23 January 1907 and at the Admiralty from 12 April 1908. Benn found his time at the Admiralty the most rewarding. He felt that he was 'right at the centre' with a place in the private office, where it was his 'duty to watch with tender care the relations' of his chief.[9]

The key issue of the period for the Admiralty was the drive to increase the pace of warship construction, promoted by McKenna and supported by Asquith, but opposed by Lloyd George and Churchill. The First Sea Lord, Fisher, had convinced McKenna that supremacy over Germany, Britain's chief rival, depended on building state-of-the-art *Dreadnought* warships, with steam turbines and heavy guns. McKenna belonged to the 'blue water school', which predicated defence policy on a 'wall of ships', avoiding continental military commitments. Although always economy-minded, McKenna viewed the warship construction as a patriotic necessity. He was successful in accelerating the pace of construction from four to six *Dreadnoughts* per year in the three years from 1909.

Like Benn, McKenna had received part of his schooling in France and was multi-lingual. He had then gone on to obtain a first class degree in maths at Cambridge and had been called to the Bar, after which he had built up a lucrative legal practice. Also like Benn, McKenna was initially (but not always) an admirer of Lloyd George. McKenna was fourteen years Benn's senior and in many ways acted like an older brother to him. A close friendship developed between the two, with McKenna later writing to Benn as 'My Beloved Wedgwood'.[10] McKenna's waspish public demeanour and his appearance (with a single long tuft of hair on his balding forehead) created the impression of a tall, bookish, aloof man, but in private he was kindly and charming.[11]

The two shared an interest in water sports. Benn had become a competent sailor during his holidays at Stansgate, and after the house had been sold he had kept a boat at Heybridge, further up the Blackwater, for a couple of years.[12] McKenna had been part of the winning Cambridge team in the 1887 boat race. An added attraction of McKenna's post was that he had the use of the Admiralty yacht, the *Enchantress*, and he invited Benn on several cruises. Benn had not just one, but two cabins to himself and a 'whole marine to polish the pewter bath'.

On 3 June 1908, at the age of forty-four, after a short engagement, McKenna married Pamela Jekyll. Pamela, twenty-six years McKenna's junior was the daughter of Dame Agnes and Sir Herbert Jekyll, brother of the garden designer, Gertrude. Pamela encouraged a friendship between Benn and her older sister, Barbara. Benn was invited by the Jekylls to stay at their Surrey home, *Munstead House*, where Asquith was also an occasional visitor. Barbara accompanied her sister and brother-in-law on one of the cruises on the *Enchantress*. The boat lived up to its name and on 20 January 1909 Benn proposed marriage to Barbara. But his suggestion was not met with the hoped-for reaction: Barbara burst into tears and ran away. Whilst Barbara's feelings for Benn were positive, her mother's were not, on account of Benn's lack of money. She influenced her daughter to reject Benn's proposal. Had Barbara been determined enough, she could probably have persuaded her mother to drop her opposition to the marriage. The fact that money was an obstacle suggests that the relationship was probably not a very soundly-based emotional match. Benn was not motivated by money: in fact he abhorred it and would almost certainly have been unhappy if he had been persuaded to make career choices based on financial considerations, rather than on interest and moral concerns. Instead, Barbara married the Liberal MP Francis McLaren in 1911. They had two children, one of whom, Martin, later became Conservative MP for Bristol North-West.[13]

Although McKenna's sister-in-law did not become Benn's wife, there was always a strong possibility that Benn would meet his prospective life partner through his work. A sister or daughter of another MP was always the most likely future partner for Benn, whose social life revolved around politics. The rejection by Barbara Jekyll did not deter Benn from keeping an eye out for a prospective wife among the relatives of his political circle of friends and eventually this did happen, but not for many years.[14] Benn continued to entertain a variety of friends and their families at the House of Commons, but not always in the most conventional of ways. In the days before health and safety concerns, one of his favourite treats was to let his friends' children ride in the small trucks which were used to carry fuel to the heating stoves around Parliament.

After his failed romance of the previous year, political and legal problems sprung up which led Benn to describe 1910 as being 'the most difficult year of my life [from a] political and personal point of view'.[15]

Lloyd George's People's Budget was rejected by the House of Lords, causing a constitutional crisis. An election was called in order for the government to win a mandate to pass the budget. The general election usually referred to as the January 1910 election, was actually held over a period of twenty-seven days between 14 January and 9 February 1910. The outcome of the election was the return of a minority Liberal government with 275 seats, just two seats ahead of the Conservatives. However, with the support of the Irish Nationalists with eighty-two seats and the Labour Party's forty, the Liberals were able to form a government. The Liberal and Labour parties had been in alliance under the Gladstone-MacDonald pact since 1903.

Benn faced a different opponent from his 1906 victory. His new contender was the Conservative, Percy Simmons, a Municipal Reform member of the LCC. (Conservatives on the LCC stood under the label of Moderates until 1906, when they changed their designation to Municipal Reform. The term Progressive was used by Liberal and Labour candidates.)

1910 January general election Tower Hamlets, St. George:

W.W. Benn	Liberal	1,568
P.C. Simmons	Conservative	1,134
	Lib majority	434 (16.0 per cent)

Although Benn was safely returned, his father was defeated by a margin of just 140 votes at Devonport, the seat which he had represented since June 1904. The Benns' father and son team in Parliament was broken up after the January 1910 election, as were all the others of the six who had dined together in the last Parliament.[16]

The new parliament resumed on 15 February 1910. Five days later Benn was appointed a whip (officially a junior lord of the Treasury – a misleading title, as these posts are in the Commons, not the Lords, and exist to enforce party discipline rather than assist at the Treasury). Benn's remit was to orchestrate the votes of the London MPs. Benn moved out from under the wing of his mentor, McKenna, and now reported to the newly-appointed government chief whip, the Master of Elibank. Elibank – Alexander William Charles Oliphant Murray – was heir to the Viscountcy of Elibank, hence the title Master of Elibank. Elibank was a talented organiser, and he needed to be, as the Liberals were dependent on support from the Irish Nationalists and Labour. His smooth operation earned him the nickname 'Oilybanks'.[17] Benn was now, for the first time, to be paid for his parliamentary work; the post of whip carried a salary of £1,000 per year. He still also continued to receive his Benn Brothers salary.

Under the rules in force at the time, Benn was obliged to seek re-election in his constituency on taking up the post of whip. (In 1919 the requirement to seek re-election was removed for ministerial appointments made within nine months of a general election. It was dropped completely in 1926.) So, in Benn's case in 1910, a by-election had to be called in Tower Hamlets, St. George. The date was set for 1 March – only just over three weeks after the last election had ended. It was the first by-election test of the new parliament. The outcome of such by-elections was not always a foregone conclusion. Voters might feel that they had only recently done their constitutional duty and would not bother to vote again so soon, or they could decide that the new post would take their MP's attention away from the constituency and that they would rather be represented by a backbencher without other responsibilities. Churchill had been defeated in his North West Manchester seat in April 1908, after he was appointed President of the Board of Trade. He decamped to Dundee to secure his return to the Commons. Benn's friend, later dubbed the 'Unluckiest Man in British Politics', Charles Masterman was to be defeated twice after his appointment to the cabinet and was forced to resign his post.

Between 1900 and 1914 there were 274 by-elections, of which twenty-three per cent were uncontested.[18] The proportion of unopposed by-elections was falling, but by 1910 there were still significant numbers which did not entail the cost and emotional energy of a contest.[19] When by-elections were contested, the time, money and effort could be considerable. One party alone could hold over 500 meetings, and twelve leaflets or letters per elector per party per week could be delivered.[20] The leafleting probably compares with the most intensive by-elections today, but the number of meetings far exceeded anything now seen.

In terms of contenders, the by-election turned out to be a repeat of the general election contest: Benn faced the same Conservative opponent, Percy Simmons. However, it was not a straightforward re-run of the campaign. Benn tried to keep the focus of the campaign on himself and the honour for his constituency of his appointment. Some bitterness from the January election spilled over into the by-election – particularly Simmons' anger that Benn had accused him of voting on the LCC 'against feeding poor children'. Benn had been referring to Simmons' vote against the provision of school meals on the rates for 'necessitous children'. Simmons' objection was that a public appeal had been launched, which had raised money for providing poor children with lunches. The appeal had raised sufficient funds for foreseeable needs and Simmons had felt that, if the cost had been transferred to the rates, then the voluntary public subscriptions would stop.

The involvement of pressure groups such as women's suffrage campaigners, the temperance movement and campaigners for and against free trade was common in by-elections of the time. The Edwardian years were the highpoint of the 'battles of the leagues', some of which had a very narrow focus, such as the Anti-Cocoa Duty League or the Sporting League. The Liberals bemoaned the facts that the leagues fell outside the spending restrictions of the 1883 Corrupt Practices Act and that most of the richer leagues supported the Conservatives.

The Women's Social and Political Union attempted to persuade the Irish voters in the constituency, (reckoned to number around 750), to vote against Benn. This was perverse, as Benn was strongly in favour of women's votes. However, their opposition was due not to the issue of the franchise, but to the Union's scepticism over the government's commitment to Irish home rule. This, too, was ironic, as Benn's only opponent was a Conservative, whose party was much less likely to deliver home rule for Ireland than were the Liberals. Benn was not being singled out by the Women's Social and Political Union. The organisation was applying pressure to Liberal candidates and ministers wherever it had the opportunity. Benn also found that he had active opposition from the local Catholic priests. Added to this, the socialists put up a large poster urging their supporters not to vote for Benn 'as a protest against the Government's insincerity with regard to the veto of the House of Lords.'[21] Benn was sincere about women's votes, Irish home rule and removing the House of Lords' veto, but he had overstepped the mark with his comments about Simmons' attitude to feeding children, or, as the *Times* sub-heading put it, that Simmons was a 'Kid Starver'.[22] The press also chipped in at by-elections, more often on the side of the Conservatives too, sometimes giving away free copies of their newspapers.

Turnout in by-elections of the period was typically on a par with general elections, unlike the lower rates in today's by-elections.[23] There was also by then the established pattern for by-election results to show a brief honeymoon for a recently-elected national government, followed by mid-term blues and a return to more favourable results nearer to the following general election. In the event, none of the activity and excitement did any serious harm to Benn and his by-election result conformed to the general pattern for a contest held soon after a general election. His majority increased from 434 (16 per cent) to 509 (19 per cent).

By-election 1 March 1910 Tower Hamlets, St. George, on Benn's appointment as a whip:

W.W. Benn	Liberal	1,598
P.C. Simmons	Conservative	1, 089
	Lib majority	509 (19 per cent)

However, the row over the feeding of poor children was later to escalate and nearly to cause Benn's departure from politics. Simmons issued a writ for libel over Benn's claim that he had voted 'against the feeding of school children'. The timing of the case was difficult for the Benn family finances, as Benn's father was also issued with a writ for libel, slander and disparagement of goods in connection with his LCC work. The goods in question were parts of the London tram system. In terms of timing of the legal process, the two cases overlapped.

Sir John Benn's case reached court on 15 November 1910. The plaintiffs were the owners of patents for a system of studs set into the road to power electric trams. They claimed that they had been 'virtually ruined' by Sir John Benn's remarks about their system, which had been included in a letter to the *Times* and an article in the *Daily Chronicle*. In court Benn Senior defended his position, citing three horses and two men who had received shocks from the system. On 1 December 1910, a judgement was entered for £12,000 against Sir John Benn.[24] Benn Senior decided to appeal, but in the meantime had a bailiff appointed, who drew up an inventory of the family belongings. On 9 December 1910, while Benn Senior was awaiting his appeal, the trial started over his son's dispute about the feeding of children.[25] In the first stage of the process Simmons won his case against the *Daily Chronicle* and was awarded £5,000.[26] Simmons then won another £5,000 from *Liberal Opinion*, which had also published the offending allegations.[27]

The legal proceedings were still unresolved when another general election was called. The People's Budget had been passed after the January 1910 election, but the long-term battle for supremacy between the Commons and the Lords was still to be resolved. Thus, 1910 became one of two years in the twentieth century to see two general elections – the other being 1974. Benn had to stand for re-election for the third time in less than a year, as he had had to fight the by-election too. However, it was to be the last election for eight years and the last which his father was ever to fight. Parliament was dissolved on 28 November 1910 and polling was set for 2-19 December. It was to be the last election held over several days.

The Conservative manifesto complained that: 'In less than a year since the last General Election the Government has resolved again to appeal to the country. They have selected the season at which the register least accurately represents the constituencies, and which is most inconvenient to trade; and have done so without the excuse of a Parliamentary defeat in either House, and with no visible breach in the strange coalition of parties which keeps them in office.... Now, as then, we are resolved that the party of revolution shall not, under the thin disguise of an attack on the Upper House, impair the liberties of the people.... Behind the Single Chamber conspiracy lurk Socialism and Home Rule.'

Benn arranged for a bill-poster to put up election material around the constituency, in the belief that the electors would be motivated by the opportunity to remove the House of Lords veto on bills passed by the Commons. Benn was somewhat disabused of their likely impact when the bill-poster asked him: 'This vetto [sic], what is it?', suggesting instead that a poster along the lines of 'Vote for Benn' would probably have been more effective.[28]

1910 December general election Tower Hamlets, St. George:

W.W. Benn	Liberal	1,401
D. Clifton Brown	Conservative	1,022
	Lib majority	379 (15.6 per cent)

So, Benn was yet again endorsed by his electorate in Tower Hamlets, St.George, but his father was again rejected in his attempt to return to Parliament, this time at Clapham.

Benn's feeling that 1910 was his most difficult year, both personally and politically, was well-founded. He was still recovering from the rejection of his marriage proposal, he had had to fight three elections in one year to retain his own seat, his father had lost his seat, breaking up their father and son partnership in the Commons, and at the year's end both were still embroiled in legal disputes, which could have bankrupted either or both of them.

Faced with the overwhelming likelihood that he would suffer the same fate as the two publications, Benn Junior was persuaded to settle his own case out of court in mid-February 1911, for an agreed sum of £2,500 and an apology.[29] Benn Junior thought he would have to go through the bankruptcy court, which would have entailed leaving Parliament. His father, showing quite a bit of nerve under the circumstances of his own perilous financial situation, refused to hear of it. Perhaps he felt that it would be better to bail out his son first, even if he went bankrupt himself leaving little for his creditors. At least then one of them would have had his career intact. However, on 20 March 1911 Sir John Benn won his appeal and costs, although in the event the costs were never paid.[30] Benn Junior summed up the conclusion: 'Everything therefore ended well except that the family pot had been scraped, the Liberal Party made some contribution [and] I had learned a bitter lesson to be duly careful in what I said.'[31]

In Benn's first eight years in Parliament he had become a master of political organisation, but he was still a novice at policy-making and implementation. 'During those years from 1906 to 1914, I learned nothing whatever about politics. I learned a good deal about political organisation, but nothing about the principles or causes involved ... Politics was quite simple for me. If I wanted to make a speech, I did it with a "liberal" outlook. I got a pamphlet.'[32] If Benn wanted to delve further into a particular topic, he would consult one of the longer policy texts produced by his neighbour and Liberal Party Publications Department head, the appropriately-named, Charles Geake. This pattern to Benn's strengths and weaknesses was to remain throughout his career. He showed good instinctive judgment on the big issues and was an assiduous organiser and motivator, but he never really developed the intermediate skill of detailed policy-making. He thoroughly enjoyed debating and political intrigue.

Benn gradually increased the number of times he spoke in the House of Commons, from eight times in his first year to fourteen in 1909, concentrating on issues which affected his constituency. On 16 February 1909 Benn, in full court regalia, seconded the motion on the address. After his appointment as a whip, Benn's opportunities to speak in the Commons were initially limited. However, on 3 November 1910, Earl Beauchamp was appointed First Commissioner of Works and Benn was given responsibility for answering questions on his behalf in the House of Commons; Beauchamp's predecessor, Lewis Vernon 'Loulou' Harcourt had been in the Commons. Benn's appearances increased rapidly in frequency and in 1912 he spoke in 107 debates and provided written answers to forty-one questions. Among the topics which Benn had to address was whether the proposed electric lighting in the House of Commons would more harmful to the eyes than the existing gas lighting and whether the royal park keepers were given a weekly day off: they were not. They had to work for six and a half days per week.

Benn also took on responsibility for answering Commons questions on 1911 National Insurance Bill. The bill was unpopular because of the 4d per week levy on workers' wages, the poorest of whom only earned around 12s or less per week. Lloyd George's claim was that with government and employers' contributions it was '9d for 4d', but this did not quell the opposition. As a whip, Benn was able to observe Lloyd George at close quarters. At this stage, Lloyd George was his 'hero' and he 'conceived a great admiration' for him. Benn was a frequent visitor to Number 11 Downing Street, trying to make himself 'useful, in order, no doubt, to secure favour and possible promotion'. A bonus was that he could be a recipient of bacon and eggs dispensed from the fender in the dining room by Margaret Lloyd George. On one occasion, Benn was invited round for what he expected to be a quiet chat, only to discover that twenty-two Baptist ministers were also invited. Benn fled.[33]

The admiration which Benn felt for Lloyd George received a severe dent as a result of the Marconi scandal in the summer of 1912. Benn disliked money and he disliked people who were interested in accumulating money, especially if it were not as the result of their own efforts. He was, therefore, not at all sympathetic when it emerged that Lloyd George, together with Herbert Samuel, Rufus Isaacs and the Master of Elibank had been caught trying to profit from insider dealing in shares in the Marconi company, which was to be awarded a large government contract. Those implicated were let off the hook by their fellow Liberal Party members on the committee set up to investigate the scandal, but the members of the other parties were not convinced of their innocence.

In 1914, Benn's father received a baronetcy. The upgrade meant that his parents still remained Sir John and Lady Benn, but his father became suffixed with 'Bart.' and the new title was hereditary. Ernest, as the eldest son, was therefore in line to inherit the baronetcy, as the second baronet. Ernest was married in 1903 and he and his wife, Gwen, had five children.

Their eldest son, John, was therefore in line to become the third baronet. So, another aspect of a dynasty was put into place. The family had now had two generations in parliament and had a title and a business to be handed on.

Chapter Three

To War with a Parachute and a Box of Pigeons 1914–18

T he outbreak of the First World War in August 1914 had immediate repercussions for British politics. The lasting impression is of the damage done to the Liberals, but initially the party remained in government with Asquith still at the helm. Patriotic instinct kept the Conservative Party united, while the Labour Party appeared to implode.

Labour had come last in all twenty three-cornered by-elections held between 1911 and the outbreak of war in 1914. However, where Labour candidates stood for the first time in a constituency, their votes had come almost entirely from former Liberal voters, rather than from Conservatives or non-voters. In three-cornered by-elections held between 1903 and 1914, where Labour had not stood in the previous general election, on average the Conservative vote rose by 0.6 per cent and the Liberals' fell by 18.8 per cent.[1] So, what was an apparent weakness of the Labour Party, was also a less-obvious threat to the Liberals.

The declaration of war split the Parliamentary Labour Party down the middle. The trade unionists were generally behind the war effort, due to patriotism and economic advantage for their members. However, Ramsay MacDonald resigned the Labour leadership, objecting to the lack of parliamentary control over the treaties and entanglements which had triggered the conflict, lamenting that it 'was no use remaining as the Party was divided and nothing but futility could result … the Party was no party in reality'.[2]

The influence of Parliament over war in 1914 was much the same as the position had been two hundred years earlier, and it still remains so today. In 1689 the Bill of Rights declared that 'the raising or keeping of a standing army within the kingdom in time of peace unless it be with the consent of Parliament is against the law'.[3] However, beyond these provisions,

Parliament's powers amount to very little. Declaration of war is effectively the decision of the prime minister, using the powers delegated under the royal prerogative. The impact of the two world wars and the backlash over the 2003 Iraq invasion have still not resulted in the removal of this royal prerogative. Although David Cameron allowed a Commons vote on military action in Syria in 2013, he could still have over-ruled the MPs' decision by using the royal prerogative.

The British Parliament is unusually weak by comparison with other European countries when it comes to powers to declare, or prevent, war.[4] The issue of the royal prerogative is one which continued to exercise the Benn family many decades later.

When the First World War started, the Liberal Party also began to fragment. Within the party there was a spectrum of views ranging from pacifists on religious grounds, such as the Quakers, Edmund (Ted) Harvey and Arnold Rowntree, to ardent militarists such as Freddie Guest, who immediately returned to military service. Between these extremes were objectors on economic grounds such as Reginald McKenna, and objectors on managerial grounds, such as John Simon. Many believed that Liberalism and compulsion to fight were incompatible. Others, who had been opposed to the Boer War, were determined this time to prosecute an all-out military conflict. This was the view of both Lloyd George and of William Wedgwood Benn. However, agreement on war policy did not mean that the relationship between the two was close. Benn, although initially admiring Lloyd George, had become very suspicious of his character after the 1912 Marconi share scandal.

Benn's work as a whip changed as soon as war broke out. An electoral truce was agreed between the main parties and inter-party co-operation increased. Benn felt that the task of organising conflict between the parties in parliament had become 'ridiculous and distasteful'. He kept his post, but began to look for something more constructive to do. For the first two months of the war, when enlistment was both voluntary and voluminous, Benn organised and chaired the National Relief Fund, which provided separation allowances for the wives and children of workers who had volunteered for the armed forces. He had gained valuable experience of fundraising for the families of striking dockers in 1912 and he put this to good use in the new wartime circumstances. In the course of soliciting help from the press, Benn had his only encounter with Lord Northcliffe, owner of the *Times* and the *Daily Mail*. The meeting was not a success: Benn was not even offered a seat. He found that Northcliffe's opinion 'was easily grasped and often repeated', namely that it would have to be the *Times'* Fund. Afterwards, Benn tactfully commented that he 'couldn't pretend that [he] attempted to form any appreciation' of Northcliffe.[5] However, Benn was more successful in attracting other high profile patrons, enlisting the help of the 'stone blind' Arthur Pearson, owner of the *Daily Express* and of Balfour, MacDonald, Asquith and the Prince of Wales, who arranged for the Buckingham Palace stables to become the fund's post office. Eventually it raised over £5 million. Benn concluded that it was actually easier to collect money than to spend it. In doing so, one of his greatest concerns was to guard against the imposition of moralistic conditions, which would have prevented payments to children born out of wedlock.

By October 1914 Benn felt that the Fund was operating on a sustainable basis and he began to feel that his skills were being under-used. So he volunteered for the army, writing to chief whip, Percy Illingworth, to resign his position as a whip.[6] Illingworth did not accept the resignation, believing, along with so many others, that the war would be brief and that Benn would soon be available to resume his duties. In the event, Benn nominally remained a whip until Asquith reorganised his government as a coalition in May 1915. Benn remained an MP throughout the war, although he did not speak at all in the Commons between 1915 and 1918 and inevitably he neglected his constituency.

For the 37-year-old Benn, this was his first taste of military service. As if this was not enough of a challenge, he chose to join the Middlesex Yeomanry – a cavalry regiment. Benn could not ride and did not even like animals. He was given a horse by his parliamentary colleague, Freddie Guest, but he was to have great difficulty with the beast. It unseated him into a barbed wire fence.

As a rather old, teetotal, first-class honours graduate and an MP, becoming a second lieutenant among a coterie of mainly wealthy, younger cavalry officers was not the easiest of transitions for Benn. He belonged to a rather different social circle from his new colleagues and the contrast between them and his constituents could hardly have been more stark. He found many of his fellow officers to be under-educated, narrow in outlook, unimaginative and obsessively keen on, what Benn saw as, pointless details and rituals. (The uniform was prescribed to the last detail. The jodhpurs had to be bought from one particular shop on Savile Row and the cloth had to have a slight pink tinge.) Benn felt contempt at the quality of education of some of the officers and privately mocked their errors of historical knowledge. He was frustrated by regulations and the constant aim of finding enough work for the troops, rather than finding efficient ways of achieving results with fewer resources. He noted disparagingly that the senior officers never considered the size of the wages bill, which they had no role in paying. His business background meant that he was out of sympathy with their waste of resources. His political contacts meant that he did not feel constrained by the chain of command. His position as an MP gave him standing beyond his rank and this was resented by some of his fellow officers.

Benn did not have a particularly high regard either for the regular troops who had joined in peacetime. He felt that they generally had low ambitions and abilities and had signed up largely to be fed and housed. He felt that the main role of the army had been little more than to instil in them rigorous standards of hygiene and discipline. He had most empathy with those recruits who had joined the ranks during the war. He valued the intelligence and generally higher personal standards of the 'middle class Londoners, bank clerks, architects' assistants, solicitors' clerks [and] young business men'. Benn probably considered his origins to be amongst this group, but that his achievements had placed him on a level with the most senior officers and their political masters – a rather dissonant situation. Benn wryly observed that the older officers had difficulty coping with the initiative shown by some of those recruited into the wartime ranks.

By no means did Benn end his contact with parliamentarians when he joined up. His commanding officer was Sir Mathew 'Scatters' Wilson, less than two years older than Benn. Wilson was the Conservative MP for Bethnal Green South West, the seat which he had won in a by-election in February 1914. Apart from the party-political differences, Benn had a particular reason to resent Wilson's election, as he had won the seat by defeating Benn's friend, Charles Masterman, in the by-election resulting from Masterman's appointment to the cabinet. Political balance was restored, however, as the second-in-command of the regiment was Harry Brodie, who had been the Liberal MP for Reigate from 1906 to January 1910.

Benn received about two pounds ten shillings per week salary from the army and was in a quandary over whether to continue to accept his MP's salary. Some of his constituency costs continued, but he was essentially being paid for a job that he was not doing. However, he did not want to set an awkward precedent for his colleagues.

Benn's initial months in the army involved the usual military experience of hanging around, sorting out kit and training – with more of the first than the second or third. Benn's initial posting was near Reading, moving on after a few weeks to the Grand Hotel at Mundesley on the Norfolk coast – not a good preparation for the hot and difficult conditions that he was going to confront. From Mundesley, Benn managed to arrange to go, unauthorised, on a machine-gun course at Bisley. He obtained a distinction from the course, but also a black mark against his record for attending without permission.

News came through that the regiment was to be sent to the Dardanelles. Unlike most of the company, Benn celebrated the news by learning some Turkish. The journey to the Dardanelles started in April 1915 with the first stop-off being Avonmouth. While waiting on the quayside, news came through that the ship preceding his regiment's, the *Wayfarer*, had been torpedoed just outside the Bristol Channel.[7] Benn sailed on the *Nile*, along with a small convoy of other ships, some of which had been converted to horse-boats. Morale at that stage was high. In Benn's words 'We were living to the full. For us the War had begun at last.'[8]

A stop-over in a camp by the Suez Canal did give Benn a chance to acclimatise to the oppressive heat and, perhaps fortunately, there was even less to do here. The tedious days were enlivened by Benn's voluminous correspondence with his parents and activities such as horse-swimming sessions. Benn managed to get himself invited to Port Said, where he made an aeroplane flight, again strictly against orders. The aircraft was a monoplane, flown by a French pilot. Benn was smitten with flying and resolved to be transferred eventually to an airborne unit. He had first flown in 1910, when he had been a passenger in a Boxkite biplane at Hendon.

While he was enjoying his 'holiday', as he described it, at Port Said, Benn received the news that his younger brother, Oliver, a captain serving with the 1st Essex Regiment, was missing in action. Oliver, ten years younger than Benn, had joined the territorial army on leaving school and had been commissioned in May 1911. He had also worked in the family publishing business in Manchester, as the Northern Branch Manager. Oliver had set sail from England on 10 May 1915, shortly after his older brother, but had taken a more direct route and had arrived earlier in the Dardanelles.

The telegram received by his parents told them that Oliver was missing, but (as was common practice) suggested that he could have been taken prisoner. Using their contacts, the family pursued many different avenues to try and find out what had happened to Oliver. His name did not appear on any list of prisoners. His mother continued to write to him daily, but after the end of the war all the letters were returned to her, unopened.

Research by the authorities and the family over the following years did not manage to find a conclusive answer about Oliver's fate.[9] The two most detailed accounts date the events to the Turkish attack early on 6 June 1915, but in other respects they seemed to contradict each other. One witness, Private Merrick, said that he had seen Oliver lying in a trench, apparently dead or unconscious. Merrick said that he had been told the following day that Oliver had been shot through the head.[10] The other witness, a stretcher-bearer, later reported he had treated Oliver after he been very badly wounded in the thigh at about 06.00 during the Turkish attack on a trench, but that Oliver might have been taken prisoner.[11] It is possible that both were accurate and that Oliver was shot in the head, after having earlier been injured in the thigh. Allowing for the confusion of battle though, it is also possible that neither report was accurate.

It seems fairly certain that Oliver had only been in action for five days, during which he had repulsed a Turkish attack, led his men in an advance and then attempted to retreat from an exposed position. Such a quick ending was unfortunately not unusual. By the end of 6 June 1915 only four of the twenty-five 1st Essex officers who had left England at the start of the campaign remained on roll – all the others were dead, missing or wounded.

Benn's elder brother, Ernest, had not joined the military, but instead became a voluntary civil servant at the Ministry of Munitions and later at the

Ministry of Reconstruction.[12] Benn also heard of the death of Gladstone's grandson, William, who was the sitting Liberal MP for Kilmarnock Burghs.

During the war the Liberal Party was also to lose Charles Lyell (MP for Edinburgh South), Thomas Agar-Robartes (St. Austell), brothers Harold Cawley (Heywood) and Oswald Cawley (Prestwich), Neil Primrose (Wisbech MP and son of Lord Rosebery) and Francis McLaren (Spalding), who had married Barbara Jekyll, Benn's proposed fiancée. Raymond, son of Liberal Prime Minister Herbert Asquith, but not himself an MP, was also killed in action at the age of 37. They were just a few examples of what came to be considered as the 'lost generation' of future political leaders.

After the early failed allied landings at Gallipoli, a plan was drawn up to send troops further north on the peninsula to Suvla on 9 August 1915. Benn's brigade was to be included in the first landing, but as an infantry unit. The horses, having been transported all the way from England, were left behind in Egypt with one third of the officers and men. There was much jealousy among the troops over who should be chosen to go and fight and who should stay to look after the horses. At the time, fighting was generally the preferred option, as it certainly was for Benn.

Large quantities of unfamiliar infantry equipment were delivered to the camp, but no orders for departure arrived. Benn's brigade was eventually brought in as part of the plan to recover the situation after the initial Suvla landing had failed. They set off on 13 August, sailing on the *Caledonia* from Alexandria to the Greek Island of Lemnos, about forty miles off the coast of Gallipoli. Here the troops were to get their first sight of one of the realities of war – hospital ships – and they received the news that the transport preceding theirs had been sunk. The last leg of the voyage started on 17 August 1915 aboard the *Doris*, so packed that there was literally not room to stretch.[13] The ship arrived at Suvla just before dawn the following day. The troops were under fire from the moment they disembarked. Benn and his batman dug a hole for the night on the hillside above the beach and proudly named their new home *Battle View*. They spent two days in residence, before being ordered into action on 20 August 1915.

Benn, with his organising efficiency and willingness to please, but his limited military experience, was adjutant for his regiment, which had been reduced in size with the loss of the horse-minders in Egypt. His role was to liaise with the commanding officer, disseminate orders and maintain morale. The troops set off in darkness and confusion, struggling to carry their machine guns by hand along the beach to the designated attack point.

Benn's regiment went into action, introducing the men to the sight of dead and maimed comrades. Benn's account simply stated that the 'horror of that scene will bear no describing.'[14] In the confusion, Benn mistakenly reported the death of his troop's harmonica player, who had been keeping up the men's morale. In the end, the man whom Benn saw shot through the head, turned out to be a different soldier. Bush fires swept across parts of the battle arena and many corpses were consumed in the flames. The implications of the report of his brother being 'missing' in action were soon brought home to Benn. The transformation in Benn's own circumstances was highlighted when he had to fix his bayonet as the closeness of the enemy became clear and his euphemistically-named 'trench-digging' party found out that they were really grave-diggers.

Benn displayed calmness and courage in battle and his ability to connect with, and maintain morale among, the troops was noted. He once set off to crawl several miles under fire to deliver orders – his men thinking that they would never see him again. Benn's parting words to his troop were 'have a cup of tea ready for me when I come back'.[15] His commanding officer wrote in appreciation:

'I'd like to bring to notice the conduct of … Lt W. Benn who was acting Adjutant, and was very cool and gallant and spent the whole afternoon and evening cheering up everyone with whom he came in contact, in particular some of the Munsters who had been terribly knocked about.'[16]

The first advance achieved nothing. The troops were ordered to retreat and then advance again. The fruitless campaign dragged on for weeks with the troops huddled in their trenches, morale sinking, at the mercy of parasites and disease, as well as from Turkish shells; dysentery, jaundice and other diseases became rife among the troops. One of the lasting effects of Benn's war experience was to be a life-long aversion to flies. Food 'could only be eaten with one hand. The other was required for defence. Myriads of beautiful large bronze-green creatures settled on everything ... if a piece of meat was uncovered to be cut there was scarcely room for the knife edge, so many were the flies that instantly settled on it.'[17]

Benn developed jaundice, causing yellowing of the skin and eyes, symptomatic of underlying liver problems. In October 1915 he was given permission to go for recuperation to the sparsely-inhabited 100 square mile Greek-controlled island of Imbros, ten miles off the Gallipoli coast and used as a staging post by Australian and New Zealand forces. He travelled there by trawler with an officer friend, Captain Gubbins. The trip was brief and unsuccessful from a health-restoring point of view, but it provided respite from three months of mud and gave the officers the chance to dine on partridge and omelette. On their return, Benn found out that his division was to be sent for recuperation to the (rather inappropriately named) Mudros on the island of Lemnos. From there the division was withdrawn to Egypt; but fewer than 1,000 of the original 3,000 troops returned.[18]

Benn's jaundice worsened and he was instead sent by the doctor to the hospital ship *Valdivia*, a French-built liner only launched in 1911, re-liveried in white with red crosses. Aboard, he gratefully enjoyed the luxuries of a bath and a bed. He hoped to return to Egypt, but discovered that the ship was bound for Malta. He resolved to choose his own destination, recruiting the support of the doctor in charge and of the ward sister, who it turned out had campaigned against him at the last election. He landed on Malta and badgered away at the authorities until he managed to secure a passage with an Australian padre on a West Indian fruit ship bound for Port Said.

Benn re-joined his regiment near Cairo, but as soon as he had arrived back in Egypt he started trying to secure a posting to the air service. While he was waiting for approval, he enjoyed the life in Cairo, where most of the staff evacuated from the failed Gallipoli adventure were gathered. He travelled extensively around Egypt, but as the months passed he became increasingly impatient to find a new role.

Life was highly-compartmentalised. Benn realised this more than most and made a much greater effort to engage with others than did most of his fellow officers. However, there was almost complete segregation – men from women, nationality from nationality and, to a large extent, officers from men. Even within the male British officer contingent, there were the dividing lines of rank, social background, age and between regular officers and wartime recruits.

After several refused requests, in mid-April 1916 Benn finally received orders from London to report to the East Indies and Egypt Seaplane Station at Port Said. This was to prove the most interesting part of Benn's war and to give him freedom from the constraints of serving in a long chain of command. Benn realised that attachment to a small unit with big ambitions, 'with no very definite place in anyone's schemes and without acknowledged parentage, enjoyed … unequalled opportunity for originality and initiative'.[19] In the days before the formation of the Royal Air Force in 1918 neither the army nor the navy appreciated the full potential of their air power, especially in a theatre of war against the Turks who had few aircraft.

The British front line was just to the east of the Suez Canal. The role of the seaplanes was to support the French Navy in the East Mediterranean, defending against submarine attack and disrupting seaborne supplies to the Turks. They also monitored and attacked the railways which the Turks relied on to bring in overland supplies.

The centre of the operation was HMS *Ben-my-Chree*, an Isle of Man packet steamer built in 1908: the name meaning 'woman of my heart' in Manx. The *Ben-my-Chree* had a crew of 250 and had returned from service in the Dardanelles. She had been converted to a sea-plane carrier in 1915 and could transport up to six (folded) aircraft (sometimes with their tails off). The conversion took the form of a large hangar installed aft of her two funnels, and derricks for lifting the seaplanes in and out of the water. The net result was inelegant, but functional. The ship looked like a cross-channel ferry with a large industrial shed perched on the back. A dismountable 18m flying-off platform with a trolley and rails was also available to enable seaplanes to take off from a solid base. At that stage no plane had yet been landed back onto a moving ship.[20] She was originally designed for short, fast, ferry crossings and therefore had limited space for storing the large quantities of coal needed for longer voyages. Several cabins had been converted to coal stores and large piles of coal adorned the decks during longer journeys. The picture of inelegance was complete, when at sea, by air outlets which blew snorts of black coal dust off the decks. Two captured German ships, the *Raven* and *Anne*, were also temporarily used as seaplane carriers at the base, but they were slow and not well-suited to the task and were later reconverted to cargo ships. The unit also had a collection of huts on shore in a one-acre compound of reclaimed land.

Seaplane design and manufacture had developed rapidly since the first successful flight in 1910. By mid-1916 the *Ben-my-Chree* hosted a collection of British-built seaplanes – all single-engined biplanes from Sopwith or Shorts. Sopwith alone made 16,000 planes during the war, either directly or via sub-contractors, but after the war became a victim of its own success when the market was swamped with decommissioned planes. Shorts managed to avoid this fate: it had been the first company in the world to make production aircraft and it survives to this day. The *Ben-my-Chree* had the single-seat Sopwith Baby and the two-bay Sopwith 860, which could carry a torpedo under the fuselage. From Shorts there were the Admiralty Type 184, a folding-wing two-seater, which had been the first type of plane to sink a ship using a torpedo and the Short 830, a two-seat reconnaissance seaplane.[21] The flying speeds of the planes were generally a sedate 65-88 mph. Also at Port Said were Nieuport VI-Gs – French-built and operated monoplanes, which had returned from Gallipoli. Part of the seaplanes' work was 'spotting' – seeing how close to their intended target the allied artillery shells were landing and relaying the information by wireless telegraphy. They were also used for bombing raids.

Command of the *Ben-my-Chree* changed hands just as Benn arrived. Colonel Cecil L'Estrange Malone had taken command in 1915. Although only 24, he had, by then, been in the Navy for ten years and had held his Royal Aero Club flying certificate for three years. Their paths were to cross again in the House of Commons after the war. Malone was replaced on 14 May 1916 by Charles Samson, six years Benn's junior. He had achieved his flying certificate in 1911, after only six weeks' experience and the following year he had become the first person to take off from a moving ship.[22] Benn found Samson's company congenial, although he learned to be wary of his publicity-seeking instincts and his sensitivity to criticism. Benn was eventually put in an interesting position vis-à-vis his commander, when he was asked to vouch for Samson's suitability as a husband by his prospective father-in-law. Benn was happy to oblige, despite recording in his own recollections that 'Samson was not a man with a benign temperament'.

Samson felt that he had found 'gold' in Benn's organisational skills. Benn's love of filing and retrieval systems proved ideal for his role in organising the intelligence on each of their combat areas. While others often valued the output of Benn's exemplary record-keeping, Benn himself seemed to derive equal satisfaction from the filing systems themselves. Reflecting back on this, Benn was interviewed for BBC Television towards the end of his life. He delivered a brisk and entertaining overview of his understanding of world affairs and how he had accumulated his knowledge, but he could not resist sharing with his viewers the details of how his filing systems worked and the massive scale of his archives of news cuttings. They eventually came to occupy their own building – a disused slaughterhouse.

When in the air, Benn took the role of observer. He had to sit among a selection of bombs, piled up with a camera, notebook, map and Verey pistol. The bombs were typically fifteen-pounders, either tied to the fuselage's frame with string or balanced on the observer's lap. Benn had to remove the safety pin, throw the bomb (there were no bomb sights) and photograph the resulting explosion.

Benn frequently flew with Samson.[23] They shared a disregard for danger which could lead them into trouble, such as when they nearly sank one of the planes. Despite being warned about the strength of the wind and the height of the waves, Benn and Samson had their plane lowered onto the sea. The plane managed to get some lift, but the floats were met by the tops of the waves and burst. The machine stood on its head in the water due to the weight of the engine, but initially floated, buoyed up by the airtight wings. The aviators climbed onto the wings, still dry at this stage, to await rescue. Then the plane started to sink. A motorboat from the *Ben-my-Chree* came to the rescue. Benn managed to get a rope onto the plane's tail and it was hauled back.

Other expeditions were more successful, including bombing raids which disrupted Turkish railway supply routes by inflicting damage on stations and bridges and on one occasion resulted in Benn's machine chasing, and catching from behind, a moving train. The similar speeds of train and plane aided accurate bomb aiming. For the benefit of others caught in the same situation, Benn's advice was 'Engine drivers, when attacked by an aeroplane, stop!'[24]

At home in political circles, Benn had not been forgotten. In January 1915, the Liberal chief whip, Percy Illingworth had died – not killed by the enemy, but by a mollusc. He had eaten a bad oyster and died from food poisoning. Benn's name had been considered then as a possible replacement, as part of a pair with John Gulland. Asquith wanted Gulland to deal with the House and Benn with organisation and the country. He felt that it would work effectively, offend no-one[25] and Lloyd George approved the plan.[26] But Benn had not been tempted and Asquith had reported: 'Gulland has seen little Benn, who absolutely declines to take on the organising job. He is eaten up with martial ardours, & determined to risk everything at the front. It is a great bore, for he was far the best man for the post.'[27] Gulland took on the role of chief whip, while Benn at that stage still nominally retained his existing role as junior whip. Benn remained in this role until Asquith formed his coalition government on 25 May 1915, bringing the other parties into his government in the aftermath of the scandal over the shortage of shells. From this point Gulland became joint chief whip with the Conservative Edmund Talbot, and Benn relinquished the title.

The prolonged debate over conscription prised open the fissures within the Liberal Party. However, a majority of the Parliamentary Liberal Party did support all the military recruitment measures – the Registration Bill (5 July 1915), the Bachelors' Bill (6 January 1916) and the Conscription Bill (4 May 1916). Benn missed all of these divisions, as he was away on active service.

After Kitchener drowned in the sinking of the HMS *Hampshire* en route to Russia, Asquith carried out a ministerial reshuffle within the coalition on 6 July 1916. Lloyd George was moved from the Ministry of Munitions to succeed Kitchener as War Minister. Edwin Montagu, who took over Lloyd George's old post, wrote to Benn to ask if he would be interested in becoming his parliamentary secretary at the Ministry of Munitions. Benn declined.

In a move which further alienated him from Benn, Lloyd George ousted Asquith as prime minister on 16 December 1916, heading a new coalition with the other parties and resulting in almost a total change of Liberal personnel in the government. Two days after being commissioned to form his coalition, Lloyd George telegrammed Benn at the seaplane base: 'Will you accept the post of joint [chief] whip with Talbot ... urgently need [your] help … you can render greater [service] to war here now by serving in new government.'[28]

Benn appears to have been Lloyd George's first, and, at that stage, only, choice as the Liberal chief whip to serve alongside Talbot. Benn did not reject this offer out of hand, and even believed that a better position could come his way. His first instinct was to consult his close friend, Reginald McKenna to find out how his former colleagues were responding to the unexpected changes in the administration. On 8 December 1916, Benn wired McKenna: 'Invited chief whip ignorant you[r] position decide loyalty to you.'[29] To be sure of getting the advice he most needed, Benn also telegrammed his father the following day: 'offered chief whip consult McKenna urgent.'[30] McKenna's reply sealed Benn's decision: 'Asquith and all [his] late liberal colleagues are absent from [new] government.'[31] This was all that Benn needed to know and that day he replied to Lloyd George: 'deeply grateful but prefer remain here godspeed new government.'[32] Benn's father, clearly still considering the possibility that his son might join the government in some senior capacity, suggested that a better offer might be forthcoming.[33] But, after talking to McKenna, eventually advised Benn that there was 'nothing worth accepting'.[34]

The advice which Benn received was far from impartial, and his decision was influenced more by personal feelings than by the interests of the country, or of the Liberal Party. McKenna was one of Lloyd George's keenest critics and probably the least likely of all the former Liberal ministers to have transferred his allegiance to the new prime minister. He and Benn's father also concluded that on a purely personal level, Benn 'would not be happy as Chief Whip'.[35] On the basis of this advice (and it appears from the surviving records, this advice alone), Benn rejected the post of joint chief whip. He had been tempted by the importance of the role and the thought that 'my father and mother had lost their younger son a few months before and were naturally anxious about me'.[36]

After Benn's rejection, Neil Primrose reluctantly took on the post of joint chief whip on a temporary basis in December 1916, while he waited to return to military service. He held the post for less than three months, then Lloyd George again sought Benn's return to government. Benn again politely declined, writing back on 28 February 1917: 'My dear Prime Minister, I hope you will not be angry with me & I need not tell you how much I thank you. But when the war broke out I resigned my office because at my age & with my health it was unendurable not to be in the fighting line.'[37] Primrose headed back to the war and his untimely death and Lloyd George instead appointed Freddie Guest, as his third choice of chief whip.

This one decision, perhaps above all others, could have changed the course of Liberal Party history. Had Benn accepted the position of chief whip, he could have provided a vital link between the Asquithians and the Lloyd George Liberals, thus holding the party together. He would have provided a symbolic, as well as a practical, link between the diverging wings of the party. Both Lloyd George and Asquith had shown their confidence in his abilities. He had experience in the whips' office and he was a natural morale-raiser with zealous organisational skills. He would have prevented Freddie Guest, who became probably the single most divisive figure in the disintegration of the party, from holding the post. Benn's refusal of the post helped to give a significant long-term advantage to the Labour Party which managed to reunite in 1917, while the Liberals were to take another crucial six years.

Instead Benn remained at his seaplane posting. In January 1917 the *Ben-my-Chree* was sent to the French-occupied island of Kastellorizo – the easternmost inhabited Greek island, only one mile off the south Turkish coast. With a strong wind catching the *Ben-my-Chree's* superstructure, but with the aid of a French pilot, the ship managed to enter the island's harbour. The Greek islanders were wealthy and well-fed, the French very hospitable, so the British arrivals' first impressions were heartening. However, this was not to last. The harbour and surrounding town of 10,000 faced the Turkish shore and the *Ben-my-Chree* provided a readily-identifiable and much-prized target for a Turkish gun battery which had set up secretly on the shore opposite. The first Benn knew of the guns was when a large explosion next to the ship sent a column of water shooting into the air. The next couple of shells also missed. Benn had been resting in his cabin but rushed onto the main deck to find Samson, just as a shell hit the hangar, followed by another which set fire to the petrol store. It soon became clear that the *Ben-my-Chree* would have to be abandoned. One possible means of escape was removed when another shell caught one of the boats slung from davits on the deck. The boat disintegrated, leaving only the bow, hanging like a 'leg of mutton'.[38]

Benn was sent to the engine room to check for casualties, but miraculously none of the crew had been killed. Either swimming or by motor boat, the men reached the shore, only to be drenched by rain and further shells which hit the buildings around the harbour. One officer was missing. Benn took out a motor boat, under fire, to search for him on the *Ben-my-Chree* and in the harbour. He had in fact, as Benn found out on his return, swum safely ashore.

An invasion of the island by the Turks seemed likely and militarily feasible. As part of a plan agreed between the French governor of the island and the captain of the, now sinking, *Ben-my-Chree*, Benn was given command of a detachment charged with the defence of the town. Most of the British crew and many of the local inhabitants moved to safer ground inland.

For eleven days, during which a Turkish attack was expected, Benn had charge of a unit comprising seventeen crew from the *Ben-my-Chree* and forty-six French sailors. Benn was very proud to be given command of this sixty-four-strong international force, armed with French machine guns, rifles and bayonets. He particularly relished the fact that his orders came directly from the French governor. This was a far cry from the intermediate role he had played as a messenger in the Dardanelles. The men were housed discreetly in a tiny whitewashed church, not risking being seen by the Turkish forces opposite. Benn's French came in useful not just for orders, but also for language lessons to pass the time during daylight hours when the troops were confined to base. His life-long love of France was reaffirmed. The priorities of a highly intelligent, bi-lingual, efficiency-seeking, 39-year-old in his first command were probably rather different from those of an aspiring officer half his age with less experience of humankind. Benn prioritised the men's welfare and avoided the practice, which he so hated in his early army days, of wasting the men's energies on pointless physical tasks. All night Benn kept watch, lying on a mattress in the attic of a shed next to the church. Fears of an attack were heightened by the sight of 150 camels going to the Turkish gun emplacement, but no assault materialised. Benn gradually came to the conclusion that the Turkish aim was to prevent the use of the harbour from afar, but not to attempt a landing.

Most of the crew from the *Ben-my-Chree* had by now been evacuated by sea from the far side of the island, out of sight of the Turks. As well as

Benn's detachment, a few others including Samson, had remained to salvage the *Ben-my-Chree's* usable equipment. The salvage party also rescued the ship's mascots – a cat and a dog, which had survived the attack.[39] Anything of value which remained on board was then destroyed. The *Ben-my-Chree's* brown and blistered corpse lay in the harbour, listing to starboard, sunk in the shallow water. She remained there until 1920, when she was re-floated and towed to Piraeus. However, she was beyond economic repair and was later taken to Venice, where she was broken up in 1923.[40]

When orders eventually came through for the re-posting of the remaining British forces, Benn held a departure ceremony for his troop. He used his language skills to present a slightly different version of the ceremony to each of the nationalities – the French version having a more emotional content. The French commander-in-chief of the island bade farewell to Benn with a hug and a kiss on both cheeks – a gesture hard to imagine from an equivalent British official and one that rather embarrassed Benn. The British contingent embarked a trawler in a hidden cove, bound for Port Said, leaving behind the wreck of their mother ship.

Benn's search under fire for the missing officer and his command of the Anglo-British church defence contingent were recognised with mentions in French and British dispatches and the awards of the Croix de Guerre, Legion d'honneur and the Distinguished Service Order (DSO).

After two years abroad, Benn applied for leave. Within two hours of arriving back in London, he had been offered a new posting by Commander Murray Sueter, on the Adriatic Barrage. Sueter shared Benn's approach to his work – inventive, organised, risk-taking and careless of formal hierarchy. Benn was later to claim that 'no man could have been a better Chief than Commodore Sueter'.[41] Sueter had been involved in the design and construction of airships before the war. After the outbreak of hostilities he was instrumental in building up the Royal Naval Air Service. He was also responsible for the development and manufacture of non-rigid airships used to attack submarines. Among his other projects had been the development of torpedo-carrying aircraft and caterpillar-track driven armoured vehicles – the forerunners of tanks. Differences of opinion with Admiralty had led to this new posting to Italy in 1917, where Benn was to accompany him. Later Sueter again fell out with his service masters after writing directly to the King. From January 1918 to early 1920 he was given no assignments, but was promoted to rear-admiral and retired.[42] Sueter, however, did not share Benn's political outlook. In 1921 he was elected to Parliament with the backing of Horatio Bottomley's Independent Parliamentary Group and the right-wing, Rothermere-funded, Anti-Waste League. He later became a Conservative MP, but remained a friend of Benn's.

Before taking up the new post, Benn made a tour of English airfields and plane factories and determined that he should obtain his wings. He managed to get himself posted to Calshot Air Station on the edge of Southampton Water opposite the Isle of Wight. He flew his first solo flight on 28 April 1917 and on 25 May 1917 he achieved enough flying hours (thirty-one hours five minutes dual and twenty hours solo) to be awarded his flying certificate on a Short seaplane. However, this was at the cost of five aircraft damaged or destroyed. Benn unashamedly commented that he fell into the class technically known as 'the World's Worst Crashers'.[43] His attitude to personal danger remained indifferent. During his time at Calshot, Benn developed a passion for larger aircraft. He was particularly smitten with the Curtiss H12 seaplane, dubbed the 'America'. The names alone give an idea of the difference in scale between the 'America' and the Sopwith 'Baby'.

Benn sailed for Taranto in southern Italy in August 1917 – just over two years after Italy had entered the war, on the Allies' side. The Adriatic Barrage was intended to create an obstruction to enemy Austrian submarines between the heel of Italy and the coast of Albania across the Adriatic Sea at its narrowest point. The Austro-Hungarian Empire extended down to the east coast of the Adriatic and had a submarine base at Kotor, in modern-day Montenegro. The aim was to kettle the submarines in the Adriatic to prevent their travelling south into the Mediterranean. The physical manifestation of the barrage comprised drifters, nets and seaplanes, but the scheme was under-resourced and never became fully effective. Benn's work on the Adriatic Barrage was interrupted by illness. This time he had malaria and was sent to Rome to recover. Initially his illness worsened and Benn was sent on to a hospital run by Blue Nuns, before eventually returning to his unit.

The tide of war meant that Benn did not remain with the Adriatic Barrage, but was instead posted as an observer and intelligence officer near the north-eastern border of Italy with Austria-Hungary, where the Italians had suffered a major defeat in the Battle of Caporetto (Kobarid) between 24 October and 19 November 1917 (in modern day Slovenia).[44] However, the speed of the combined Austro-Hungarian and German advance had stretched their supply lines to breaking point. French and British forces, including air power, were sent to reinforce the Italians and the Central Powers' advance was halted. Winter froze the frontlines. At Benn's camp, heating fuel was in short supply, so night-time lorry excursions were organised to the nearby abandoned, shell-ravaged, town of Nervesa. Here, window frames, doors and furniture, regardless of ownership or antiquity, were collected to be sacrificed in the stove at the airbase.

As an observer, Benn was involved in sorties behind enemy lines to photograph and count vehicle, train and troop movements and encampments. When the planes were met with enemy fire, the pilots had to twist and turn or rapidly lose height by stalling. Despite the gyrations to avoid ground fire and interventions from enemy fighter planes, Benn had to remain focused on his primary role with his camera. His plane was often hit, but never disabled in the air; the first task on landing was always to inspect the damage.

Concentration was undermined by the enemy, not just while in the air, but at night. Benn, along with his colleagues, lost many hours' sleep due to night-time air raids on the aerodrome where his unit was based. Some nights there were as many as three raids and the Italians' hangars were burnt down. Some of the bombs remained unexploded, including two 300-pounders, four feet high, which remained embedded in the airfield, marked only by white flags to warn off approaching pilots.

Benn took part in retaliatory day and night bombing sorties on Austrian bases at captured former-Italian airfields. On one of these raids, Benn was observer in the leader of twelve bombers, which should have been accompanied by fifteen fighter escorts. He was disconcerted to find that by the time that his plane had crossed the enemy front line, only half the bombers and none of the fighters remained. Having got this far, Benn decided that they should press on, even though they were now unprotected and the Austrians on the ground were alerting their forces along the line in the direction in which the bombers were flying. Having to fly over half a dozen enemy airfields to reach their target, the bombers also attracted three fighters who, although bothering them like wasps, failed to down any of the bombers. Amazingly, the six bombers all returned safely to base. The only damage to Benn's plane was from spent cartridges which had dropped into the fuselage.

Although locked in mortal combat, (in six months the fifty-four scouts from Benn's operation brought down almost 300 enemy)[45], the air units on both sides had a healthy respect for each other and maintained direct contact. When Austrian aviators were captured or known to be have been killed behind the Italian front line, a respectful and detailed account of their incarceration or demise was delivered by letter, dropped at an Austrian airbase. The Austrians reciprocated and even enclosed photographs of graves and funeral ceremonies, which they had held with military honours for downed allied aviators. In one unfortunate incident, the pilot of an Austrian plane bearing news of lost allied airmen was shot and killed at the controls of his plane – as Benn commented, this was 'the cruel romance of conflict'. Benn maintained a detached view of death and recorded that for him 'the war was chiefly a back-ground'. Benn felt strongly that opponents should be respected rather than vilified and this was a sentiment which he carried into his political life, especially when some of his comrades-in-arms later became his political opponents.

On 1 April 1918 the Royal Air Force came into being as an amalgamation of the Royal Naval Air Service, in which Benn was serving, and the army's Royal Flying Corps, creating the world's first air force to be independent of army or navy control. Benn was involved in the co-ordination of the two wings in Italy, which he claimed gave him an opportunity to bustle about and generally make himself 'important'. Sueter understood that Benn 'was grown-up' and they agreed that a certain amount of 'liaison' could provide Benn with an excuse for 'a perfect tour of many Italian cities'. Benn enjoyed these trips more than any other aspect of his war service. He joined the officers' club in Taranto and particularly savoured his time in Ancona, which he considered 'one of the most romantic cities of Italy'.[46] Whether it was the architecture, the people generally, or perhaps a particular person, who led him to feel this, he left no record.

A complete contrast to the noise and speed of the planes was balloon flight, something which Benn also had the opportunity to experience in northern Italy. Excited by this new sensation, he was trussed up in a rope parachute harness and launched skywards to 3,000 feet in the balloon's basket with one colleague for a four-hour watch. The balloon was in telephone contact with a gun battery which they were directing on the ground and with the neighbouring balloon three miles down the line. Benn was struck by the way sounds from the ground carried – a dog barking or a cycle horn, but mainly the silence. So relaxing did he find the experience that he dozed off at one point. When the operation was complete, the balloon was hauled down to 100 feet, attached to a lorry and towed at that altitude to the balloon sheds, where a soft clean landing had been prepared. Within three minutes of its return, the crew and the telephone were out and the balloon was walked to bed in its hangar.

In the summer of 1918 another experience arose, which was new, not just to Benn but to aviation, in the form of his participation in the first attempt at dropping a parachutist from a plane behind enemy lines. Benn was seconded to the Italian army for the assignment. The aim of the mission was to drop an Italian agent, Lieutenant Alessandro Tandura, on a moonless night back near his home town near Vittorio, which was now in Austrian-occupied territory. He was then to gather intelligence on enemy troop dispositions and to get in touch with escaped Italian prisoners. The results of his harvest were to be relayed by signal and by pigeon to Italian headquarters. A box of pigeons for the purpose was included in the luggage.

This was to be Tandura's first flight and, as if the whole operation was not risky enough, screwed to the floor of the plane between Benn and the pilot was a quantity of explosive, large enough to destroy the plane if it were forced to land in enemy territory. For good measure they also took a couple of bombs, to be dropped as a distraction from the true purpose of the flight. Despite the minute planning of the whole operation, an errant cow nearly disrupted their plans on take-off. Benn likened the nighttime navigation to Columbus's voyage – passing from a country he could see, to one he merely believed in. Benn had wireless contact with navigation lights on the ground (via 200 feet of dangling aerial), but otherwise could see nothing; the Earth disappeared to be replaced by an 'excellent loneliness'.[47] A quick-release harness had been invented for rapid divestment before the parachute could be caught by a gust of wind after landing. But the more complicated issue was the departure from the aircraft. This required a means of storage for the parachute during the flight, which would leave no risk of its becoming entangled in the plane on departure and also some form of exit door for the parachutist. The solution to the first was a metal parachute housing, which could be lowered during the flight to hang below the lowest part of the plane. The solution to the second was a hole in the floor. The agent was to be seated above the void, which had two hinged flaps, opening in the middle. Benn, as observer, was charged with pulling a rope to release bolts on the flaps, at what he calculated to be the right moment to launch the agent into the 'future'.[48] When the launch was done, and for weeks afterwards, Benn had no idea whether the agent had enjoyed any future at all. In fact, Tandura landed, alive, feet in the air on a grape vine in the pouring rain. He had to swim a river and was forced to shed his knapsack in order to cope with the current. He was sheltered and hidden for weeks by his countryfolk, but then arrested by the Austrians. He escaped by climbing over the wall of his prison, under fire. Back in operation, he received further deliveries of pigeons and money, but one consignment was found and held to ransom by a local. He was then re-arrested, but re-escaped. He survived the last weeks of the war and was awarded the highest Italian award for bravery – the Gold Medal for Valour. Benn, too, was rewarded, receiving the Italian bronze medal for valour and the British Distinguished Flying Cross. He also had a baby named after him – Wedgwood Benn Tandura.

Many gallantry awards, but few promotions, had come Benn's way. His brother, Oliver, had reached the rank of captain before his death in June 1915: Benn had reached the same rank by the end of the war. This placed him on a level with Anthony Eden, and a rank below Clement Attlee. Benn had twice been mentioned in despatches, appointed to the DSO, awarded the DFC, made a chevalier of the Légion d'honneur, received the Croix de Guerre, the Italian war cross and the Italian bronze medal for valour. Benn also became a published author, when his brief and engaging but modest account of his wartime activities appeared in print as *In the Sideshows*. Benn's First World War service spanned a greater variety than most. His time in the Dardanelles was equally horrific to service in the trenches on the Western Front, but once this was over, although not out of danger, he had the opportunity to travel, to learn to fly and to apply his inventive mind to the technology of warfare. He certainly proved that he was adaptable and brave – almost to the point of recklessness, but he also decided that a military life in peacetime would not be for him. He used a surprising set of adjectives to describe his last year of the war: 'romantic, happy and buoyant'. He escaped the war without serious physical injury (the un-saddling onto the barbed wire fence did more damage than the shells and bullets of the Dardanelles or the half dozen plane crashes), but he carried a legacy of intermittent ill-health from the malaria for the rest of his life.

It was ironic that the Dreadnought battleships which had been the main focus of the arms build-up during Benn's time at the Admiralty, played little part in the war, with the indecisive Battle of Jutland in 1916 being the only major naval encounter of the whole conflict. It was also ironic that Benn had joined a cavalry regiment, which then exported their horses all the way to Egypt, only to leave them there before they went into battle. The home-made aircraft carriers and parachute systems ended up playing as great a role as the Dreadnoughts and the horses.

Military success had done nothing to heal the rift in the Liberal Party, split between Asquith's supporters and Lloyd George's Liberals who intended to fight the next election in alliance with their Conservative coalition partners. However, the Labour Party had regrouped at the end of 1917 around a statement on war aims and peace policy. The new Labour policy bridged the gap between the trades unions and former leader, Ramsay MacDonald, whose successor, Arthur Henderson, had served as Labour's first cabinet minister from 1915 to 1917, but was now outside the government. He put his organisational skills into building up the Labour Party in the constituencies. This was to give the Labour Party a critical advantage at the next election.

For Benn, the war ended prematurely. He was on leave when the armistice was signed. He had taken his accrued leave and returned to England to deal with 'a whole pack of trouble', particularly the urgent need to find a seat in time for the imminent general election. His constituency of Tower Hamlets, St. George was to disappear. Smaller constituencies were to be amalgamated and boundaries redrawn in an attempt to equalise the electorate between seats. At the last election, in December 1910, Tower Hamlets, St. George had the fourth smallest electorate of any constituency in the country – just 3,133 voters.[49] At the other end of the scale, Romford had 53,002 – nearly seventeen times as many. The discrepancies were so huge that the case for reorganisation was unanswerable. The redistribution was to be brought in with the Representation of the People Act of 1918, which enfranchised almost all men over 21 and women over 30. The previous reform in 1884 had only enfranchised sixty per cent of male householders and no women.

Benn's seat was to be amalgamated with the neighbouring constituency of Tower Hamlets, Whitechapel, which had an electorate of just over 4,000 at the last election. This seat was also held by an Asquithian Liberal, James Kiley. He had been elected unopposed on 28 December 1916, under the wartime electoral truce. Kiley was a local councillor and a director of a Houndsditch warehousing company. This was his first term in Parliament, but he had been active in the constituency and in the House of Commons.

The new combined seat was to be known as Stepney, Whitechapel and St.George's. With the amalgamation of the constituencies, the enfranchisement of more men and some women and the movements of population, the new seat was to have an electorate of over 23,000. Benn's war service was turning out to be more of an impediment than an asset. He had inevitably neglected his constituency work and would be unknown to many of the electors in the combined constituency. He was faced with an uncomfortable set of options and time was very short. Parliament was dissolved on 28 November 1918, just seventeen days after the end of the war, with polling day set for Saturday 14 December.

The most promising avenue for Benn was to compete for the Asquithian Liberal nomination for the combined seat, but this would have to involve persuading the new combined constituency Liberal organisation to drop Kiley in favour of Benn. Kiley had been active and was popular in his constituency; and it included the larger portion of the combined electorate. Benn attempted to win the nomination, but things did not go according to plan. Benn, acknowledging that he was not an 'impartial judge in this matter', admitted that there was 'a great deal to be said for Mr Kiley [but] on the other hand you won't be surprised to know that I felt strongly that there was a great deal to be said for me'. Both were Free Trading Liberals, opposed to the idea of a peacetime coalition. Benn called a meeting of the committee members of the two seats at the town hall in Cable Street, hoping to settle the Liberal candidacy for the merged seat. Kiley had assured Benn that he did not intend to put his name forward as a candidate, if Benn wished to stand. In the event, Kiley's name was not put forward, but Benn's name was nonetheless rejected. He was shocked and forty years later reflected: 'I could not believe then, and I can't understand now, what happened. My feelings were extremely strong.' It was 'sheer agony'. He walked back from the meeting with Ernest to their office in Finsbury Square and 'had a shake-down on the floor'.[50] But, Benn was not prepared to give up. He no longer had a base in the constituency, as Gladstone House had been given up during the war, so he managed to negotiate accommodation at Toynbee Hall, where one of his abiding memories was the sight of William Beveridge with his coat off trying to teach a group of dockers how to do Elizabethan dancing. The lesson seemed to be making some progress – until the pubs opened. From this new political base, Benn sent a post card to every elector in Whitechapel and received an encouraging response. However, he also received a letter from Kiley to say that after the meeting he had been invited by a deputation from the Asquithian constituency association to submit his name for the still-vacant Liberal candidacy. All that Kiley offered as a concession to Benn was that if he chose to fight on, which Kiley thought he might, he would endeavour to keep personalities out of the contest.

The election was to be a coupon election. In each constituency one candidate, either a Conservative or a Liberal who supported the coalition, was to be offered the coupon – a letter of support and recommendation jointly from Lloyd George and Bonar Law. Many electors regarded the coupon as an endorsement of the candidate's patriotism. In general, a couponed candidate could expect to garner almost all of the Conservative vote and a proportion of the Liberal support in the constituency. Benn was reluctant even to consider seeking the coalition coupon, but he explored the possibility and its implications. It would have meant that he would not have faced an official Conservative opponent, but he would have ended up in a contest with Kiley and potentially a Labour candidate too. In such circumstances Benn would probably have been able to gather the majority of the Conservative voters and perhaps around half of the Liberal voters. In December 1910 the Conservatives had attracted over forty per cent of the vote in both seats, so on paper, the seat was winnable by a Coalition Liberal candidate. The problem for Benn was not the potential result, nor the chances of being offered the coupon, but the unpalatability of accepting the coupon and of standing against Kiley, his former parliamentary colleague.

Benn had missed the divisive Maurice Debate in May 1918, generally regarded as crystallising the division within the Liberal Party between the supporters of Asquith and those of Lloyd George. The debate on General Maurice's allegations about the inaccuracy of Lloyd George's figures on military strength was essentially futile – with varying definitions, constantly changing troop deployments, and no real means of establishing the truth. However, it was the first time that Asquith had led his faction in a division in opposition to Lloyd George. There was no doubt in anyone's mind that Benn's allegiance was to Asquith but, by his absence on military service, he had avoided the taint from the Maurice Debate. Benn had tried to be tactful in declining Lloyd George's job offers, but his refusals had generated no goodwill from Lloyd George's camp. Benn went to see his 'old friend' Freddie Guest, the Coalition Liberal chief whip who had given him the wayward pony. Guest was the key figure in drawing up the list of Liberals who would be put forward for the coupon, with the agreement of the Conservatives. Benn's name was not on Guest's list of coalition supporters, but nor was he beyond the pale as he had missed the Maurice Debate. (Only four Liberal MPs who had voted with Asquith in the debate were given the coupon.) Benn's name had been included in a list of forty-four 'Unknowns'.[51] Although their personal relationship was still cordial, Benn came away troubled after the interview with Guest. To Benn, who hated the idea of coalitions and couponed elections, the whole thing 'just stuck in [his] gizzard'.[52] He made it clear that he could not bring himself to support what he felt would be a 'nominated Parliament'. As a result, Benn's relationship with Guest and Lloyd George inevitably became a step more distant. The coalition whips went ahead and selected a couponed Conservative candidate for the merged seat, George Cohen, who was fighting his first election.

This left the possibility of Benn's standing as an independent candidate against the couponed Conservative and against Kiley, but it was not a promising option. Benn would have appeared as a party outcast. He claimed to have been sure that he would have won. But, in reality, the Liberal vote (just under sixty per cent at the last election) would have been split and the

Conservative vote would mainly have gone to the couponed candidate, who would likely have emerged the winner.

Benn's political courage was now put to the test. He agonised over his situation, 'thinking of nothing else day and night'. Invited to a lunch party by Reginald McKenna, Benn cornered some of his parliamentary colleagues and poured out his troubles. It was Augustine Birrell who provided the most compelling advice, to 'Do the High Sublime'. Birrell had resigned the post of Chief Secretary for Ireland in 1916 in the wake of the Easter Rising, he had nursed his terminally ill wife and had decided not to contest the 1918 election. He therefore knew the relief of escape from torment and was an example of someone who had emerged from some dark places with his dignity and sanity intact. After another couple of days of turmoil, Benn took Birrell's advice, writing to Kiley to 'hand over ... if you will take them as a gift, my organization, my committee rooms, my canvas cards, and ... the services of my agent'. With the election two weeks away, Captain Benn was convinced that politically he was 'sunk'.[53]

Chapter Four

From Leith to Obscurity 1918–27

Relinquishing his claim to the candidacy of the new constituency at Stepney, Whitechapel and St.George's was 'a bit of a gulp' for Benn, but he realised that it 'did impart tone to what was becoming a nasty little quarrel'. Once he was free of agonising over his old seat, Benn was able to focus on the future. He went to the Asquithian Liberal headquarters and a week later heard that the Leith constituency was looking for a candidate.

Benn headed north from London's port to Edinburgh's. Leith was usually a safe Liberal seat and under the 1918 reorganisation the constituency was to be shorn of the more Conservative-voting towns of Musselburgh and Portobello. Leith had been represented by a Liberal MP since 1832, apart from two exceptions under unusual circumstances. In June 1886 the sitting Liberal MP, William Jacks, had voted against the second reading of the Irish Home Rule Bill, even though he was in favour of home rule for Scotland.[1] When the general election was called for the following month, Liberal Leader William Gladstone stood in Leith as well as in his existing seat of Midlothian, in order to prevent Jacks' being re-elected.[2] The ploy worked; Jacks stood down. Gladstone was elected for both seats, but he relinquished Leith to a by-election in August, which was won by Gladstone's supporter, Ronald Munro Ferguson, who held the seat until his appointment as Governor-General of Australia in 1914.[3] A by-election was called for 26 February 1914, which was won by the Conservative, George Currie, by a margin of just sixteen votes. Currie was to be Benn's opponent in the 1918 election, standing as a Coalition Conservative. Also in the field was a Labour candidate.

Although geographically more restricted in 1918, the Leith electorate grew, primarily due to the Representation of the People Act of 1918. The numbers increased from under 18,000 to over 42,000 – more than thirteen times Benn's former electorate at Tower Hamlets, St. George. This, plus the shortage of time, inevitably had an effect on canvassing and individual contact with voters.

Leith was a major centre of the drinks trade, including many bonded warehouses and liquor shops. As the trade was traditionally allied to the Conservative Party, this made Benn's task rather difficult, not just as a Liberal, but as a teetotal English Liberal of the 'neither touch, taste-nor-handle' variety, as he described himself. The best accommodation that he could manage with the trade was a respectful disagreement.

Across the country as a whole the electorate nearly tripled. However, due to the Spanish flu epidemic and the impact of war injuries and disruption, the turnout fell from 81.1 per cent in December 1910 to only 58.9 per cent in 1918 – lower even than the nadir of the 2001 election. Even so, the number of people who actually voted just over doubled. Far from creating battles between Lloyd George and Asquithian Liberals, many seats had no Liberal candidate at all. In total only 411 Liberal candidates stood throughout the 707 constituencies and there were just thirteen seats where a Lloyd George coalition Liberal was pitted against an Asquithian.[4]

The success rates for the two factions of the Liberals diverged significantly. Lloyd George's supporters, sheltered from Conservative opposition by the coupon, managed to return 133 of their 158 candidates (eighty-four per cent), while only twenty-eight Asquithians were successful, from a field of 253 candidates (eleven per cent). However, Benn won Leith by a comfortable margin.

1918 general election Leith:

W.W. Benn	Liberal	10,338
G.W. Currie	Coalition Con	7,613
S. Burgess	Labour	4,251
	Liberal majority	2,725 (12.3 per cent)

Kiley, with the benefit of Benn's file cards and local intelligence, won in Stepney, Whitechapel and St.George's.[5] However, Asquith lost his seat at East Fife. For a party leader to lose his seat was remarkable, but not unprecedented. Conservative leader, Balfour, had suffered the same fate in

1906 and the Liberals were to lose successive leaders, Samuel in 1935 and Sinclair in 1945.

Lloyd George returned as prime minister, in coalition with the Conservatives. But, as his 133-strong Liberal faction was far outnumbered by his 335 Conservative colleagues, his position was precarious. The Labour Party advanced from forty-two seats in 1910 to sixty-three in 1918, although both Henderson and MacDonald lost their seats. William Adamson now led the Labour Party, which significantly outnumbered the Asquithian Liberals on the Commons opposition benches.

The issue of the interim leadership of the surviving twenty-eight Asquithian Liberal MPs needed to be settled. Asquith seemed convinced, as did most other party members, that he would soon return. A portrait of Asquith painted around this time and now hanging in the Reform Club shows him holding a book with his finger marking a place near the middle, as though conveying the message that his story still had a long way to run. Benn was now one of the most senior Asquithian Liberals in the Commons. Only four others had first sat in Parliament before he had arrived in 1906. One of these, Thomas Bramsdon, had only served a six month term in 1900, prior to his re-election in 1906 and he was out of Parliament again from January 1910 to 1918. (The others were George Lambert, John Wilson and John Macdonald). Benn visited Asquith at Sutton Courtenay to be sounded out about taking on the interim leadership, but in the end the role passed to Sir Donald Maclean.[6]

Benn described the parliamentary activities in the aftermath of the 1918 election as a state of 'continuous warfare'.[7] However, he thrived in guerrilla politics. Hostilities escalated when Asquith returned to Parliament fourteen months later at the Paisley by-election on 12 February 1920. Asquith had a majority of 2,834 over the second-placed Labour candidate, with the Coalition Conservative candidate coming in third and last and losing his deposit. The by-election had been caused by the death of the Asquithian Liberal MP, John McCallum, who had held the seat in 1918 with a majority of just 106. The euphoria over Asquith's return was therefore tempered by the fact that his followers' numerical strength was only restored to its former level and that the seat was by no means a safe Liberal seat. However, the by-election result was a personal fillip for Benn, as his beloved leader had returned, and it was a significant morale boost for the Asquithians, at the expense of the Coalition.

The overall pattern of changes in party strength during the 1918 parliament was of recovery for the Labour Party and the Asquithian Liberals, to the detriment of the coalition parties. During the parliament Labour increased their representation from sixty-three to seventy-six MPs, while the Asquithians recovered from twenty-eight to thirty-five seats.[8] Asquith's return followed less than two months after the Coalition had lost the Spen Valley by-election to Labour, where the Asquithain Liberal candidate, John Simon had come a close second. Earlier in the previous year Joseph Kenworthy had been elected as the Asquithian Liberal MP for Hull Central at a by-election caused by the death from Spanish flu of the sitting Coalition Conservative member.

The Coalition Liberals' poor showing in post-war by-elections added urgency and impetus to attempts at fusion between the Lloyd George Liberals and the Conservatives. The Conservatives reluctantly supported Lloyd George's merger proposals, but by 18 March 1920 the scheme was killed off by the Liberal coalitionists, many of whom wanted to keep open the possibility of reunion with the Asquthians. Among the coalition ministers, Mond, Montagu and Fisher opposed the plan. Back-bench feeling was even more strongly against fusion, and Lloyd George was forced to abandon it.

The collapse of the fusion project meant that the Lloyd George Liberals were distanced from their Conservative coalition colleagues. To make their positions more isolated still, several of them then deliberately undermined their tenuous relationship with the Asquithians. Feeling that they were in the ascendancy after Asquith's victory, his supporters had organised a conference in Leamington Spa in May 1920. One of their resolutions welcomed 'Asquith's return to the House of Commons and reaffirm[ed] its unabated confidence in him as Leader of the Liberal Party.' A group of senior Coalition Liberals, including Addison, Hewart, Macnamara, Kellaway, Edge and Ward, took the train to Leamington and sparked a row with the Asquithians at their conference. Amid scenes of chaos, the Asquithians shouted down the coalitionists. Addison was heard to denounce the 'sentence of excommunication' which had been passed on the coalitionists, before his group left, fired up with emotion. Their provocative interruption had only served to damage the dwindling prospects for their party's reunification.

The collapse of the post-war boom and the forced curtailment of many of the coalition's most liberal policies, such as house-building, caused a steep decline in the popularity of the coalition government and the prestige of its senior Liberal ministers. Benn's opinion of Lloyd George was commensurately deteriorating, exacerbated by Lloyd George's accumulation of his fund from the sale of honours and his handling of the situation in Ireland, with the ruthless deployment of the Black and Tans in the Irish War of Independence. Benn moved an amendment to the King's Speech in 1921, condemning the Lloyd George coalition for having 'handed over to the military authorities an unrestricted discretion in the definition and punishment of offences, and frustrated the prospects of an agreed settlement of the problem of Irish self-government.[9]

Lloyd George may well have behaved immorally and implemented policies which Benn disliked, but he had not personally ill-treated Benn. Although Benn had plenty of political reasons for disagreeing with Lloyd George, for him the rift was starting to become personal. Benn looked forward to the demise of the coalition and the end of Lloyd George's premiership, gloating that there were 'plenty of heroes getting ready to dance on his corpse'.[10] Freddie Guest wrote to Lloyd George pointing out the 'that the Independent Liberals (inspired by Hogge and Benn) would not accept any terms of reunion'.[11]

Having been absent from Parliament for almost the entire war, Benn was extremely active in the Commons once the war was over, speaking or asking written questions on around 300 different occasions in each of the first two years. Among many others, one of his specialist subjects was, not unnaturally, aviation. Before the First World War flying had been a recreation. The war had accelerated technological development and had demonstrated that planes could be effective weapons. After the war they started to become instruments of Empire administration, foreign policy and commercial opportunity. When the war ended Britain had the world's largest air force with 103 airships, 22,647 planes, 26,000 trained pilots and 700 aerodromes.[12] Cachet, commercial opportunity and adventurism spurred many of the demobbed aviators to use their skills in opening up a whole new industry of civil aviation. Benn was enthusiastic about opportunities and relatively cavalier about the risks. In February 1919 he spoke in the Air Navigation Bill debate, in which 'baby of the House' and new Conservative MP, Oswald Mosley, made his maiden speech. Benn argued that there was 'a danger that unimaginative officials will not give either the encouragement or the scope to the private adventurer. [It] must be remembered that the danger primarily is to the pilot and passenger in the machine rather than to the public, and we might suppose that alone would be a sufficient guarantee that no excessively dangerous experiments would be made.'[13] Benn was particularly keen on the development of airships. Glossing over the potential dangers, he set out his reasons for being so enthusiastic about their commercial possibilities: 'Everybody knows that the airship possesses certain great advantages over the aeroplane. It possesses much greater endurance and a much greater lifting power. It can stop easily, alter its speed, and all these qualities give it very great advantages. It can be navigated in bad weather, and can grope its way to its moorings, while under similar conditions the aeroplane is in constant danger. For these reasons the airship has got a very great commercial future.'[14] Among the businesses which were keen to exploit the potential was Boulton and Paul, the company which had built the kit for the 'ancestral home' at Stansgate. The company went on to build the structure of the R101 airship.

Benn later claimed, perhaps surprisingly in view of the intra-party hostility, that the 1918 to 1922 parliament was 'the happiest in which I ever served'.[15] But, he was in a cheerful frame of mind, largely because he was on the verge of finally being married – to Margaret Eadie Holmes, daughter of his former parliamentary colleague, Daniel Turner Holmes, Liberal MP from 1911 to 1918. However their overlapping service in the Commons had ended when Holmes was decisively beaten in the 1918 election, defending his seat at Glasgow Govan as an Asquithian Liberal. He had come third and last with only 1,678 votes, compared to the Labour victor's 9,577.

Like Benn, Holmes had a first class degree from London University. He was a cultured man of letters – a wit, a poet and a writer, who had worked as a schoolmaster. His intelligence was counterbalanced by a total lack of practicality: 'What a brain, and he can hardly tie his own shoelaces!', commented his brother. He was unable to shut a window without jamming it, according to his daughter.[16] His love of books did not extend to their physical care: If he went for a walk, he would tear a chapter out of a book to take with him. While some of his senses were finely developed, his ear for music was so limited that he only recognised the national anthem when everybody stood up. To him any sound, including music, was just noise and he would put up with no noise when he was writing.

Holmes was a Conservative who had converted to Liberalism, but who was eventually to drift back in that direction.[17] He was an opponent of women's suffrage, but married to a feminist and with a feminist daughter. Holmes was given one final chance to return to Parliament, standing for the Asquithian Liberals in a by-election at Edinburgh South in April 1920, less than two months after Asquith's victory at Paisley. The by-election was one of those occasioned by the appointment of the sitting Coalition Conservative MP to a ministerial post, in this case Solicitor-General for Scotland. Holmes managed to reduce the incumbent's majority from 9,908 at the 1918 election, to 2,999. This was to be the last parliamentary contest for Holmes and after the by-election defeat, the Holmes family moved to the Sussex coast to live in an architect-designed house at Seaford.

Margaret's mother was the daughter of Peter Eadie, who was Provost of Paisley and the founder of Eadie Brothers, which manufactured equipment for the textile industry. 'She was a woman of great beauty, charm and vitality, but she had an unstable character and was quite unpredictable.' Her general unease with the world could not have been helped by the fact that, after her mother's death, her father married a young women whom he had met on holiday in Damascus. She was young to the extent that she was born in the same month of the same year as her new step-daughter. The two women took an instant dislike to each other, which only deepened with time.[18] As a result of this marriage, Margaret ended up with an uncle and aunt who were younger than herself.

Margaret knew that her parents had wanted a daughter – her mother because she was an ardent feminist who wanted support for her cause, and her father because he was an ardent anti-feminist who wanted his home to be made comfortable for him. He would have liked twelve daughters. In this he was to be somewhat disappointed. They had two – Margaret and her younger sister, Hermione. Like Benn, Margaret had spent part of her childhood in

Paris and had learned French, but she only started school at the age of seven, when the family was back in Scotland. Having been unhappy and behind at school, Margaret was then taught at home for a while by a governess. Her education was further disrupted by the family's move to London after her father's election to Parliament in 1911. Margaret had started at St. Columba's School at Kilmalcolm in Renfrewshire, Scotland, but moved to St. Mary's, Lancaster Gate in London, which she then left because she disagreed with the school's high church headmistress.[19] Margaret showed some of the same spirited awkwardness as Benn with regard to schooling. Her mother had warned Margaret when she was about to change schools: 'when you know you are not coming back ... you must not go about the school talking about it and looking pleased'.[20] But, Margaret was pleased. She attended one more school in Holland Park, before abandoning her schooling in 1915, but her zest for learning was nowhere near satisfied. However, her parents refused her the opportunity to study for a diploma in theology at St. Hugh's College, Oxford. Instead, she had had to settle for a secretarial course. Margaret's relationship with her parents, particularly her mother, rarely ran smoothly and she was keen to escape from their constricting and inconsistent influence.

Benn's marriage to Margaret was a successful and enduring partnership. They had some lively arguments at the beginning, but they had the essential ingredients for a happy marriage, although one founded initially more on comradeship and intellectual spark than on romantic love. 'It almost felt like one of those "sensible" arranged marriages of long ago', Margaret later wrote, 'It cannot be said that we were in love, but we were strongly mutually attracted to each other and we felt sure that we could fall in love and be happy together.'[21] Where their heads led them initially, their hearts did follow. To Benn, his marriage was 'the most important thing of all that ever happened to me in my life'. 'Home for me has meant everything which is represented by such words as love, comradeship, fortress, refuge.'[22]

Whilst Benn's sentiments may have been clear to him, his recollection of his first meeting with Margaret was remarkably vague. The typed version of his draft autobiography says 'In 1912 ... on the occasion of the great reception at the Foreign Office, I first met my wife, a young girl, in her early teens, with flaxen pigtails'. However, he later (perhaps, after consulting Margaret) corrected the account to read 'Just before the war … my colleague John Gulland got married. I was best man … the wedding reception took place at Lord Inverforth's house on Hampstead Heath. There I first met my future wife, a young girl, with flaxen pigtails in her early teens.'[23] Margaret's youth and pigtails were clearly seared into Benn's memory, even if the location and the event were not. John Gulland was married in December 1912, so the year of their first meeting seems fairly certain.[24] Margaret had her fifteenth birthday that year, and Benn his thirty-fifth. They were not to meet again until after the war, on the occasion of Asquith's by-election campaign in Paisley in early 1920. Shortly afterwards, Benn wrote to Holmes to invite himself to tea at their new house while he was on a cycling tour with his nephew. Holmes, assuming that he was to be the centre of attraction for the visit, suggested that his daughter keep out of the way. But, Margaret had other ideas, as did Benn. After tea, Benn invited Margaret and Hermione, to accompany him and his nephew on the last leg of their journey for that day to Alfriston. Once they arrived, Benn chivalrously decided that he should accompany the young women back to Seaford, before finally returning to Alfriston for the night.

Their accounts of their courtship and proposal have an endearing ring of adolescent naivety about them, despite the fact that Benn was a war veteran and an MP of fourteen years' standing and Margaret had lived on her own and travelled to her work as a temporary civil servant in the Ministry of Labour through wartime *Zeppelin* raids. Benn proposed to Margaret the first time they went out alone together. They went to the theatre and during the play, *The Grain of Mustard Seed*, Benn took hold of Margaret's hand. The culinary theme of the evening continued in Benn's unorthodox proposal to Margaret, which she said consisted of being told: 'We could live round the corner and you could have a chop at the House every night.' His suggestion and her reply illustrate how little they really knew each other at that stage. Margaret did not actually like chops. Her reply was: 'What shall I call you – Captain Benn?' Having established that Benn wanted Margaret to call him William and that she did not like chops, the rest of the arrangement seemed to fall smoothly into place. Benn was so happy that he dropped a half-crown into the pocket of a man sitting on a bench in the street, although the pocket had a hole in it and the coin clattered to the pavement. Their engagement was to last eight weeks, their marriage forty years to the day.

The slightly haphazard progress of the romance continued. Benn stuck to the traditions of his Victorian upbringing and decided that he should seek the consent of his intended's parents. Holmes lodged at the National Liberal Club during the week, as did Benn. So, Benn pushed a note under Holmes's door one night, asking to see him in the morning. Benn lurked in the corridor the following day until Holmes appeared. He nervously made his request, to which Holmes's only reply was, 'She's a good girl and now I must catch a train to Brighton.' Benn was keen to share his good news, recalling, 'I remember now with a certain feeling of shame ... I sent out Ronco'd letters to a number of my close friends saying that I was going to be married but omitted to say who I was going to marry.' In view of both his own and his fiancée's feminist instincts, Benn went to see the Bishop of London to ask if he would omit the word 'obey' from their wedding ceremony, but he failed to get the service changed. Margaret's mother's reaction to the announcement of the engagement was, 'Oh, dear, I wish you wouldn't get married. I'll have to be polite to Sir John and Lady Benn.'

On 17 November 1920, Margaret sent her husband-to-be a note in the form of a three-line whip, 'Wake up, Captain Benn. It's your wedding day!'[25] The service took place at St. Margaret's Church, Westminster, the Anglican parish church for the House of Commons – appropriate in name, if not in denomination. Benn was a Congregationalist, but not very devout. Margaret was on a journey of religious discovery, with a destination still unknown, which had already taken her from her parents' agnostic humanism, to a period when she had considered becoming a nun.

Whilst McKenna's pre-war attempt at match-making for Benn had failed, in the end Benn was to follow McKenna's example in marrying in his mid-forties a woman twenty years his junior. The McKennas loaned the Benns their car, chauffeur and butler for their wedding day.

McKenna and Asquith signed the marriage certificate. The wedding was certainly not a private family affair; there were large crowds and mounted police outside. It was certainly not a wedding dominated by the bride's mother's aspiration for her daughter's big day; Margaret's mother hated big occasions and disapproved of the marriage. She wandered off instead of attending the wedding. It was, as Benn later admitted, a political event, and an Asquithian Liberal event at that. 'I suppose that in my imagination

I had seen this as representing a bringing together of all the Parties, of course, against Lloyd George. Nowadays I blush to think that Lloyd George was purposely kept off the list of guests. But he was.' Nonetheless, he sent them a handsome present of books. Ramsay MacDonald, Stanley Baldwin, George Lansbury, Freddie Guest, William Beveridge and several journalists were among the hundreds who were invited.

A baker from Leith designed the wedding cake – four feet high with an aeroplane on top. He accompanied his creation to London in the guard's van of a train. When they visited Leith afterwards, the couple were thronged by well-wishers, particularly pleased that their English MP had married a Scots girl (even if she had moved to the far south of England). The age difference was not missed by Benn's constituents. He and Margaret visited one of the local schools, where the teacher asked, 'And who has Captain Benn brought with him today?', to which the pupils replied, 'His daughter'![26]

Benn decided that for their honeymoon they should 'get away from it all' – by attending the first session of the League of Nations in Geneva. They then travelled on to Italy. Instead of taking the twenty minute train journey from Brig to Domodossola, the couple boarded a horse-drawn post sleigh before dawn, climbed the Simplon Pass arriving at their destination just before dark. Despite the Alpine mid-winter cold and snow, the journey went fairly smoothly, apart from a can of paraffin being spilt on Margaret's luggage. At Milan the newly-weds had their first marital disagreements – over tariff reform and whether buses were better than trams.

Margaret was keen to visit Rome to discover whether there was any prospect that her religious destiny might have been within the Catholic Church. Much to Benn's relief, the visit confirmed to her that it would not; Margaret eventually became President Emeritus of the Congregational Federation. However, she did feel that Catholicism could have been therapeutic for her husband. She felt that 'an understanding father confessor could have absolved Benn of his own perceived failings and released him from the torments of his relentless conscience'. But it was not to be for Benn either. Raised in the tradition of the Congregational Church, all his life he was in active antipathy to Catholicism. His puritanical streak ran deep, his self-direction was too strong and in any case he did not seek an easy life, preferring the motivation of harsh self-discipline, much as Gladstone had.

Also, Margaret's notion of Catholicism as a potential relief from guilt is one that is certainly open to question by many brought up in the faith.

Revealing his intellectual curiosity and his attraction to danger, but also his naivety, when they arrived in Sicily Benn tried to learn more about the Mafia, by asking the locals. Rather predictably, he was met with a wall of silence. At the end of the trip Benn suffered a recurrence of his malaria and the pair headed for home. Margaret reflected that, despite his illness and their minor disagreements, her new husband was 'in every way the best of company'.[27] Benn had waited until he was forty-three to marry and Margaret commented that initially he had difficulty thinking for two.[28] She considered them to be of different, but compatible, temperaments – both 'left-of-centre Liberal-radicals, working for a more just society'. They shared a similar sense of humour. Benn was very witty – not so much of a story teller, but an amusing interjector. Margaret was patient, tolerant and tactful, and she softened Benn's frantic desire for perfection. Although they treated each other as intellectual equals, the couple organised their practical lives along fairly traditional lines, with Margaret taking responsibility for their home and providing as much opportunity as possible for her husband's work to be uninterrupted. However, she was not by any means totally submissive. She even persuaded Benn to remove the chart of how he spent each day from the bedroom, to his study.

It seems a fairly safe assumption that the 23-year-old Margaret, a debutante who had considered becoming a nun and who had been inculcated with her parents' 'severe sexual ethics', was a virgin at the time of her marriage.[29] As for her 43-year-old husband, this is less certain, but Benn never revealed anything so private in his records. He did not even record his rejected marriage proposal in his draft autobiography and Margaret, who presumably knew about it, did not mention it either in her memoirs. Benn may possibly have left the merest of clues about his personal history in his First World War reminiscences, where he talked of being allowed to go off on 'liaison' visits to a 'romantic' city in Italy, because his superiors understood that he was a 'grown up'. Also an ambiguous reference survives in a fragment of a letter written by Benn during the war declaring 'if only you ... had been with me to see the beauties' in Italy.[30] However, perhaps the absence of direct references was because there was no history to record.

Their first home together was a flat at Westminster Mansions opposite Church House in Westminster, although Benn's parents persuaded the couple to spend most weekends with them in the country at their home *Stone Wall* at Limpsfield in Surrey, at the foot of the North Downs.[31] This house had replaced the cottages at Crowborough, which had in turn replaced Stansgate. Benn's parents had kept the Crowborough weekend home for fourteen years – a long time for the family to have kept any of their homes. Their cramped London home and the weekends away with the canine-averse Benn family meant that Margaret had to give away her beloved West Highland terrier, Dugald. The terrier was quite a character and had even helped in the upbringing of a litter of kittens by taking them into the garden for a play while their mother had a rest.[32] He went to live with neighbours of her parents' in Seaford. When they were not 'in the country' with the family, the Benns' social life centred on the other Asquithian Liberals, but it also extended to the Mosleys and the Astors, including parties at Cliveden – not exactly renowned as examples of the highest moral standards. Among the Liberals, Walter Runciman and Sir John Simon (generally regarded as being at the opposite end of the spectrum from the Astors when it came to sociability) were particularly active in providing hospitality. Margaret was amused when Simon's chauffeur, named Kingdom, arrived one day, to be announced by the maid with the words, 'Kingdom's come'.

Benn seemed to be able to put aside moral and political differences when it came to choosing his friends. He did not seem fully to understand or empathise with the more wayward morals of others, but nor was he generally all that censorious of those outside the family, other than over financial wrongdoing. Within the family, he expected the highest standards of moral *and* financial probity. The Lloyd George Fund and the Marconi Affair weighed heavily in Benn's balance of opinion of Lloyd George, although the Black and Tans and the peacetime coalition pressed harder on the scales. As with many who are over-concerned with money, Benn was liable to make false economies and to worry, as others would see it, unnecessarily. He was far from alone in this however; the memoirs of many figures who could reasonably be judged to be well off are littered with near-panic over their finances. Benn's family history of wealth accumulated over a relatively short period by his father's business from a rather impoverished start, the ups and downs of the publishing world, the precariousness of a parliamentary career and the brushes with the courts all left their imprint on Benn's feeling of financial insecurity.

The Benns planned to try and find a larger home within 500 yards of Parliament. This gave them two options – south of the Thames (which was cheaper) or Westminster Village (which they felt was beyond their means). As with most house-hunters, they settled for the option which was supposedly too expensive. They just needed to convince themselves of the benefits, which Benn summarised as being that 'you could have a division bell in your house and with a good pair of legs govern the country from your own fireside'.

In early 1921 the Benns moved to a tall, narrow Georgian house at 15 Cowley Street in the heart of Westminster village. Opposite lived Sir Harry Brittain, a pioneer of the motor car. He had a Ford, which he sometimes left running all night in the street. The Benn's house was rather small and there were problems getting some of the furniture up the stairs to the top floor. Margaret was alerted that her husband had found a solution, by the cook's shouting 'Don't look! Don't look!' Of course, as anyone would, Margaret did look up, to see Benn climbing the fire escape with a table strapped around his waist.[33]

On 5 September 1921 the Benns became parents for the first time, when Margaret gave birth to their son, Michael. While Benn was a rather elderly father at the age of 44, Margaret was a relatively young mother at 24. By this time they had been married for nine months and nineteen days, suggesting that Michael was probably conceived during his parents' honeymoon. Benn declared that Michael was going to be his 'best friend'. Michael was christened in the crypt chapel of the House of Commons. His godparents were John Whitley, the Speaker of the House of Commons, Reginald McKenna and Benn's younger sister, Irene. His other sister, Margaret, was much less involved in their lives.

Benn's father had been weakened by a bout of pneumonia during the war and had been forced to resign from the leadership of the Progressive Party on the LCC. He had celebrated his seventieth birthday in November 1920, but died less than eighteen months later on 10 April 1922. Benn was always close to his mother, and she was even more devoted to him, displaying a 'possessive affection'.[34] She leaned heavily on Ernest, as her eldest son, but liked to imagine that her younger son leaned on her.[35] After his father died, Benn's mother wondered aloud why she had been 'spared', concluding that it was because 'Will … needs me'. Margaret, however, felt that she herself was 'quite adequate for the job'.[36] After their father's death, Benn's elder brother, Ernest shouldered the greatest responsibility for their mother's welfare, although she continued to be stoical, protective of her four surviving offspring and rather interfering. (Four of Elizabeth Benn's six children were still living – Ernest, William, Irene and Margaret. Christopher had died in infancy and Oliver had been killed in the war.) Within the family, Lady Benn felt no reservation about offering her (unsought) advice on any aspect of housekeeping or family life, while at the same time holding a rather disdainful and dismissive attitude towards 'the Outside World'.

By the beginning of 1922 the Asquithians were contemplating the next election – or at least some of them were. Convinced that an election would be 'political suicide' for Lloyd George, Asquith showed little urgency about drawing up policies.[37] Benn was disconcerted to learn over dinner with Herbert Gladstone that the cost of the 1906 General Election had been £100,000, but that the coalition was supposed to have a war chest of £3,000,000 towards the next contest.[38]

The 1922 general election was called precipitately for 15 November, in the aftermath of the Carlton Club meeting at which the Conservatives decided to drop Lloyd George and fight the next election alone. Lloyd George managed to reach a last-minute agreement with his former coalition partners to protect some of his supporters from Conservative opposition. They fought under the label of National Liberals. It was the first election after the departure of the MPs representing seats in what had become the Irish Free State, although Northern Ireland MPs (as today) remained at Westminster.

The 1922 election reversed the fortunes of the two branches of Liberalism. The Asquithians nearly doubled their number of seats from twenty-eight to fifty-four, while the Lloyd George National Liberals' total was worse than halved from 133 to 62, despite the protective arrangement with the Conservatives in some of their seats. So, while Lloyd George's followers still slightly outnumbered the Asquithians (and could easily out-spend them), a near-parity in Parliament resulted. Across the country the Asquithians spoke for 2.5m voters, while the Lloyd George Liberals, with only half as many candidates, had garnered just under 1.7m. Significantly though, for the first time the Labour Party out-polled the combined forces of Liberalism by a slim margin and won more seats – 142 compared to the combined Liberal total of 115.[39] Ramsay MacDonald returned to Parliament and took up the role of Leader of the Opposition. Asquith and Lloyd George both held their seats and Benn was returned with a comfortable majority in Leith.

1922 general election Leith:

W.W. Benn	Liberal	13,971
A.M. MacRobert	Conservative	7,372
R.F. Wilson	Labour	6,567
	Liberal majority	6,599 (23.7 per cent)

Nationally, the 1922 election result led to a majority Conservative government under the leadership of Bonar Law. However, in May 1923, only seven months into his premiership, he was forced to resign on health grounds. He was suffering from throat cancer, from which he died in October 1923. Baldwin succeeded as prime minister and decided that the ailing British economy would benefit from protective import tariffs, for which he did not feel he had a mandate. Therefore, he wanted to put the policy to the test at an election. If there was any policy which could have united the Asquithian and Lloyd George Liberals, it was the issue of free trade. So, an uneasy alliance was established within the Liberal Party just in time for the 1923 election, with Asquith nominally still the leader. Lloyd George and Asquith managed to present a united image, posing at Asquith's home, *The Wharf* at Sutton Courtenay, for a photographer. However, the image glossed over a lot of cracks.

Another general election was called for Thursday 6 December 1923, only one year and three weeks since the country last went to the polls. This election and its immediate aftermath were to prove crucial for the future of British politics.

Benn again improved his majority at Leith.

1923 general election Leith:

W.W. Benn	Liberal	15,004
R.F. Wilson	Labour	8,267
	Liberal majority	6,737 (29 per cent)

Nationally, the Liberal Party seemed to be resurgent, winning 159 seats and 29.6 per cent of the vote. However, the Liberals were in third place, just behind Labour on 191 seats and 30.5 per cent, who in turn were behind the Conservatives on 258 seats and 38.1 per cent of the vote. It was to be the nearest election to a three-way split which the country has ever seen and it left no party with an overall majority.

Asquith was put in a position where the stakes were high. He could quite reasonably have joined forces with the Labour Party to defeat the Conservatives, on the grounds that the two parties had opposed protection and that this key policy had not received a majority in the country or in the House of Commons. The two parties could jointly have prevented a Conservative government. Beyond this, though, there were several possibilities. One was to allow a minority Labour government for the first time in the hope, from Asquith's point of view, that the party would prove to be incapable of governing. Another would have been some form of alliance or coalition between the Liberal and Labour parties and the third would have been to press the case for a minority Liberal administration. Asquith, cerebral, patient, old and somewhat ailing, decided not to press the claim for a Liberal minority administration. The relationship between the parties did not favour a Liberal-Labour alliance and so, as Asquith put it: 'If a Labour government is ever to be tried ... it could hardly be tried under safer conditions'. Asquith's decision, whilst lacking in vim and vigour, was not obviously wrong at the time, but with hindsight, it certainly was.

Incumbent prime minister, Baldwin, did not resign immediately and presented his own King's Speech to Parliament, but on 21 January 1924 he was defeated in a vote of no confidence. Ten Liberal MPs defied the party whip and voted with the Conservatives and a further seven did not vote.[40] Benn voted along with Asquith, Lloyd George and the vast majority of other Liberals against the Conservatives and brought their putative government to an end. The Liberals who were not in favour of trying the Labour experiment, harboured continuing resentment from this point on.

Ramsay MacDonald was able to form a government, for which he relied quite heavily on former Liberal MPs. Benn watched as several of his former Liberal colleagues who had defected to Labour were called into MacDonald's government. Within the cabinet, Viscount Haldane was appointed Lord Chancellor, Noel Buxton went to Agriculture and Fisheries, Charles Trevelyan went to Education and Josiah Wedgwood became Chancellor of the Duchy of Lancaster – between them comprising one fifth of the first Labour cabinet. Arthur Ponsonby was appointed under-secretary at the Treasury and the ennobled Sydney Arnold held the equivalent position in the Colonial Office. However, two other former Liberal MPs who had made the jump – Christopher Addison, who had only defected in November 1923 and did not stand in the election and Bertie Lees-Smith, who had been defeated – were out of Parliament and missed their opportunity to be included. The only former Liberal MPs who had defected to Labour and who were in Parliament but not rewarded with office were Percy Alden and Edward Hemmerde. The lesson that defectors increased their prospects of ministerial office was a pattern which was to persist throughout the century and applied to defectors to the Conservatives as well.[41]

After the 1923 election Benn was concerned that the façade of the Liberal Party reunion hid a rather ugly interior. It was nothing like the 'band of brothers' feeling among the Asquithians before the election.[42] Both Lloyd George and Asquith were opposed to holding party meetings unless absolutely necessary. This avoided some potentially fractious encounters, but it meant that the more radical left of the party (including Benn) became increasingly detached from the party management.[43] Benn felt that Lloyd George was too interested in tactics, rather than principles. In the short run this may well have been true, but overall Lloyd George's record was one of radical policy-making, more so than Asquith's. Benn responded keenly to a suggestion from Asquith that a research department be set up to include himself and Ernest Simon. The question of funding presented the stumbling block, with Lloyd George keeping a tight grip on his money.[44] Benn also gauged his standing with the Lloyd George family after an encounter with Lloyd George's wife and daughter. Benn confided the unsurprising conclusion to his diary: 'both very chilly. Evidently I am out of favour with the family.'[45]

Benn was, by this time, beginning to weigh up the pros and cons of defecting from the Liberal Party. It was now clear that the Liberals were not really reunited and that if they did genuinely reintegrate at all levels, it would be Lloyd George, not the decade-older Asquith, who would be the leader. Added to this was the now-proven fact that Labour was a party of government and that most of the former Liberal MPs who had defected were rewarded with office. On the other hand, his view of the Labour Party's conduct in office was not entirely positive: 'The Labour Party accept our help in the House, but ... send down people to abuse us in our constituencies. I think we shall blow them out of the water when we attack. We shall attack on the ground of pure hypocrisy: they are making no attempt whatever to carry out the programme they advertised.'[46] 'Feeling in the House is becoming very bitter ... I hate the whole place.'[47] Despite his growing discontent, Benn saw 'no point in abandoning the Party at this moment.'[48]

Another factor which complicated any decision over future party allegiance was whether the same three major parties would be the only contenders for power in the future. Churchill, who had lost his seat at Dundee in 1922, and had failed to return as a Liberal in the 1923 election, was clearly on manoeuvres in the undergrowth between the Liberal and Conservative parties, culminating in his candidature as a Constitutionalist in the Westminster Abbey by-election in March 1924. Benn's analysis was that: 'Churchill's idea is to accumulate Centre Party followers ... We should be left with the Radicals. In the meantime the Labour Government may lose their Left Wing ... So five Parties may prepare for the next Election.'[49]

The Constitutionalist label did not disappear after Churchill narrowly failed to be elected in the Abbey by-election and the boundaries between the right of the Liberal Party and the Conservative Party began to blur, as Benn noted after a Liberal Party meeting on 15 April 1924: 'The trouble began with a very frank statement from Freddie Guest saying ... that he has been offered a seat where he would have Tory support; he was prepared to accept this, and wished to see the Liberal Party as a wing of the Tory Party.' Asquith followed, saying that 'we should all be in a stronger position when we had come in touch with our constituencies (he is off to the Riviera tomorrow!) and that he was confident, convinced, etc, that the Party would be unimpaired, united, and anything else that begins with a "u2".'[50] Benn clearly detected the ironic disconnect between Asquith's words and his actions, but his loyalty to his leader remained undiminished. There were moves to expel Freddie Guest, but Asquith 'asked that the motion should not be pressed, which I think was quite right as we never drum people out ... I should think Guest will take steps. He is, of course, working with Churchill to make Liberalism a wing of Toryism: that is the real offence.'[51]

As has been common over the decades with parties facing internal division, leaks of party meetings appeared in the press. Benn busied himself with his constituency work, but the activity seemed somewhat perfunctory and his diary records relatively little about Leith. His real fondness for his old St. George's constituency did not seem to have transferred fully to his new seat: 'eight days in Leith: fulfilled about twenty-five engagements ... addressed ... nearly 3,000 people ... Leith visit always does me good ... But after eight days, one gets rather tired of the sight of the place.'[52]

At a party meeting at the beginning of the parliament, Asquith had expressed his opinion that, constitutionally, the King would be compelled to turn to the Liberals if the Labour government fell.[53] But, by May 1924, with Labour having been in power for over four months, it was clear that the Liberal Party was no longer the default government in the eyes of the monarch, the people, or even the Liberal Party itself. Asquith admitted to Benn that 'the prospect of the formation of a Liberal Government if MacDonald is defeated is a phantasy [sic]'.[54]

After the Labour Chancellor of the Exchequer, Philip Snowden, had presented his budget in April 1924, the Liberal Party's stance towards the Labour government warmed, partly as a result of the actual measures which encouraged free trade and partly in the hope that the government would allow a bill for electoral reform to be passed. Liberal MP Athelstan Rendall had introduced a Proportional Representation bill, which was to receive its second reading on 2 May 1924. The Labour Party decided not to support the bill, but to allow a free vote in the Commons. However, it was defeated by ninety-four votes and relations between the Labour and Liberal parties deteriorated again. The first-past-the-post system survived this and future challenges. This was not to be the last time that party differences erupted over proposals for its replacement, as was demonstrated in 2011.

There was to be only the one budget introduced by the first Labour government, an administration which did not even last the full year. The immediate cause of the government's demise was the Campbell Case – a case which illustrated how apparently isolated events can cause a chain of unforeseen consequences and how the worst of the damage can accrue to relatively passive bystanders – in this case the Liberals. J.R. Campbell was acting editor of the Communist Party's magazine, *Workers Weekly*. In the 25 July 1924 edition he published 'An open letter to the Fighting Forces' inciting the military to refuse to fight against members of the working class during a hypothetical war or industrial dispute. On 6 August the attorney general initiated a prosecution against Campbell under the Incitement to Mutiny Act of 1797. A week later the case was dropped, leaving a public impression of government interference in the legal process and opening it up to allegations of Communist sympathies.

The Conservatives, confident of their electoral prospects, prepared a motion of censure on the government in the hope of precipitating a general election. The Liberals were left in an invidious position. They could have helped the Conservatives to force an election, which they certainly did not want. Alternatively, they could have supported the Labour Party in its apparently underhand manoeuvres in interfering with the legal process. Faced with this dilemma, the Liberals proposed what appeared to be a sensible compromise – an inquiry (i.e. delay and diffusion of attention in the hope that other events would overshadow the case). The Liberals felt that their motion for an inquiry would give them enough reason to refuse to vote for the Conservative censure motion. But the sensible compromise turned into the Liberals' own petard. The whole plan unravelled when the Conservatives decided to withdraw their censure and instead support the Liberal motion for an inquiry and the Labour Party declared that the Liberal motion would be considered a vote of no confidence in the government, precipitating a general election if it were passed. The Liberals were then faced with the ugly fact that their own motion was likely to blow up in their faces and lead to a general election, if they continued to support it. Twelve Liberals voted against the motion, while most of the rest, including Benn and Asquith, felt that they had no moral alternative to supporting it.[55] On 8 October the resolution was carried by 364 to 198 votes and another general election was called for 29 October 1924 – the third in less than two years.

In most respects the Labour Party had fulfilled its important, but limited, objectives for its first term in office. It had taken office and behaved conventionally and moderately, neutralising scare stories of extremism. The party, particularly with the augmentation of the defectors from the Liberals, had shown itself to be capable, serious and relatively united. Nine months in office had been sufficient to demonstrate this and it was also enough time to make the Liberal Party appear close to irrelevant. MacDonald, near-exhausted having performed the roles of prime minister and foreign secretary, was more relieved than sorry at the calling of the election.

Benn was only too aware of the prognosis for his own party: 'This is the story, as I see it, of the suicide of the Liberal Party. Perhaps it is better boldly to commit hara kiri than to await senile decay. The Elections will probably result in a considerable increase for Labour, and a larger increase for the Tories, both at the expense of the Liberal Party which cannot, I should say, exceed a hundred.'[56] Benn was concerned not only about the likely sharp reduction in the number of Liberal MPs, but also about the balance of survivors between Asquithians and Lloyd George followers. He knew that the proceeds of the 'honours scandal' had not been exhausted and that they had not been shared equally across the party.[57]

In the election campaign its opponents tried to paint the Labour Party as sleazy over the Campbell Case and the so-called 'biscuits scandal', in which MacDonald had received financial support and a car from Alexander Grant, a biscuit magnate. These issues did not do much damage to the Labour Party among its supporters, but the Zinoviev letter incident was more serious. A letter purporting to come from the Communist International was published by the *Daily Mail* four days before the election, calling for Communist agitation in Britain. Benn had his doubts about the letter's authenticity and two weeks after the election was acknowledging that 'It is possible that if it was a forgery, it was a forgery concocted in Russia by agents of Rothermere [chairman of the *Daily Mail's* parent company].'[58] The Zinoviev letter did relatively little damage among Labour's supporters, but it helped to harden opinion among its opponents, leading some Liberal support to polarise towards the Conservatives.

1924 general election Leith:

W.W. Benn	Liberal	16,569
R.F. Wilson	Labour	11,250
	Liberal majority	5,319 (19.2 per cent)

Although Benn's majority fell, his result – a winning margin of over 5,000 votes – was good by comparison with the Liberal Party's performance nationally. The Liberals only fielded candidates in 340 seats, a drop of 113. Partly as a consequence, the party's share of the vote fell from 29.6 per cent to 17.6 per cent. Benn's prediction of a hundred seats for the Liberals turned out to be wildly optimistic. The party ended up with only forty (down from 159 at the 1923 election, held only eleven months earlier). The fragility of the party was illustrated by the fact that the surviving Liberal MPs divided fairly evenly between the supporters of Lloyd George and those of Asquith. However, Asquith had lost his seat at Paisley, while Lloyd George was re-elected in Caernarvon. Among the forty Liberal MPs, only Lloyd George and David Davies had also sat continuously since Benn had entered Parliament in 1906.[59]

The result for the Labour Party was mixed. With ninety more candidates than in the previous election, the party increased its total vote by over one million, but lost forty seats. It was now even more emphatically the second party, while the Conservatives emerged as the clear winners, with a large overall majority and a large increase in their vote. Stanley Baldwin was back in Number 10 for what was to prove to be the only single-party government to last nearly a full term in the inter-war years.

The flow of defections from the Liberals continued. Three former Liberal MPs were elected under Conservative colours in 1924.[60] Five former Liberal MPs were elected for Labour.[61] Additionally, seven former Liberal MPs were elected as Constitutionalists; although four of them did later retake the Liberal whip,[62] three became Conservatives.[63] One of these three was Churchill, who was appointed to the Treasury. However, no other former Liberal MPs gained office in the Conservative government, as there was a plentiful supply of ministerial experience within the party, unlike the situation with the first Labour administration.

The ambiguous position of the Liberals after the 1924 election was captured by Trevelyan Thomson, one of the forty surviving Liberal MPs. He had actually been returned unopposed. Thomson raised the question as to 'whether or not we were an Opposition Party'. As Benn commented, it was 'a strange question to be raised in the Liberal Party under a Tory Government.'[64] Both Asquith and Lloyd George suggested Benn's name for the position of Liberal whip, but when Benn was telephoned by the former whip, Vivian Phillipps, who had lost his seat at the election, he 'let [himself] go' about Lloyd George and declined this latest offer.[65] Benn went along to the Liberal Party meeting at the Reform Club, expecting that Asquith would propose Lloyd George as leader in the Commons. Benn had prepared a statement repudiating the proposal. 'I had no notion of what support I should get ... I thought the moment had arrived, and recapitulated my points mentally. Not a single word, however, about [Lloyd George]. I felt like an anarchist with a bomb in his hand who learns that the route of the Royal procession has been altered.'[66]

The press reported the new session of Parliament with a damning indictment of the Liberals' position, noting that Lloyd George 'entered the House unobserved [sic]' after Baldwin and MacDonald had made their choreographed entrances. Then, 'as if to fill the cup of his bitterness' he found that Benn, 'the impetuous leader of the Liberal revolt' had 'captured' the corner seat which he expected to take. Benn then offered Lloyd George the seat, but 'the condescension was too obvious to be accepted.'[67] Benn later protested that he had checked first that Lloyd George had not intended to take that particular seat, but the public impression of antagonism had been reinforced.[68]

The teetotal and scrupulously moral Benn's allegiance to Asquith never wavered even in the face of mounting evidence of his leader's weakness for alcohol, whereas his nemesis, Lloyd George was a model of sobriety. Benn had once found Asquith wandering around the corridors of Parliament drunk and seemingly unable to find his own way back to his room. Margaret also became aware (and so presumably did Benn) of Asquith's reputation for liking young women. Margaret astutely observed some aspects of the

Asquiths' lifestyle and personality, which only became public knowledge much later. On one of their visits to *The Wharf*, Margot took Margaret to her suite of rooms above Asquith's garden library and confided that she more or less lived there on her own and that a sexual relationship with her husband was not important to her. Some light was shed on the double (or higher multiple) life which Asquith was leading when his relationship with Venetia Stanley was eventually established with the publication of the letters between them.[69] Though on this score, of course, Lloyd George's reputation was worse than Asquith's.

Among others, Benn sought the opinions about the political situation not just of those like himself on the left of the party, but also of those on the right. He went to see Arthur Murray, the son of the exotically-named Montolieu Fox Oliphant Murray, first Viscount Murray and brother of the Master of Elibank, former Liberal chief whip. Benn visited Lord Beauchamp, 'knee-deep in condolences and tears' and also lunched with Lord and Lady Wimborne: Lord Wimborne [Ivor Guest] was the elder brother of Freddie Guest and cousin of Winston Churchill. Benn wryly noted, (from what evidence he does not tell us), that the Wimbornes had 'resumed their married life'.[70] Typically, Benn would report uncritically on people's private lives, affairs or alcoholism, but could be roused to vitriol over politics and financial wrongdoing. The discussions included the supposed manoeuvres by Lloyd George before the last election to engineer another Liberal-Tory coalition.[71] Eventually Murray drifted over to the Liberal Nationals and four Guest brothers – Ivor, Freddie, Oscar and Henry – all followed their cousin, Winston Churchill, in defecting from the Liberal Party to the Conservatives.[72]

While a putative group of defectors was simmering with discontent on the right of the party, Benn's activities stirred up a potential leftward breakaway group. Benn organised the Radical Group, under the nominal leadership of Walter Runciman.[73] The group was in no way clandestine and an announcement of the group's formation appeared in the press on 4 December 1924. During parliamentary sessions, Benn organised weekly lunch parties for the Radical Group in a private room on the terrace floor of the House of Commons. Speakers included William Beveridge. The Radical Group (rather unconvincingly) protested that it was 'far from being actuated by any personal considerations', but tellingly 'lamented' the absence of Asquith and announced that it was 'forced to declare' that Lloyd George did 'not possess the qualifications required as leader of the Liberal Party'.[74]

Benn had a letter published in the *Daily News* on 14 November 1924, stating that 'The people have no confidence, and rightly so, in Mr. Lloyd George'. He received some hostile response, but also dozens of letters of support from around the country, including one from Christopher Addison who wrote: 'I take my hat off to you for your letter in the *Daily News* ... Liberalism is a living thing, but there is no hope for the Liberal Party as it is'. He also later had an open letter to the Leith Liberal Club and Association published in the local paper, saying that he did not support Lloyd George's leadership. Again, Benn reported a mixed response: 'Letters from Leith show very considerable differences of opinion. Whatever the outward effects may be, they don't in the least shake my own convictions. In no circumstances will I become an acknowledged follower' of Lloyd George.[75]

Surprisingly, given the dire state of the Liberal Party, Margaret later reflected that Benn enjoyed the period after the 1924 election and that in some ways this was the 'happiest of his parliamentary life.' Benn was a natural fighter and enjoyed being in opposition far more than being in government.[76] But, to some extent, his happiness was to do with his home life rather than his work. Margaret was expecting their second child in 1925 and the family moved to a larger house at 40 Grosvenor Road (since renamed Millbank). It was a tall, narrow five-storey house built in the 1880s. The Benns took a thirty-three-year lease for £2,000, at the end of which the house was demolished to make way for Millbank Tower. For Benn, who had lived at over a dozen different addresses before moving to Grosvenor Road, the thirty-three year stay was to represent a significant period of stability.

The following year, the Benns also acquired a holiday home, back at Stansgate – they rented the farmhouse next door to the property which had been the family's holiday home from 1899 to 1903. In the meantime the family's old house had passed from the merchant banker who had bought it from Benn's father and it had ended up in the hands of a formidable and unfriendly merchant seaman, Captain Grey. However, Benn had ambitions to re-acquire the house which his father had built. It had been on his mind ever since his father had sold it. Crossing the Mesapotamian desert, he had even remarked to Margaret that it reminded him of Stansgate!

The Benns' second son, Anthony, was born on 3 April 1925. His parents were alert to the possibility that his name would 'degenerate' into 'Tony', which was not what they wanted.[77] However, they went ahead with the name, adding Neil along with Wedgwood as middle names. (Michael had been given Wedgwood as his middle name too.) Within the family, Anthony became known as Jim, which in turn was lengthened to James. So Anthony became Tony, then Jim, then James and eventually back to Tony. Benn was an 'alongside' parent, well ahead of his time. He had a natural authority over his children, without being at all authoritarian. He did not insist that his children chart the way they spent their time, but he did want them to grow up to be teetotal and careful with money. The boys were expected to keep accounts of their pocket money, leading them to be overheard one day by their mother asking each other, 'Have you "made up" your accounts for Dad?' As was normal for many middle class families of the time, the Benns employed a nurse to carry out most of the childcare. She was assisted by a succession of live-in nursery maids. The children's upbringing was rich in discussion of politics and religion, but surprisingly devoid of reading or the arts. Even the Tate Gallery, next door to their home in Grosvenor Road, remained unvisited. Pets were definitely out of the question; the children tried to smuggle a local kitten from Stansgate in the car on the way back to London. Unfortunately, Fluffy was discovered on the journey and had to be handed over immediately to a woman who lived in a cottage en route. So, Fluffy went the way of Margaret's dog, Dugald, and was re-homed. Other aspects of the children's upbringing were also rather patchy. The boys were brought up with the example of a mother who was able to hold her own in debate and who was the expert of the family on topics such as religion. However, interaction with young women was limited and discussion of sex education was not on the agenda. Tony once came across an unfamiliar word and asked his father what the term 'buggery' meant. Benn deftly came up with the definition of 'two men trying to have a baby' and then referred Tony on to his mother before he could ask any more awkward questions.[78] The boys went on to be educated at Westminster School, as were seven prime ministers (but none of them Labour), philosopher John Locke, architect Christopher Wren, actor John Gielgud, broadcaster Matt Frei, entrepreneur Martha Lane Fox, impresario Andrew Lloyd Webber and Liberal Democrat leader Nick Clegg. The school was chosen to provide the boys with an education which would equip them to 'deal with the Tories', as their mother put it. This meant that they could walk to school from Grosvenor Road, even if they were rather self-conscious in their top hats and morning coats.

Benn was one of the most active parliamentarians and contributed to between 100 and 300 debates per year after the war, either with speeches or written questions. He intervened on a wide range of issues, but particularly foreign affairs, the air force and matters concerning Leith. However, Benn's constituency was not bringing him much cheer, as he recorded in his diary: 'Resumed work after a fortnight's visit to Leith. The impression I gathered at the outset was one of intense gloom among Liberals, and of a steady almost overwhelming slide to Labour. [But as] regards the women, I don't see signs yet of their capture by Labour.'[79] It was significant that Benn did not regard his visit to his constituency as part of his 'work'. The main focus of his attention was the guerrilla war within the Liberal Party. Confirming Margaret's feeling that Benn rather enjoyed this party strife, he wrote that 'the row in the Party goes on merrily. The trouble is that large grants have been made since 1922 by [Lloyd George], and it is now rather late in the day to say that that they won't touch his money.'[80] 'The real issue is whether it is consistent with the dignity, or even the life, of a Party to go on as the pensioner of a single man.'[81] In January 1926 Alfred Mond defected from the Liberals to the Conservatives. Benn was disgusted at Lloyd George's anti-Semitic outburst over Mond's departure, commenting that his 'vulgar taunt about the race that must be on the winning side is the sort of thing that drives all decent-minded people away from the Party. This little dog fight on the old wreck makes the whole situation very pitiful.'[82]

However, Benn felt a sea-change in relations with the Labour Party. In the previous parliament, Liberals had complained that the Labour Party treated them as 'patient oxen', expected to pull the Labour cart and then be slaughtered.[83] But, after the 1924 election, Benn felt that 'relations between ourselves and Labour have completely changed. In place of the pin pricks and suspicions of the last Parliament, there is a very warm feeling of friendship.'[84] 'The great feature of this Parliament is the amazingly good relations between the Radicals and the Labour Party.'[85] Benn could now envisage himself comfortably in the Labour Party.

When Ernest learned that his brother was seriously thinking of leaving the Liberals, he assumed that his judgment had been affected by over-work. Ernest decided that the best way to try and ensure that Benn did not defect was to send him and Margaret away on an all-expenses paid holiday to the Mediterranean. Ernest and his wife Gwen offered to look after Michael and Tony for a few weeks. In the end the weeks turned into months and the trip to the Mediterranean turned into a journey through France, Italy, Greece, Turkey, Egypt, modern-day Israel, Lebanon, Syria, Iraq and the Soviet Union. Having set off in February 1926, the couple returned in May, having missed Tony's first birthday; he had forgotten who his parents were when they returned. Surprisingly, for a family who were so close and loyal to each other, this extended absence was not to be the last. The lure of travel was to prove that it could outshine both politics and family on several occasions.

The General Strike of May 1926 was inevitably a serious problem for Baldwin's Conservative government and naturally it was also a sensitive issue for the Labour Party because of its links to the trades unions. However, it was the relatively disinterested Liberal Party which managed to come out of the events with the worst damage – and most of this was self-inflicted. The Asquith-Lloyd George split once again emerged. Asquith, now in the Lords but still Liberal Party leader, condemned the strike, while Lloyd George expressed his sympathy for the strikers. Acrimonious correspondence seeped into the press. Benn made a short speech saying that it was 'inconceivable that the so-called Parliamentary Liberal Party should pass a public vote of censure on [Asquith] who for forty years had stood by Liberalism, not always, perhaps, going fast or far enough, but always down the straight road.' However, the leadership question was settled when Asquith suffered a serious stroke in October 1926, which meant that he finally relinquished the party leadership to Lloyd George. Asquith survived for another sixteen months, but needed a wheelchair to move around and was limited in his ability to contribute politically. This was the tipping point for Benn's future allegiance to the Liberal Party.

Benn was not the only Liberal MP on the verge of defection. Ironically, Joseph Kenworthy, who usually opposed Lloyd George, supported him on the Strike but still defected to Labour in October 1926, commenting that: 'The collapse of the General Strike left the Labour Party ... in an extremely weak position ... their moment of defeat, was, I felt, the time to join them'.[86] Kenworthy initially held to the line that he would not resign his seat and trigger a by-election.[87] However, the local Labour leaders, believing that the seat was winnable, persuaded Kenworthy to resign and re-contest the seat under Labour colours. Kenworthy had never faced a Labour opponent in his four contests at Hull and no other prospective Labour candidate had been adopted for a future contest, so he did not have to deal with the complication of displacing an incumbent prospective Labour candidate. Kenworthy had seen off a Conservative challenger at each election and, as long as the Liberals could not mount a strong challenge, he had a good prospect of success as a Labour candidate. In the event, Kenworthy won the by-election on 29 November 1926, by a margin of 4,679 votes over his Conservative challenger, increasing his majority compared to his last contest. The Liberal candidate lost his deposit. After his defection, John Simon had commented wryly that 'Kenworthy having thus forced his fat body through the hedge you may be sure that a large number of sheep will go dribbling through the gap'.[88] As it turned out, Simon's unflattering analysis did have a ring of truth to it. Kenworthy was bulky – he had been a heavy-weight boxer; others did follow his path and their exit from the Liberal field did resemble the behaviour of sheep in some respects – they tended to move in a common direction, but without an obvious leader or any significant communication between them.

Benn decided the time had come for him to cross into pastures new in the Labour Party. On 5 February 1927 he wrote to the Leith constituency Liberal Association, asking for a meeting to announce his defection. Margaret insisted on coming up with him. As Benn remembered it: 'It was a painful occasion. I can't remember anything that was more saddening. I understood exactly how my friends felt. They regarded me as having been guilty of treason'. When the Benns rose to leave the meeting 'we passed ... people who had been kind to us, who had put us up and had given us meals ... not one hand was held out ... very, very bitter and very sad'.[89]

A man of principle, Benn felt that he would be honour-bound to resign his seat on changing his party allegiance. The problem for Benn was that Leith already had a Labour candidate in place, whereas Kenworthy had not had a Labour opponent in any of his four previous elections. Benn resigned his seat, accepting that he would have to wait for an opportunity to return to the Commons in a different seat. Benn and Margaret left Edinburgh 'extremely downcast' and only then began to decide what to do next. Benn took his seat on the Labour benches in the House of Commons, but six days later applied for the Chiltern Hundreds – the sinecure post which compels the holder to leave the Commons – 'the only public appointment for which I had ever asked'. He wrote to the Leith Liberal association, confirming that his decision involved 'the honourable obligation to resign my seat. I have always considered that obligation as being unconditional; it has never been part of any bargain. The choice of a candidate rests with the Leith Labour Party ... Whoever is selected to advance the Labour Cause will have my goodwishes and support'.[90]

Benn wrote sadly to Asquith, 'the only leader I have ever had',[91] and received the baleful reply: 'I regret more than I can say the decision which you have persuaded yourself to take.'[92]

Chapter Five

Turbulent Times in the Labour Party 1927–31

B enn's resignation from the Commons was a brave and honourable move. He was giving up his chosen career, with no certainty of a return to parliament. He knew that it would spell financial hardship, but not ruin. He gave up his parliamentary salary of £400 per year, but he still received an annual income from Benn Brothers of £500. This meant a forty-five per cent reduction in his income, but it still left the family with enough to live on, if they were frugal. Benn ensured that the family was (in reality, remained) frugal, re-using stationery and switching off unnecessary lights.[1]

Kenworthy, in his easier electoral position with no previous Labour opponent, had risked his seat but managed to remain in the Commons under his new party colours. Benn completely sacrificed his. Very few others have resigned their seats on changing party allegiance. William Jowitt was to cause a by-election in 1929 when defecting from the Liberals to Labour, but he held his seat, as did Dick Taverne on leaving the Labour Party to stand as an Independent Democratic Labour candidate in the 1970s. In the 1980s Bruce Douglas-Mann became the only defector from Labour to the SDP to resign his seat and stand again in the resulting by-election, but he lost. In 2014 Douglas Carswell and Mark Reckless resigned their seats on defection from the Conservatives to UKIP. However, these are the rare exceptions; the pattern has been for most defectors to remain in their seats and to weather the inevitable storms of protest.

Benn's defection was part of a wider trend of departures from the Liberal Party. Before the First Word War, the party had been the net recipient of defectors. The war did not directly cause an immediate exodus: only two former Liberal MPs stood as Labour candidates in the 1918 election and these were rather unusual individuals. Leo Chiozza Money defected over the issue of nationalisation of shipping and Edward John over Welsh nationalism. However, a series of connected events had begun to unfold after the war, which did lead to a significant outflow. In total, one in six people elected for the party between 1910 and 2010 eventually defected, with the majority of the departures in the period 1918 to 1931.[2] The Lloyd George-Asquith split distracted the leaders from managing the party, damaging the party's morale and its electoral fortunes in the 1918 and 1922 elections, at a crucial time when the Labour Party was reunited and reorganised. Alexander MacCallum Scott, who had defected to the Labour Party in 1924, summed up the feeling: 'If Lloyd George, or … the Asquith crowd had shown any disposition to consult me … I would have recognised the obligation to play the team game … But they held out no hand'.[3]

More defectors were motivated by enhanced prospects in their new party – in terms of electoral advantage, ministerial office and peerages – than for any other reason. They were primarily concerned about their own career prospects and judged (correctly in a majority of cases) that they would be more likely to achieve office and honours within another party – whether Labour or Conservative. Disagreement or disillusion over policy accounted for the next largest group. The decline in the Liberal Party's prospects encouraged some to look for another political home where they could see progressive policies implemented. The diminishing prospects for the Liberal Party to be able to enact its policies had been the main reason for disillusioned progressives to defect to the Labour Party. A much smaller number, including Benn, left due primarily to personality clashes.[4]

For the duration of Asquith's leadership of the party up to 1926, his detractors always had Lloyd George present as a leader-in-waiting and source of solace. After Asquith's death, the Lloyd George detractors had no such alternative spiritual or potential leader to turn to within the party. There is no doubt that Benn was primarily motivated by his personal distrust of Lloyd George. He did not particularly disagree with party policy and by the later 1920s Lloyd George was the leader who was arguably promoting the most radical policies in any party. Benn was certainly not motivated by personal advantage. In fact he was prepared to sacrifice almost anything for his beliefs. Benn was, therefore, unusual in his motivation and very rare, but not unique, in terms of resigning his seat. However, he was fairly typical in terms of his timing and the direction of his move. Defectors left the Liberals in roughly equal numbers to go to the right and to the left. In total forty-seven former Liberal MPs defected to the Labour Party, while thirty-four went to the Conservatives.[5] The directions of departure were not always obvious beforehand. There was a natural inclination for Lloyd George supporters who had grown close to the Conservatives in coalition from 1916 to 1922 to defect to the Conservatives, and many did. However, six Lloyd George supporters did defect to the Labour Party. Conversely, although a larger proportion of the Asquithian defectors went to Labour, eight went to the Conservatives.

Although Benn had a strong instinct for social reform, it was not a totally foregone conclusion that his dissatisfaction with the Liberals would result in his joining the Labour Party. In 1922, when the Lloyd George Coalition had been crumbling, Benn had even harboured fleeting thoughts of an alignment between the Asquithians and the Conservatives who were opposed to the Coalition. In a passing exchange with Bonar Law, Benn cheekily said that he hoped that Bonar Law was arranging a new coalition with the Asquithians and that it would introduce a little 'ginger' into that 'effete' group.[6]

Benn's closest parliamentary colleague, Reginald McKenna, defected to the Conservatives, as did his predecessor as Liberal MP for Leith, Ronald Munro Ferguson. They were the first of the eight Asquithians to defect to the Conservatives.[7] Reginald McKenna was offered the position of Chancellor of the Exchequer under two Conservative prime ministers – Bonar Law and Baldwin. He had served as Chancellor in the Asquith Coalition. McKenna, standing as an Asquithian Liberal, lost his seat in 1918. Instead, he took up a directorship, then later the chairmanship, of the Midland Bank. After the fall of the Lloyd George Coalition, but before the 1922 election, possibly in the hope of establishing an alliance with the Asquithian Liberals, Bonar Law had offered McKenna the chancellorship. Although McKenna never acknowledged that he made a political defection, a former supporter wrote to him: '[M]y political idol has fallen!!! I find it impossible to believe you have abandoned … Liberal principles [by] appearing on a … Tory platform'.[8] In the end, McKenna's health, his success at the bank and his distaste for the personality-driven aspects of politics, led him to focus on his business career instead of taking up either offer of the chancellorship. He never returned to politics and came to be regarded by some as a prime minister-manqué. In reality, he was a highly-skilled technical expert with business acumen and wealth, but limited in his political skills and following.

Always feeling that he was short of money, Benn's predecessor at Leith, Munro Ferguson had left domestic Liberal politics in 1914 to take up the post of Governor-General of Australia. He returned in 1920, was ennobled as Viscount Novar, and accepted the post of Secretary of State for Scotland in Bonar Law's Conservative government in October 1922. He held the post until January 1924, but was not reappointed when Baldwin returned to power later that year.

Ernest Benn remained a Liberal until 1929, but in that year he publicly supported the Conservatives because of what he considered to be their sounder position on individualism.[9] When Ernest had first thought that his brother was considering leaving the Liberal Party, he assumed that his judgement was faulty through over-work. However, Ernest, normally having no doubts about the rightness of his own decisions, had joined the exodus – only he went to the right and in the process changed many of his political views. Ernest went on not only to support the Conservatives, but to promulgate a whole raft of right of centre policies and was a monetarist long before Margaret Thatcher.[10] His changing political views emerged in a series of books which he published. The first three advocated collaboration between government, trades unions and business, but in 1925 he published *Confessions of a Capitalist,* emphasising the public benefit of wealth-creators. He made sure that he benefitted from his own wealth creation. A family joke was; 'What's the difference between travelling with Ernest Benn and travelling with William Benn?' 'With Ernest it's all creature comforts. With William it's all creatures and no comforts!'[11] The family also enjoyed a Christmas play which made fun of the relationship between the brothers and their attitude to money. The performance ended with the line: 'The eldest was rich and respected, the youngest was wretched and poor.' An ironic twist was included as Ernest played the younger, poorer of the brothers.[12] However, despite his acquisitiveness, Ernest always retained a paternalistic attitude towards his employees and his family (and several people fell into both categories). He enjoyed using his business as a platform for public pronouncements and public works, but he was much more in the mould of a business leader than a politician. He changed the name of the family business from Benn Brothers to Ernest Benn Ltd, but continued to support several family members financially. From their father, William had inherited the political mindset and Ernest had inherited the business acumen. John Benn was quite successful in both fields, but his sons each surpassed his achievements in the one area in which they specialised. In Ernest's view, business was of much more practical value, as politics was 'the art of looking for trouble, finding it whether it exists or not, diagnosing it incorrectly, and applying the wrong remedy'.

Whilst some might have believed that there was a very slight prospect that Benn could have been tempted along the rightward path of McKenna, Novar and his brother Ernest, Benn 'had always cherished the hope that there might be perhaps some sort of alliance or understanding between the left wing of the Liberal Party and the Labour Party'.[13] When this was clearly not going to transpire, he was drawn to the path taken by his distant relative, Josiah Wedgwood, by Joseph Kenworthy and by his friend Christopher Addison.

Christopher Addison had been a loyal supporter of Lloyd George and was the member of the coalition government responsible for the 1919 Housing and Town Planning Act. As the economy worsened during the Lloyd George Coalition's term of office, Addison's department faced severe financial restrictions. Addison's policies were amongst the most expensive and the most socialist of the government's programmes. This made him particularly vulnerable to demands for budget cuts, the clamour for which increased significantly with the popular support for the Anti-Waste League, sponsored by Lord Rothermere. In April 1921, Addison was moved to become minister without portfolio, but he resigned in July. His estrangement from Lloyd George and from his Conservative former colleagues left him without a political home. Addison had been one of the chief protagonists of fusion until the scheme collapsed. He then left the coalition and crossed the floor; although he was hardly welcomed or comfortable among the Asquithians, especially after his pugnacious behaviour at the Leamington Conference in 1920. Benn had had 'a long heart-to-heart talk with Addison as to his political future' and had persuaded him to remain in politics.[14] In 1922 Addison was third in a three-cornered contest and was called upon to pay over a thousand pounds in election expenses. He was almost driven to insolvency. After this financial and personal rebuff and the loss of his seat, Addison was in limbo between political parties and he did not contest the 1923 election. His policy positions, and his lack of an alternative political base, steered him towards the Labour Party. In November 1923 he decided to 'throw in his lot with the Labour Party.'[15] Addison stood unsuccessfully for Labour in 1924, but eventually returned to Parliament as Labour MP for Swindon in 1929.

Also already in the Labour Party when Benn arrived were, among others, his former Liberal parliamentary colleagues Charles Trevelyan, Arthur Ponsonby, Percy Alden, Hastings (Bertie) Lees-Smith, Noel Buxton, Sydney Arnold and Athelstan Rendall.

Benn's transition to the Labour Party did not involve him in a significant abandonment of old policies, nor the adoption of many new ones. Until 1914 Labour policies had been almost identical to Liberal policies. The two parties had been in alliance – the Gladstone-MacDonald Pact – since 1903 and the Labour Party had supported the Liberals in office after the 1906 and January and December 1910 elections. The war had seen serious splits within both the Liberal and Labour parties; however, while the Liberals remained divided until 1923, the Labour Party had managed to reunite in 1917 around a set of policies contained in 'The Memorandum on War Aims'. MacDonald, Webb and Henderson had all played a role in its formulation. It was the party's first independent foreign policy, focusing on the establishment of a League of Nations, mediation of international disputes, international trusteeship of African colonies and international co-operation on the supply of raw materials. In office in 1924 Labour foreign policy had been very much MacDonald's personal project: he had served as foreign secretary as well as prime minister. MacDonald had recognised the Communist government in Russia and had instigated bilateral trade agreements, but he was no admirer of the realities of the Communist regime and 'at home' was keen to maintain a distance from Communists, to the extent that the 1921 Labour Party conference had endorsed the exclusion of Communists from the party. With regard to Communist or other left-wing dictatorships, Benn did not turn a blind eye to their repressive methods, but always drew a moral distinction between right-wing dictatorships aimed at serving an elite and left-wing dictatorships which seemed to be aimed at promoting the interests of the poor.[16]

On the domestic front, Snowden, as chancellor, had adopted orthodox policies – less radical than Lloyd George's. Government spending had been held in check in order to balance the budget. Benn certainly did not find Labour economic policy too advanced, and, if anything, rather too timid for an old radical. So, a radical Liberal such as Benn could find an acceptable home near the centre of Labour policies, or if anything even slightly to the left of centre. He felt that his 'opinions were practically unchanged' by his transfer to the Labour Party. Henderson and Webb had drawn up a new constitution for the Labour Party, which had been adopted in February 1918. The totemic Clause 4 had in fact been drawn up at the Webbs' house next door to the Benns' and was eventually replaced by a new watered down version during Tony Blair's premiership, devised on the same spot, but by then the houses had been replaced with the Millbank Tower office complex. The new membership arrangements were more to Benn's liking than the old. Membership of local Labour parties had been opened up to individuals. Previously, membership had to be obtained through an affiliated socialist society, such as the Independent Labour Party, or via a trade union. Benn never developed close links to the trades unions and never received any significant union backing.

The most significant difference between the Labour and Liberal parties was in terms of representation. The Liberals were keen to see improvements for all sections of society, but were content for these changes to be brought about by a largely middle-class, well-educated elite, while the Labour Party was determined that working-class representatives played a full role in policy-making. However, in reality, many of the Labour Party's key figures such as Benn's neighbours, the Webbs, were middle-class intellectuals too. Socially, the Parliamentary Labour Party had become much more middle class, particularly after the 1922 election, when among the 142 MPs returned, twenty-one were graduates, nine had attended public school and twenty-six had worked in the professions.[17] The Labour Party had matured very rapidly since the end of the war. MacDonald had lost his seat in 1918, but had returned in 1922 to become not only the first person to hold the title of Labour leader (previously the role was only entitled 'chairman'), but also to become the official Leader of the Opposition. The 1922 election had seen the Labour Party for the first time win more seats (142) than the two wings of the divided Liberal Party combined (sixty-two Lloyd George supporters and fifty-four Asquithians). After the 1924 election, despite their removal from office, Labour still held 151 seats to the Liberals' forty.

Benn, with his London University education and East End upbringing, could comfortably straddle the class divide and would have been content for an even greater working-class representation in politics, subject to ability (but not education). Whilst policy differences would not have presented a significant barrier to defectors from the Liberal Party to Labour, social attitudes and tribalism could cause discomfort for some. Benn was better placed than most to overcome this and his direct, lively and engaging personality could bridge cultural divides. This had already been clear with the relationships he had established within both his constituencies, in the air force and with the many foreigners he had encountered. Socially, the main gulf which he had found hard to span was with the regular cavalry officers, whom he had encountered early in the First World War. Overall though, all the Liberal defectors to the Conservatives remained happily in their new party, while half of those who defected to Labour became dissatisfied, or even left the Labour Party. In an enduring pattern which was brought clearly into focus in the 2010 coalition negotiations, the Liberal-Labour policy gap was small, but the cultural gap larger. The Labour Party's stricter discipline and tighter rules made it a more efficient political machine, but a less comfortable home for refugees from other parties. Benn was sometimes irked, but never repulsed, by Labour's tighter discipline.[18] He never regretted joining that 'warm-hearted fellowship', as he described the Labour Party.[19]

In Benn's case, his defection had been directly prompted by his distrust of Lloyd George. His admiration for Asquith had anchored him to the Liberal Party until Lloyd George took over the leadership in October 1926, but from then onwards it was almost inevitable that he would drift away. The current of 'push' factors from the Liberal Party was carrying him away. As Benn recorded, once 'it became clear that [Asquith] did not intend to return, when a few days later it was announced that he had received an earldom, then the situation as far as I was concerned, became completely intolerable.' Benn's view of the prospects for the Liberal Party turned out to be over-pessimistic, but not by a large margin. 'Was it possible after what had occurred between 1918 and 1927 for the Liberal Party to survive? My answer

... is perfectly clear, it was impossible.'[20] The Labour Party was not a strong attraction in itself, but rather it provided an acceptable alternative political home for Benn and one which already contained some of his former-Liberal colleagues. Once inside the Labour Party, however, the former-Liberals did not particularly act in concert.

After Lloyd George assumed the leadership of the Liberals in October 1926, the party did actually see some improvement in its prospects. The leadership question was settled, not to everyone's satisfaction admittedly, but for the time being there was no serious challenger to Lloyd George. The Liberals had not captured a new seat at a by-election since 1923, but in the period from March 1927 to March 1929 the party won by-elections at Southwark North, Bosworth, Lancaster, St. Ives, Eddisbury and Holland with Boston. The encouraging features of these victories for the Liberals were that they included gains from Labour and from the Conservatives, they involved urban and rural seats, they were geographically distributed from Cornwall to Lancashire and not all the victors were male. These victories were all in England, but in many respects they appeared to be indications of a broad-based recovery in Liberal fortunes. The Liberals also held Leith at the by-election resulting from Benn's resignation, which was held on 23 March 1927. Ernest Brown won for the Liberals, but with a much reduced majority – down from over 5,000 in Benn's last contest to just 111.

23 March 1927 by-election Leith:

A.E. Brown	Liberal	12,461
R.F. Wilson	Labour	12,350
A. Beaton	Conservative	4,607
	Liberal majority	111 (0.3 per cent)

Brown held Leith again as a Liberal in 1929 and as a Liberal National in 1931 and 1935, but lost the seat to Labour in 1945. Had Benn fought the by-election as the Labour candidate, he might well have won, being likely to have received the vast majority of the Labour votes and also a personal vote from some former Liberals. But it would have meant ousting the incumbent prospective Labour candidate and campaigning against his old Liberal friends, and he did not want to do either of these. While Benn had no designs on standing as the Labour candidate, had the local Labour Party accepted his help, he could almost certainly have swung enough voters to Labour in the by-election to ensure Wilson's victory. However, his help was not sought. Benn had made no advances to the local Labour Party. 'The fact was that the existing Labour candidate ... had even less respect for me than my late Liberal associates. He was an ardent left-wing believer, quite sincere, but no idea of getting my help at the forthcoming election ... His fear had always been that I was after the seat ... I had no intention' of contesting it.[21]

Benn now found himself in the same political party as his friend and neighbour, Oswald (Tom) Mosley. In fact, Tony Benn's first ever speech was to say 'Thank you' at a Mosley birthday tea.[22] Mosley had previously been a Conservative MP, then an independent and in 1924 had joined the Labour Party. He had returned to Parliament as the Labour MP for Smethwick at a by-election in December 1926. After Benn's move to the Labour Party, he and Margaret also became more friendly with their next door neighbours at Grosvenor Road, Beatrice and Sidney Webb. The Benns were invited to stay at the Webbs' country retreat, *Passfield Corner* in Hampshire. The Benns thought that the Webbs were an odd couple, living in an oddly-furnished house. Beatrice, attracted to Sidney's brilliant mind, but physically repelled by him, had persuaded herself that she was only marrying Sidney's head.[23] She had described him as having a 'tiny tadpole body, unhealthy skin' and a cockney accent. At *Passfield Corner* they had different unmatching curtains at each window in the sitting room. When Sidney was raised to the peerage in 1929 he took the title Lord Passfield. Beatrice, declaring that she was a middle-class socialist, refused to be called either Lady Passfield or comrade, but wanted to remain Mrs Webb.[24] Sidney's father has been variously described as an accountant, hairdresser and perfumer. Beatrice shared a wealthy background with her cousin-by-marriage, Charles Booth, with whom she had collaborated on the social investigations, but despite their shared experiences of studying East End poverty, Booth moved from Liberalism to Conservatism, while Beatrice had adopted Socialism. Despite their misalignments, the Webbs gave the impression of being a happy couple. They moved from Grosvenor Road in 1929 and most of their house was taken over by the Labour MP, Susan Lawrence, who had previously been the Webbs' lodger. The Benns rented part of the house from Lawrence to provide them with a large library-cum-sitting room. They had a doorway installed between the two houses. Lawrence was a congenial neighbour, too. She had started her political life as a Conservative, serving as a Municipal Reform member of the London County Council from 1910, but two years later she resigned her seat and joined the Fabian Society, returning to the council in the Labour interest in 1913. In 1921 she was jailed for her part in the withholding of council payments in Poplar and sent to Holloway prison. She had then been elected to the Commons in 1923, as one of the first three female Labour MPs.[25]

In November 1927 Benn was chosen as the prospective Labour candidate for Renfrewshire West, the constituency in which Margaret had grown up. West Renfrew had been a marginal Tory-Liberal seat from its creation in 1885 until 1910. Labour first contested the seat in 1918 and their candidate, Robert Murray, won it at the second attempt in 1922. He held the seat at the following election in 1923, but lost it to the Conservative, Douglas MacInnes Shaw in the Conservatives' good showing in 1924, by a margin of just over 2,000 votes. Shaw had transferred to Renfrewshire West at short notice in 1924. He had been Asquith's opponent in neighbouring Paisley in 1923, but had stood aside from that seat in 1924 to give Asquith a straight fight with Labour. The same Conservative-Liberal arrangement was established in many of the Scottish seats in 1924.

At one o'clock in the morning of 8 January 1928, while Benn was away in Scotland, Margaret was woken up by their cook who announced that the Thames was in their house.[26] The river had breached the retaining wall opposite their house, and the basement, in which they had created a self-contained flat for their domestic staff, was filling with water. All the Benn family and staff survived, but fourteen people drowned in the flood, including some in the basements of their neighbours' homes on Grosvenor Road. The Benns were luckier and only had to contend with the aftermath of the insurgence of water, debris and neighbours' belongings which had entered their house, including a case full of Sidney Webb's underwear.[27] The house was made habitable again and further 'improvements' were carried out, such as building a cupboard which could be hauled up to the ceiling. It was installed outside Benn's study and housed his clothes, presumably intended to be out of sight and out of reach of flood water. Tony once took delight in showing the contraption and its contents to his father's visiting parliamentary colleagues.[28] Like his father, Benn was an incorrigible alterer of houses and designer of gadgets. Among Benn's other inventions were the design for a new type of gas cooker, which he discussed patenting,[29] and a bed on stilts, so that it was possible to admire the view out of the bedroom window without getting out of bed. In terms of space and organisation, Benn's work dominated many of the domestic arrangements. His 'study' comprised much of the basement, ground floor and first floor of the house, all connected by trapdoors and ladders. His secretary, Miss Triggs, worked on the ground floor, spending much of her time cutting up and filing articles from multiple copies of the *Times*. The equipment for this included huge guillotines and gluing machines. It was somewhat ironic that Benn, a radical and by no means a supporter of its successive owners (the Northcliffes and the Astors), almost exclusively relied on the establishment-oriented *Times* as his source of information about the world. The only telephone in the Benns' house at Grosvenor Road was an operator's headset, designed to allow Benn to work and talk on the 'phone at the same time. However, it was not conducive to social calls and Margaret did not enjoy having her hair squashed every time she used the 'phone.

After nursing West Renfrew as his future political home for eight months, an alternative route for Benn back into the Commons arose, following the death of Frank Rose, the sitting Labour MP for Aberdeen North in July 1928. The Aberdeen North constituency was compact and confined entirely within the city boundaries. (So was neighbouring Aberdeen South). As with Benn's previous constituencies, in Tower Hamlets and Leith, Aberdeen looked to the water for much of its livelihood, with fishing and shipbuilding being among its leading industries. At that time Aberdeen was Scotland's leading fishing port, employing 3,000 and providing a base for 300 trawlers. Aberdeen North had been Liberal held until 1918, when Rose had won the seat, initially as an Independent Labour candidate, eventually becoming an official Labour MP. At the last election in 1924, Rose had held the seat against his only opponent, the Conservative Dr Laura Sandeman, with a majority of 4,704 (21.6 per cent). It was the Independent Labour Party which proposed Benn for the seat, with twenty-eight members voting to put his name forward, against seven for the only other candidate considered, Fraser Macintosh. Benn's nomination was then endorsed, unopposed, by the Executive Committee of the Aberdeen Trades and Labour Council. Benn had very little time to prepare for the by-election. His Conservative opponent had stood in the constituency at the last election, but Benn was only adopted as the Labour candidate on 30 July and the by-election was set for 16 August 1928.[30]

There was disunity in left-of-centre politics in Aberdeen. At the by-election Benn was to face not only a Conservative and a Liberal opponent, but also vocal opposition from the Communists, who also put up a candidate, Aitken Ferguson. The Communists put out leaflets pointing out that their candidate was the only 'genuine trade unionist' and that Benn stood for the 'Starvation of Railway Men'.[31] Benn, responding by letter in the local press, reassured a correspondent who, as Benn cheekily pointed out, 'in his anxiety ... has forgotten to give his name and address' that 'I have never preached a "class war" and I never will'.[32]

16 August 1928 by-election Aberdeen North:

W.W. Benn	Labour	10,646
L.S. Sandeman	Conservative	4,696
A. Ferguson	Communist	2,618
J.R. Rutherford	Liberal	2,337
	Labour majority	5,950 (29.4 per cent)

Benn's victory represented an improvement in the Labour performance compared to 1924, when Rose had won the seat with a 21.6 per cent majority, against only a Conservative opponent.

Margaret was pregnant again and had been unwell during the by-election campaign. This pregnancy had been more difficult than the first two, but on 28 December 1928 she gave birth to their third son, David. The family were to receive vital help from a new nurse, Olive Winch, who was recruited via the Norland Institute just before David's birth and who became an important part of the family for two generations. She replaced a rather bullying Nurse Parker, who had frightened Margaret. Olive Winch was organised, competent, very well-liked and trusted. She took a lot of actions on her own initiative, but was diligent in letting the family know what she was doing and if they were away would write and explain what she had done and spent.

When Benn returned to the Commons, he was reunited with two of his wartime commanders: Murray Sueter and Cecil Malone, both of whom had taken unorthodox routes into Parliament. Sueter had been an MP since his by-election victory for the Anti-Waste League (in many ways the UKIP of its day) in 1921, but he had subsequently joined the Conservatives. Malone had been elected for Labour seven months before Benn was elected at Aberdeen North. Of all the convoluted career paths of former Liberals, that of Cecil L'Estrange Malone was probably the most unorthodox. Malone had gone from being elected in 1918 as a Coalition Liberal to being the UK's first Communist MP.[33] His shifting political allegiance gave rise to what must have been one of the strangest exchanges of correspondence between an MP and his constituency chairman, who wrote to Malone to say that he 'found it very difficult to form any opinion as to what your political views really were and as to what party you, in fact, belong.'[34] Malone officially joined the Communist Party in July 1920. After a speech at the Albert Hall in November that year, he was charged with sedition. He had argued that during a revolution, it would be legitimate to execute leading members of the bourgeoisie. He was convicted and sentenced to six months imprisonment. On his release, Malone returned to the House of Commons.[35] During his time in prison, he had changed his views on revolutionary politics and decided to join the ILP. The Communist Party concluded that his temporary allegiance had been genuine, despite allegations that he had been an infiltrator.[36] Malone was out of Parliament from 1922, but was re-elected for Labour at a by-election in Northampton on 9 January 1928.

Less than ten months after first being elected for the seat, Benn had to defend Aberdeen North in the 1929 general election. Labour's manifesto, entitled 'Labour and the Nation' presented a moral case for gradualist socialism, with the eventual nationalisation of land, coal, power and transport. Labour's manifesto may have sounded tame, but compared to the Conservatives' election slogan of 'Safety First', it was relatively radical. Much more radical, but to the point of implausibility in the eyes of many, was Lloyd George's library of policies brought together under the banner

'We can conquer unemployment'. A centrepiece was the plan for a vast, and improbably-quick, road building scheme. Benn again faced a Communist challenge from Aitken Ferguson in Aberdeen. MacDonald's strategy was to place every obstacle he could in the way of the survival of the three-party system.[37] This clearly had implications for his attitude to the Liberals. With Lloyd George as the Liberal leader, Benn could more comfortably subscribe to this strategy than would have been the case if certain other figures had been at the head of his old party, such as Archie Sinclair for instance.

1929 general election Aberdeen North:

W.W. Benn	Labour	17,826
R.C. Berkeley	Liberal	9,799
A. Ferguson	Communist	1,686
	Labour majority	8,027 (27.4 per cent)

The 1929 general election was the only election between the wars when the Conservative Party was not the party which won the most seats, but even then the Conservatives did attract the most votes. (The elections of 1929, 1951 and February 1974 all resulted in the party with the most votes not capturing the most seats.) The outcome saw Labour win 287 seats on 37.1 per cent of the votes and the Conservatives 260 seats with a slightly higher 38.1 per cent of the vote. The Liberals trailed in with 59 seats, although their share of the vote was 23.6 per cent – an improvement of 19 seats and 5.8 per cent more of the vote than at the last election in 1924. The Labour Party formed its second government, but still without an overall majority. Benn sailed home comfortably in Aberdeen North.

In his second premiership MacDonald relinquished the role of foreign secretary to Arthur Henderson, possibly working on the premise that the safest place for a premier's rivals is at the foreign office (i.e. mainly out of the country). Benn was appointed Secretary of State for India and on 8 June 1929 sworn of the Privy Council at Windsor Castle, along with the other cabinet ministers who were not already privy councillors. So, within ten months of first being elected as a Labour MP, Benn was in the Labour cabinet. He was one of only three members of the cabinet who had military service, one of only two who had seen action and the only one to be a decorated officer.

Albert (A.V.) Alexander had also reached the rank of captain in the army but, due to health limitations, had served as a posting and education officer. Bertie Lees-Smith had chosen to serve in the ranks and had seen action, ending the war with the rank of corporal. The new cabinet assembled in the sunlit garden of Number 10 to appear before the media. For the first time, the event was recorded in moving pictures with sound. A delighted, but nervously-shuffling, MacDonald introduced his ministers to the cameras. In a somewhat awkward piece of choreography, the ministers took it in turns to come before the cameras. Benn emerged from the group towards the end of the introductions, looking very smart in a double-breasted suit – the only one sporting a bow tie. He smiled diffidently, one hand in his pocket, while MacDonald introduced him as 'one of the young men': he was 52-years-old, but did look younger. MacDonald announced that Benn was to face a 'very trying time', and he was not to be alone. Margaret Bondfield was the last to be introduced; 'a double-first' as MacDonald explained – the first female privy councillor and the first female cabinet minister. In a touching gesture, Bondfield kissed MacDonald's hand. Presciently, MacDonald made several mentions of the challenge of unemployment which the group was to face. There was every sign of MacDonald's supremacy over the cabinet, but a noticeable degree of informality for the times and indications of a friendly rapport among the group. This was only slightly diminished by the non-appearance of Arthur Henderson and the dour demeanour of Philip Snowden, introduced first and moving with the aid of his two walking sticks.[38]

Former Liberals continued to provide a sizeable minority of the Labour government. The 1929 cabinet contained three former Liberal MPs – Benn, Trevelyan and Buxton. Outside the cabinet were Ponsonby as under secretary at the Dominions Office and Lees-Smith as Postmaster General, later to replace Trevelyan in cabinet. Addison was to replace the newly-ennobled Buxton in June 1930, but was initially outside the cabinet and temporarily junior to Benn. Missing from the second Labour cabinet were Haldane, who had died in 1928 and Josiah Wedgwood, who had a difficult relationship with MacDonald and was not included in the new administration.

Immediately after the 1929 election MacDonald asked Liberal MP William Jowitt to serve as Attorney-General. Jowitt was a highly capable and ambitious lawyer, but, in politics, even he accepted that he lacked conviction. With nine older sisters, and a vicar for a father, Jowitt seemed to have become reliant on external guidance when making major decisions. Benn recorded in his diary that Jowitt was 'tortured to know what to do ... he wants to join the Labour Party, but is afraid it would affect his briefs.'[39] Jowitt resigned his seat at Preston, which he had only just won for the first time, causing a by-election, which he won under Labour colours on 31 July 1929, without Liberal opposition. He thus became the last of the three defectors (after Kenworthy and Benn) who resigned his seat on changing party allegiance from Liberal to Labour. The Liberals were therefore deprived of Kenworthy's Hull Central and Jowitt's Preston seats, as these defectors retained their old constituencies for Labour, but the Liberals had retained Leith.

As Secretary of State for India, Benn had to maintain the link between the cabinet and the Viceroy of India, Lord Irwin. Irwin was four years younger than Benn, but his post was arguably second only to the prime minister's in terms of the breadth of executive responsibility. His grandfather had served as Secretary of State for India. Irwin (at the time known as Edward Wood) had sat as a (fairly moderate) Conservative MP for Ripon from January 1910 until the announcement by Baldwin of his appointment as Viceroy in November 1925. He had then been elevated to the peerage. Despite having a deformed left arm, Irwin had served in the army during the First World War, reaching the rank of major. He had become a fierce opponent of the continuation of the coalition under Lloyd George's leadership in 1922. After the 1922 election, He had sat in the cabinet as President of the Board of Education. On the Conservatives' return to power after the first Labour government he had held the agriculture portfolio in the cabinet until the announcement of his appointment to the viceroyalty. He took up the post in April 1926. A five-year term of office was the norm, with a return to England for a few months' break in the middle. Irwin left India for his mid-term visit to England on 27 June 1929, less than a month after Benn's appointment as Secretary of State. This provided a useful opportunity for face to face meetings between the two, as Benn did not visit India at all during his term of office.

Benn and Irwin had both served in the Commons and in the army, so they shared some valuable formative experiences. The difference in their party backgrounds was to be an advantage, with many Conservatives reluctant to disagree with Irwin, and Benn enjoying the support of the prime minister, the cabinet, most of the Labour Party and still retaining some friends in the Liberal Party. Their main opposition was to come from some radical Labour quarters, from some die-hard Conservatives and from Lloyd George together with Irwin's Liberal predecessor as Viceroy, Lord Reading (formerly Rufus Isaacs). Benn and Irwin were united in their attitudes to most of the dissenters. Both had abandoned their confidence in Lloyd George. In Benn's eyes, Reading was, like Lloyd George, tainted by the pre-war Marconi share scandal. Benn did not worry about the Labour dissenters, knowing that his views were closer to theirs than any previous Secretary of State for India. Only those on the Conservative right bothered Irwin, partly because of personal relationships and partly because they had the ear of Stanley Baldwin.

The balance of power between the two was certainly weighted in Irwin's favour, especially in Benn's early days in post. The impression was reinforced by Irwin's height of 6'5", towering over Benn by nearly a foot. Irwin was privately reassured by his friend, the Conservative Party chairman, J.C.C. Davidson, that 'Little Benn is genuinely anxious "in no way to let you down" ... I wish it meant more – he is very light weight'.[40] Six months later, Davidson's view of Benn had improved marginally, even offering faint praise: 'little Benn stood up manfully' in the Commons, but still added 'of course he is a very light weight'.[41]

The last major declaration on Indian affairs had been the 1917 Montagu Declaration, which had been embodied in the Government of India Act of 1919, promoted by Edwin Montagu as Secretary of State and passed under the Lloyd George coalition government. It had set out a policy for 'the gradual development of self-governing institutions with a view to progressive realization of responsible government in British India as an integral part of the British Empire'. It had instituted a system of dyarchy – or dual control, whereby Indian ministers were responsible for local self-government, education, public health, public works, agriculture, forests, and fisheries. Crown-appointed executive councillors still administered reserved subjects, including law and order, justice, police, land revenue and irrigation. The entity of India in the 1920s and 1930s extended over modern-day Pakistan,

India, Bangladesh and Myanmar (Burma). It comprised a patchwork of provinces of British India, each administered by a British governor and over 500 princely states, which were under the control of Indian rulers. The princes were regarded as royal, but subordinate to the British monarch, who was Emperor of India.

The only previous Labour Secretary of State for India, Lord Olivier, had left most policy undisturbed during his brief tenure in 1924. One of the 1919 act's provisions had been the setting up, within ten years, of a committee to review the operation of Indian administration. Accordingly, a commission comprising seven British MPs (but with no Indian members) had been set up under the chairmanship of Sir John Simon in 1928. The Simon Commission's report was still in preparation when Benn took up his post.

Benn was not quite out of his depth in his new role, but at first he certainly found it difficult to establish a firm foothold and was dragged by currents of opinion in different directions. Essentially Benn, MacDonald and Irwin were able to reach common ground on the policy of further devolution. In this they received valuable support from Stanley Baldwin, at least in a personal capacity. Those pulling in other directions included Lloyd George, Churchill and some Conservative allies, who wanted to preserve the maximum British control over India, and also Fenner Brockway and some Labour allies who wanted the exact opposite. However, it was not just a case of steering a middle course through the minefield of British political opinion – an almost irreconcilable range of views existed in India.

Benn and Irwin agreed to move ahead without waiting for Simon's report and on 31 October 1929, shortly after his return to India, the Viceroy announced the 'Irwin Declaration'. The main points of the declaration were that the eventual aim of British policy was for India to achieve self-governing 'dominion' status within the British Empire and that a round table conference was to be held, involving Indian representation, after the Simon Commission report had been published. The potential for differing interpretations of the term 'dominion status' had echoes of the decades of problems over the meaning and interpretation of 'home rule' in Ireland. In some respects the Irwin Declaration had similarities to the 'Hawarden Kite', when Gladstone revealed his conversion to home rule for Ireland.

The organisation of the round table conference was to absorb most of Benn's energy during his term of office. However, Benn had to respond in the House of Commons to a wide range of other issues relating to India: some of life and death importance and some detailed, but rather trivial. He contributed to 587 debates and written answers in 1930 and 435 in 1931. Benn had to give virtually daily updates to the Commons. On economic matters, Benn was able to report that, unlike the British situation, the financial position of India was very sound. The debt per head of the population of British India was approximately £3 3s 0d.[42]

He had to reply to a question about film censorship. It was a matter entirely for the local authorities, but Benn had to request a list of the forty-seven films banned over the previous two years and explain that the majority were proscribed on the grounds of 'ordinary decency and morality'.[43] He also had to deal with an in inquiry into the consumption of opium. On other occasions Benn was asked about child marriage and slavery in India and replied that 'the Government of India are satisfied that slavery in the ordinary sense of the term does not exist in any Indian State'.[44]

The state of personal relations and the scale of policy disagreement between Benn and Lloyd George was revealed in an acrimonious adjournment debate on Indian policy in the Commons on 7 November 1929, which is better remembered for an exchange of insults than for its substance.[45] Baldwin opened the debate with an explanation of his personal position. Privately, he was in agreement with the Irwin/Benn position, but he did not carry the support of the whole Conservative shadow cabinet and the *Daily Mail* had exposed the differences. Baldwin had a delicate path to tread, not wishing to derail the policy of which he actually approved, but adding caveats and conditions to his support to avoid a serious split in his own party and to undermine the press report. The state of relations between Baldwin and the *Daily Mail* had descended into a vendetta.[46] In his avuncular style, Baldwin dismissed the article as:

'merely a journalistic stunt ... Let us pass away from this rather sordid subject and give our attention to a matter of the greatest import ... To talk ... of a crisis, is absurd ... To speak of the situation as one in which there are elements which require explanation and elucidation would be true ... In our view, a blunder was made when a statement of policy was made without the assent of the Simon Commission ... We felt that there were two risks being run ... one ... was the risk of prejudicing the Report of the Simon Commission, and ... the other [is] the risk of misunderstanding in India'.

Immediately after Baldwin sat down, Lloyd George rose to his feet to launch an onslaught, not only on the policy, but also on Benn personally. The substance of Lloyd George's objection was the announcement of the Irwin Declaration in advance of the publication of the Simon report, but his tone was strongly influenced by personal feeling:

'I did not receive from the Prime Minister the honour of a letter informing me what he proposed to do ... I was the head of the Government that introduced [the 1917 Declarations]. I presided over the Imperial Cabinet that sanctioned the terms of these Declarations ... there is no question in so far as hon. Members sitting around me are concerned, of going back one single inch from these Declarations'. Lloyd George ended his denunciation by claiming that Benn had 'smashed' the 'Tables of the Covenant' and describing him as 'this pocket edition of Moses', to which Benn spontaneously replied: 'But I never worshipped the golden calf.' Lloyd George tried to snatch back the initiative with his retort that Benn had: 'shown a very shrewd appreciation of what is known as "the main chance"; and the calf which has been sacrificed for him has its golden side.' Lloyd George's initial insult was a comment on the destruction of his policy, which he sanctified as the 'Tables (tablets) of the Covenant'. (According to the Bible, Moses smashed the tablets inscribed with the Ten Commandments, when he was enraged by the sight of the Children of Israel worshiping a golden calf, which had been fashioned from molten gold.) Lloyd George was also pointing to Benn's successful emergence from the political wilderness and mocking his short stature, although Lloyd George himself was hardly a towering figure at 5'6", and Benn was not the shortest of the men in the cabinet: William Graham was shorter. In fact, Benn was usually recorded as being 5'6" tall, but according to his passport details he reached the dizzying height of 5'8" in 1929 (and again in 1941).[47] Up until Benn's appointment to the Labour cabinet, it would be fair to conclude that he had not profited

Kyverdale Road, Stoke Newington, London, William Wedgwood Benn's home from 1883.

Finsbury Square today, unrecognisable from when it was the Benn family home in 1885.

Julius Benn, William Wedgwood Benn's paternal grandfather, murdered in 1883 by his own son.

The Boulton and Paul catalogue, from which the flatpack 'ancestral home' was chosen.

The chosen design for Stansgate, number 303.

Stansgate delivered and erected 1900.

W. WEDGWOOD BENN.   GEOFFREY HOWARD.   F.E. GUEST.   HENRY WEBB.

J.W. GULLAND.   PERCY ILLINGWORTH.   WILLIAM JONES.

William Wedgwood Benn and the team of Liberal whips before the First World War.

Captain Benn DSO DFC MP after the Great War.

Cowley Street, Westminster, the Benns' home from 1921.

The wedding of William Wedgwood Benn and Margaret Eadie Holmes in 1920. He was forty-three, she was twenty-three.

40 Grosvenor Road, later renamed Millbank, the Benns' home from 1925. Sidney and Beatrice Webb lived next door.

The lease on 40 Millbank expired in 1958 and the house was demolished, to be replaced by Millbank Tower.

The growing Benn family in 1929, shortly after David's birth. Michael is on his parents' right and Tony is on the left.

Family picnic. Food was never very important to the Benn family.

The Benn family sporting the latest fashion in swimwear.

Michael, Tony and David posing for the camera during the 1937 Gorton by-election campaign.

William Wedgwood Benn, worshipped by his children.

William Wedgwood Benn taking his children for a ride on the lawnmower. Health and safety was never a major concern of his.

Captain Benn comes ashore.

The Benn family modelling the latest headgear.

Rowing home to Stansgate.

The Benns set off round the world with a kettle, but without their children, in 1934.

The Benns shortly before the outbreak of the Second World War

The Benn family prepares for war.

The Benn family in uniform after the outbreak of the Second World War.

William Wedgwood Benn, ennobled as Viscount Stansgate, in RAF uniform.

William
Wedgwood
Benn and eldest
son Michael, in
RAF uniform.

The plane in which
Michael was killed
in 1944 after an
instrument failure.

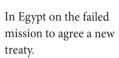

In Egypt on the failed
mission to agree a new
treaty.

Afloat again.

Reading a newspaper, particularly the *Times* even though he did not share its political outlook, was an essential part of Benn's daily routine.

The noble viscount in front of his ancestral home.

Attlee's 1945 to 1946 cabinet. Benn is fifth from the left on the middle row. Addison and Jowitt are first and second from the left on the front row. AV Alexander is third from the right on the front row. Ellen Wilkinson was the only female member of the cabinet.

The four Benn siblings who survived into middle age – from left to right William, Irene, Ernest and (Lilian) Margaret.

Caroline, Tony, Stephen and Hilary, Christmas 1956 - in case there was any doubt.

Putting the family first – health and safety still not much in evidence.

Tony inherited his father's lack of concern for health and safety.

Cook's rest house. Despite the Benn family's feminist instincts, the division of labour at home did not quite match up to modern expectations.

Hilary represents the fourth consecutive generation of Benns to sit in the House of Commons, pictured here with his father and grandmother.

The subject looks down trustingly on his biographer from his portrait at Stansgate.

The author with Stephen, the third viscount. Alcohol is now consumed at Stansgate. Note the bottle of beer for the journey home in the author's pocket.

The author with Melissa Benn, sampling the 'strong' Stansgate air. It was too much for her great-grandfather who sold the house, only for it to be bought back by her grandfather thirty years later.

The author enters the slaughterhouse. Along with four 'Welsh cottages' and six shipping containers, it houses some of the Benn family archives. William Wedgwood Benn was not joking when he described himself as a 'file merchant'.

The author on a research visit to Stansgate, somewhat surprised to find that his subject's car was still there fifty-four years after he died.

by his rejection of office under Lloyd George or his defection from the Liberal Party. However, Lloyd George for his part had been busy selling honours. Seeing Benn accept a Labour cabinet post and being in a position to overturn one of his own policies, Lloyd George let slip his personal feelings, which he had kept cloaked under an artificial politeness until then. A mental image of pots and kettles was probably conjured up in the minds of many parliamentarians by Lloyd George's claim that Benn's motivation was mercenary. It was not; but he had tried Lloyd George's patience to breaking point. Benn held the moral high ground in his decisions, but he had snubbed Lloyd George on too many occasions – over his wedding invitation, the rejected job offers, his usurpation of Lloyd George's seat in the Commons, his objection to Lloyd George's leadership of the Liberal Party and now over his lack of consultation on the plans to overturn one of Lloyd George's own policies. In most people's eyes, Lloyd George's comments rebounded on him and Benn was relieved of some measure of guilt for the manner of his past treatment of Lloyd George. It marked a very public turning of the tables in the relationship between the two.

Benn tried to steer the debate onto the process to be followed in reaching a broadly acceptable solution for India: 'I am standing here with an immense consciousness of the responsibility that rests upon one slenderly equipped ... The Liberals were against [the Irwin Declaration], the Conservatives were against it, and the Commission were unwilling to participate. What did the Government do? They governed ... We do not shelter behind the Viceroy. He offered advice and we were free to reject it. We did not reject it, because it agreed with our own convictions. [We want] to make a good atmosphere for the [Simon] Report ... the atmosphere [in India] has been growing steadily worse and worse ... The real interest in India is ... in this Conference [which] is to be fully representative of different parties and interests in British India and of the Indian States ... The problems that face us are very grave ... There are obstacles in the path, but there are two ways of regarding obstacles. You can regard them as an excuse for abandoning a pre-determined purpose, or you can regard them as merely exciting a desire to overcome them.'

Benn was followed by John Simon, who in many words and several different ways, explained at length that he really was not prepared to say anything at all, in order to preserve the independence of his commission:

'I should have thought that by this time everybody would know that it was impossible to provoke me on the subject of the Commission ... I would most earnestly ask Parliament to leave us to continue our work undisturbed without Parliamentary controversy ... Of course it is useless to pretend that the incidents leading to this Debate have not for the time being added to our own difficulties, through no fault of our own, but, in fact, these things do not make the slightest difference in the determination of the Commission'.

Simon, no friend or ally of Benn's, confined himself to this limited rebuke, but then returned to his purdah. This suited Benn.

MacDonald wound up the debate by adding force to Simon's argument that there was nothing to be gained by exploiting disagreements in Parliament, nor by pre-empting or diverting the conclusions of the Simon Commission. Effectively, the debate had been a non-event, which had let off some steam, but which had changed no minds (other than about Benn's ability to retort to Lloyd George's insults). As it was an adjournment debate called by the government, there was no vote taken. Lloyd George and a section of the Conservative right had hoped to be able to press for a division, but it was not granted by the Speaker. Baldwin thus avoided exposing the divisions within the Conservative Party to any further scrutiny. Benn had not looked completely in command of the situation, but he had managed to avoid any serious damage to the government's, or his own, position and had scored a rhetorical victory over Lloyd George. The work of the Simon Commission and the preparation for the round table conference proceeded, but the situation in India remained precarious.

Benn also had to contend with minor skirmishes within his own party, including a motion in the Commons put down by Fenner Brockway, James Maxton and others to reduce Benn's salary. Brockway explained: 'I should like to make it clear that the Motion on the Paper for a reduction of his salary [by £100 per year] is not in any way antagonistic to my right hon. Friend the Secretary of State for India. Indeed, I can claim personal friendship with him. But it is because I believe the moment has come when very strong protest should be made against the policy which he and the Government are pursuing in India.'[48] The three were arguing for faster progress, rather than a change of direction. In the event they did not proceed with the motion to reduce Benn's salary.

Overall though, there was much more than money or hurt pride at stake in terms of the impact of Indian policy. In India, people were being killed and injured in riots. Irwin survived several assassination attempts, including having his train bombed in December 1929.[49] And in the background was the Meerut conspiracy trial, which had started before Benn took office and was still in progress when he left. The authorities believed that there was a Moscow-inspired plot to encourage a Communist revolutionary spirit within India's trades unions. Thirty-two people had been charged with conspiracy to deprive the King of the sovereignty of British India. The protracted length of the trial encouraged public sympathy for the accused to grow. Against this background, Benn decided to ban the former British Communist MP, Shapurji Saklatvala, who had been defeated at the 1929 election, from returning to his native India.[50] As Benn stated in the Commons, 'I do not like doing it at all, but I have to consider a very delicate situation'.[51]

If Benn was reluctant to prevent Saklatvala returning to India, he was more reticent still about having to endorse the jailing of Gandhi. Mohandas (Mahatma) Gandhi was a very difficult figure for many British politicians to estimate. Benn, with his innate belief in equality, and Irwin, with his deeply-held religious principles, were better equipped than most (particularly Churchill) to understand Gandhi. Superficially, Gandhi was a bundle of contradictions. He was from a relatively prosperous Hindu Indian background, but he had spent much of his life in South Africa, practising as a lawyer, having qualified in London at the Inner Temple. He lived the lifestyle of a pauper. He was associated with India's oldest political party, Congress, but he was not a political office-holder. Innately, however, Gandhi was one of the most consistent political activists the world has seen. His beliefs, actions and lifestyle were all compatible, open and consistent – but very different from those of a British politician. He was a symbolic leader, who had developed a powerful following for his ability to change minds through non-violent campaigns which united people across religious and social divides. This was unprecedented in the history of the British Empire, which essentially had experience of dealing with either acquiescence or violent opposition. Gandhi's selflessness was expressed in his clothing, his lifestyle, his willingness to admit failure and his reluctance to take formal office. He was deeply religious, but respected those of other faiths on an equal basis. His power stemmed from his ability to inspire others in huge numbers, his integrity, his willingness to suffer and his complete lack of care for his personal status, meaning that he had nothing to lose in any negotiation and he was prepared to negotiate. He had been imprisoned on many occasions previously, but the immediate cause for the latest incarceration was his organisation of a peaceful boycott of the salt tax, which had been doubled in 1923 during Lord Reading's viceroyalty and was widely resented in India. It existed purely for the benefit of the Treasury, not for India or for health reasons. The British had the monopoly on the production of salt, which was obtained from the sea. On 12 March 1930, Gandhi set out for a walk of twenty-four days to the west coast of India, where he waded into the sea and picked up some salt, declaring that with his handful of salt he was proclaiming the end of the British Empire. The police arrived and arrested thousands of national leaders with Gandhi himself being arrested on 5 May 1930. Benn had to explain the decision in the Commons. His view was that 'the defiance of the Salt Law has in itself not caused much trouble. Its real significance lies in the attempt to use it as a means of rousing public sentiment to a dangerous pitch, and in one or two places the public demonstrations have, I regret to say, resulted in clashes with the police.'[52] Benn explained the rather unusual circumstances of Gandhi's incarceration to the Commons. As Gandhi had not been convicted of a violent crime and 'by social status, education and habit of life has been accustomed to a superior mode of living',[53] he was entitled to be detained in conditions, which afforded 'no analogy for the treatment of persons convicted and sentenced under the ordinary law.' 'Gandhi is occupying the same quarters as those he had during his imprisonment in 1922. He has the necessary furniture, and his rooms are provided with electric light and with wide verandas and a small garden in front. He has complete liberty to take what exercise he desires. He sleeps in the open and is not closely confined. He is being supplied with his usual diet and is in receipt of an allowance. The question of his wife's being allowed to be with him has not arisen: so far as I am aware there is no precedent for such an arrangement.'[54] Gandhi did, however, manage to give a press interview from prison.[55] In total, 80,000 Indians were imprisoned for breaking the salt laws but, eventually, Gandhi was released on 25 January 1931.

In June 1930 the long-awaited, and simply long, Simon Commission report was published – in two volumes. It set out four main recommendations: The new constitution should contain provision for its own development; dyarchy should be scrapped and ministers responsible to the legislature would be entrusted with all provincial areas of responsibility; a federal union, including both British India and the Princely States, was the only long-term solution for a united, autonomous India and finally, to help the growth of political consciousness, the franchise should be extended and the Legislature enlarged.

In a personal, political and technological blow to Benn, on 5 October 1930 Secretary of State for Air, Lord Thomson, was killed in the R101 airship disaster. Benn had been considering him as a potential successor to Irwin.[56] Instead, the Earl of Willingdon replaced Irwin as Viceroy.[57] Thomson was also a serious loss to the cabinet. Along with J.H. Thomas, he was one of MacDonald's few genuine friends in politics. However, the disaster did create an opportunity for Simon to carry out another investigation and produce a report, which had the by-product of keeping him usefully occupied during the first Indian round table conference, to which he was not invited. The R101 inquiry started on 28 October 1930 and the round table conference began on 12 November.

The first round table conference in London was opened officially by Irwin and chaired by Ramsay MacDonald. It lasted until 19 January 1931. The three British political parties were represented by sixteen delegates (eight Labour – including Benn, MacDonald, Henderson and Jowitt – and four each from the Conservatives and Liberals – including Reading, but not Lloyd George). There were fifty-seven political leaders from British India and sixteen delegates from the princely states. In total eighty-nine delegates from India attended the Conference. However, the Indian National Congress along with Indian business leaders, kept away from the conference. Many of them, including Gandhi, were in jail for their participation in the civil disobedience movement. The organisation of the conference was a mammoth task, with nine plenary sessions involving all the delegates and sub-committees considering specific regional or administrative issues.

Outside the meetings, there were extensive banquets, lunches, dinners and other diversions. Benn and Margaret were involved in many of these, having to pay careful attention to the religious, dietary, political, diplomatic and personal sensitivities of the attendees. As the conference extended over the new year of 1931, the Benns and some of the Indian delegates were treated to a traditional Scottish celebration with MacDonald at 10 Downing Street.

Considering the scale, the differing agendas, the unfamiliarity with the process and the absence of some key figures, it was something of an achievement that agreement was reached at the round table on some important areas, particularly on the creation of an all-India federation to which the princes were willing to subscribe. A second round table conference was planned, but it was clear that it could not make much headway unless Gandhi and other Congress members were to be involved. Between 1 and 4 March 1931, during several lengthy, but productive, meetings between Gandhi and the Viceroy, an agreement was reached. It became known as the Irwin-Gandhi Pact. It called off the civil disobedience campaign, accepted the principles from the first round table conference and paved the way for the Congress Party to take part in the second round table conference. Churchill was outraged 'at the nauseating and humiliating spectacle of this one-time Inner Temple lawyer, now seditious fakir, striding half-naked up the steps of the Viceroy's palace, there to negotiate and parley on equal terms with the representative of the King Emperor'.[58]

India was to be the most divisive issue within the Conservative Party for the following four years and it was the main cause of Churchill's excursion into the political wilderness. Debates on the government of India (or any of the dominions) tended to become bogged down with entrenched positions on relatively minor aspects of the overall situation. In a situation familiar to David Cameron, Stanley Baldwin had found the centre of gravity of the Conservative Party pulled to the right by the threat of losing seats to right-wing challengers, with support from some sections of the press. In the 2010 parliament UKIP personified the challenge. In the 1920s it was the Anti-Waste League, the vehicle by which Benn's former commander, Murray Sueter, had entered Parliament at a by-election in 1921. In the 1930s a similar challenge came from Beaverbrook's Empire Crusade. On 30 October 1930 vice-admiral Ernest Taylor, standing for the Empire Crusade, won the Paddington South by-election, in what had previously been a safe Conservative seat. In the event, this was to be the Crusade's only victory, but it unnerved moderate Conservatives and emboldened those on the right.

The Commons debate on India on 12 March 1931 illustrated the Conservative Party's problems vividly. Benn was not sorry to have contributed to the party's problems, but he respected Baldwin and valued his support for the Indian policies. The moderate Baldwin stood his ground and was eventually vindicated. He embodied the longstanding ideology of the Conservative Party as one which does not seek to force the pace of change and which only reluctantly, for fear of unintended consequences, disturbs the status quo. However, the party (as it has since shown with issues such as Bank of England independence or the minimum wage) usually accepts the work of opposition governments as established fact and does not try to undo history. Benn did not subscribe to Baldwin's views. He was comfortable with the position of Labour and of radical Liberals that change could, and should, be forced on society for the benefit of the most disadvantaged. However, whilst Benn and Baldwin did not share the same instincts, the two understood, respected and liked each other. Benn was very conscious that Baldwin was having far more trouble with his party than MacDonald was with the Labour Party.

Benn appreciated Baldwin's intervention, attacking the die-hards in his own party. Baldwin issued this warning to his party, and to Churchill in particular:

'I want to remind my party that we have always prided ourselves ... on putting the Empire in the forefront of our speeches. [The Declaration gives] the lie to the idea ... that the East ... must be static, however far and however fast the West may move ... I will take the [round table] Conference as an accepted fact ... we are still suffering from [the] effect of nerves and hysteria ... If there are those in our party ... who would have to have forced out of their reluctant hands one concession after another, if they be a majority, in God's name let them choose a man to lead them. If they are in minority, then let them at least refrain from throwing difficulties in the way of those who have undertaken an almost superhuman task, on the successful fulfilment of which depends the well-being, the prosperity and the duration of the whole British Empire.'

Benn followed; his first remark really summing up all that he needed to say: 'After the historic speech to which we have just listened, there is really, from the point of view of the Indian situation, nothing to add to this debate.' Benn spoke at some length, but, quite deliberately, said little. Churchill followed, said a lot, was interrupted frequently and achieved no advance for his cause. Josiah Wedgwood, unkindly but accurately, delivered the verdict: 'The House was against him [Churchill] when he started and has remained against him to the close of his speech. Never before has a Right Hon. Gentleman spoken to a House so hostile.'[59]

Baldwin's attack on his own party was to be a turning of the tide in his leadership. Next he attacked the press: 'What the proprietorship of those papers is aiming at is power, and power without responsibility – the prerogative of the harlot through the ages.' Within a week Duff Cooper had convincingly won the Westminster, St. George's by-election, standing as a Baldwin supporter against his only challenger, Ernest Petter, an Independent Conservative supported by Beaverbrook. This halted, and began to reverse, the damage done to Baldwin's leadership over the defeat at Paddington South and the constant press onslaught. In the short run, this was good news for Benn and for the Labour Party's policies on India. In the long run, it was to become part of an existential threat to the Labour government and even to the Labour Party. However, Labour was not alone in suffering from potential threats to its long-term survival.

The Conservatives began to kindle some confidence in the prospects for their eventual return to power, but they were in no hurry. It suited them to remain in opposition during the worst of the economic crisis. Meanwhile the Labour and Liberal Parties were increasingly suffering from their own problems. The Liberals did not want an early election, but they were keen to extract some price for helping to keep Labour in office. The Liberals were (and remained) in favour of a proportional voting system. The Alternative Vote (AV) was not this, but it was a compromise solution, heading in that direction. The Labour government sponsored a bill to introduce AV. It was passed in the House of Commons in March 1931, but never made it onto the statute books. (The unloved AV system reared its head again in 2011, but once again failed to be adopted.) A by-product of the 1930s machinations over the voting system was that it drove a wedge into the Liberal Party. Simon had emerged as the strongest opponent of Lloyd George's plan to sustain the minority Labour government in return for the voting reform. In June 1931, as a result of increasing dissatisfaction with the Liberal Party's stance towards the Labour government, Simon, in the company of Ernest Brown and Robert Hutchison, resigned the Liberal whip.

Despite its relatively short life, the personnel of the second Labour cabinet underwent several changes. Passfield had relinquished part of his job, that of responsibility for the dominions, which had been taken up by J.H. Thomas. Vernon Hartshorn took up Thomas's former role as Lord Privy Seal. Lord Thomson's demise in the R101 disaster brought Lord Amulree into the cabinet as Secretary of State for Air. In June 1930 Addison had joined the cabinet, replacing Noel Buxton. The changes in the cabinet had been amicably arranged or were unavoidable, as in the case of Thomson. Outside the cabinet, though the departure of Chancellor of the Duchy of Lancaster, Oswald Mosley, in May 1930 over his failure to convince his colleagues on implementing radical policies to alleviate unemployment, had not been amicable. It led to his departure from the Labour Party at the end of February 1931 and the setting up of the New Party, which attracted the adherence of four other former Labour MPs. However, in early 1931 discord crept into the cabinet.

The Education Bill caused controversy in the Commons over the funding for denominational schools and it was rejected by the Lords in February 1931, after which President of the Board of Education, Charles Trevelyan, resigned from the cabinet, alienated from MacDonald and his colleagues. Trevelyan thus managed the dubious achievement of resigning from the same department in the governments of two different parties: as a junior Liberal minister he had resigned from Asquith's government on the outbreak of the First World War. Like Benn, Trevelyan was principled, but he lacked the ability to maintain good relations with his colleagues during times of stress. After joining the Labour Party, Trevelyan had written to MacDonald in 1924 to say that 'you can rely on [Ponsonby] and myself in a different way from so many others. Nothing could shake our feeling'.[60] But by 1931 this was certainly not reciprocated. MacDonald described Trevelyan as a 'poor fussy figure + unpleasantly sophistical',[61] feeling that 'we gave you and others who were not at all acceptable to our friends … a generous welcome … they will laugh at me … all I did was to give you a chance of walking out and giving the Govt. a nasty stab in the back'.[62] In contrast however, Benn remained popular with his Labour colleagues and maintained the confidence of MacDonald, despite the stress of office making him noticeably worn and haggard to the point that Hoare worried that Benn was in such a 'state of nerves' that he might have made 'some almost fatal mistake'.[63] Benn's wartime experience navigating under fire helped him cope with the most tense of situations. He didn't make a fatal mistake then, and he didn't make one over India either.

Chapter Six

Summer of 1931

The second Labour government is doomed to be remembered for the manner of its demise. It sank Ramsay MacDonald's reputation, and others along with it. For Benn, it meant a serious setback in his parliamentary career, but not ruination. However, despite the subsequent preoccupation with seeking political scapegoats, the real blame for the situation can squarely be laid entirely outside of the British political system. With the experience of the 2008 banking crisis, the government deficit explosion and the subsequent coalition government's cuts, the events of 1931 can be interpreted with an empathy which might not have been possible before 2008. The crisis of 1931 was imported: likewise, the 2008 crisis. In both cases the problems originated in the American financial system – the US stock market crash and the sub-prime lending scandal respectively. In both cases it was the governments' response to banking failures which determined the impact on British society and politics. In scale, the two crises were similar, although in Britain the fall in GDP after the 2008 crash was actually greater than the fall of the 1930s – albeit from a more comfortable starting point. In both cases a coalition government came into being to deal with the fallout.

In the recession following the 2008 crash, unemployment nationally peaked at 8.3 per cent, but the impact was relatively evenly spread with the worst affected areas (in Birmingham) reaching a maximum rate of 12.5 per cent. In the 1930s, the unemployment rate nationally reached 16 per cent, but Jarrow recorded a rate of 73 per cent. However, London and the south-east of England, with concentrations of newer industries such as electronics and plastics, avoided the worst of the recession and even saw a housing boom fuelled by cheap building materials and land, cheap labour, low interest rates, lax planning laws and improved transport links. Bankers and journalists mainly lived in the areas least affected by the economic downturn, but if they were not fully alert to the plight of the unemployed, they were fully aware of the impact of the unemployment bill on the government's finances. Unemployment shot up from 1.5m in January 1930, to 2m in June and 2.7m in December and the bill for unemployment pay rose with it.

On 31 July 1931 the Committee on National Expenditure (the May Committee), which included members nominated by each of the three main parties, delivered its majority report on how to deal with the government's deteriorating finances. It warned of a government deficit of £120m by April 1932 and recommended new taxation to bring in £24m and spending cuts of £96m, including a twenty twenty per cent cut in unemployment benefit payments.[1] The two Labour members dissented.

The context for the cuts was deflation. It meant that, as prices had fallen, the real value of incomes and unemployment benefits had risen. The fall in prices had been in the order of 11.5 per cent since 1929. A 'cut' to unemployment benefits of ten per cent therefore could still have left recipients with greater real spending power than they would have had two years previously. A cut of twenty per cent would have been a different matter. In the 1930s the unemployed were able to survive on their dole money: no-one in Britain was actually starving. In some ways Britain in 1931 had a 'bigger society' than today and more people really were 'in it together'. Extended families and larger households offered mutual support, landlords (even if unwillingly) reduced rents on houses and farmland. Health, measured by indicators such as infant mortality, actually improved across the inter-war years.

With hindsight, the 1929 election was a good one to lose, coming as it did just before the Wall Street crash. The Labour cabinet were left holding the parcel when the music stopped in 1931. With no parliamentary majority, the second Labour government was constantly in need of support from other parties. This inevitably involved MacDonald in discussions with the other party leaders. The Labour Party's strength was concentrated in the areas of the country worst affected by unemployment – South Wales, Strathclyde, Lancashire, West Yorkshire, Derbyshire, County Durham and Tyneside, which had been hit hard by the collapse in demand for coal, shipbuilding, textiles and steel. Many, but by no means all, of the cabinet represented seats in these areas. Sankey, Amulree, Passfield and Parmoor were in the Lords and so had no constituency to represent. Sankey and Amulree had never sat as MPs. Although Passfield (as Sidney Webb) had been MacDonald's predecessor as Labour MP for Seaham, Parmoor (as Charles Cripps) had been Conservative MP for Stroud, Stretford and Wycombe. None of the cabinet represented a seat in Wales. Benn, Graham, Johnston and Adamson all represented Scottish seats – Aberdeen North, Edinburgh Central, Stirling and Clackmannan West and Fife West respectively – the last two included significant mining areas and were worse affected by unemployment than Benn's and Graham's constituencies. The rest of the cabinet represented industrialised English constituencies, many with seats in Lancashire, Yorkshire and Derbyshire – Snowden (Colne Valley), Lees-Smith (Keighley), Shaw (Preston), Clynes (Manchester Platting), Henderson (Burnley), Greenwood (Nelson and Colne), Alexander (Sheffield Hillsborough) and Thomas (Derby). Lansbury and Morrison represented seats in East London – Bromley and Bow and Hackney South respectively, where pockets of high unemployment existed within the South-East region which generally only had unemployment levels under seven per cent. Addison's seat at Swindon in Wiltshire escaped the worst of the slump. MacDonald (Seaham) and Bondfield (Wallsend) represented seats which were among the most seriously affected by the slump. MacDonald and Bondfield, due to their respective constituencies and their cabinet responsibilities, arguably represented the unemployed more closely than did the other cabinet ministers, the press, the banks or even the TUC.

The epicentre of the crisis arrived in Britain at the beginning of August 1931, just after the summer parliamentary recess had started, in the wake of the failure of the Austrian bank, the Creditanstalt, and the publication of the May Report. Hardly conducive to calm and considered solutions, the press snapped: 'Cut the talk and get on with it', 'Another Day Gone', 'Still Waiting', 'There Must be Action To-day' and 'A Matter of Hours'.[2] The resulting pace of political activity was frantic. Benn attended cabinet meetings on 19 August, 20 August, 21 August, two on 22 August (a Saturday), 23 August (Sunday) and 24 August 1931. He attended all the meetings of the full cabinet. However, his department did not have a large budget, so he could not make a substantial contribution to the solution of the financial problems, unlike Margaret Bondfield at the Ministry of Labour or Lansbury as First Commissioner of Works. He did not wield great influence at the grass roots of the party, so he was not a key figure in terms of influencing the trades unions, unlike Henderson. He was not an authority on economics and policy-making, unlike Snowden. The focus of his remit was India, which kept him extremely busy, rather than a domestic brief which could have kept his finger on the pulse of domestic opinion, unlike Morrison at Transport or Clynes at the Home Office. He was not one of MacDonald's closest confidants, so his opinion was not constantly sought by the prime minister, unlike Snowden.

The Cabinet minutes for the first of these meetings, on 19 August, set the stark scene: 'The Cabinet met in the circumstances of exceptional gravity and urgency to consider the recent serious developments in the financial situation of the country. In this connection there was circulated ... a most secret memorandum ... containing suggestions for balancing the Budget'.[3] The meeting lasted from 11.00 to 22.30 with short adjournments at midday and 19.00. The remit of the meeting was circumscribed in that it was to balance the budget via tax increases and spending cuts, effectively ruling out further borrowing as a means of maintaining government expenditure. After contributions from all the cabinet, the main decision at this meeting was to reject the May Committee's proposal for a twenty per cent cut in the rate of unemployment pay. There was however, *provisional* agreement to cuts amounting to around £58m.[4] Some of these cuts were to be the subject of further discussions between the chancellor and departmental ministers.

The cabinet agreed to meet again the following day, 20 August. In the meantime a cabinet committee comprising Margaret Bondfield, William Graham, Tom Johnston and Arthur Greenwood was delegated to devise a scheme which would relieve the Treasury of £20m of expenditure from the unemployment insurance budget without imposing the twenty per cent cut in the rate of unemployment pay. Snowden told the cabinet that the real value of unemployment benefit was over thirty per cent higher than the 1924 value and 'that value had been accepted as adequate by the then Labour Government at a time when the Budgets were showing handsome surpluses ... while the wage earner was receiving the same value as in 1924'.[5] The cabinet agreed that a meeting was also to be held with the leaders of the opposition parties. MacDonald and Snowden met with Chamberlain and Hoare from the Conservative Party and Samuel and Maclean from the Liberals. A critical misunderstanding arose from this meeting, whereby the opposition leaders left with the impression that £78m of savings were being proposed by the cabinet. They had not been familiar with the scale of the deficit or the necessary cuts beforehand and had arrived with no predetermined figures in mind, so the figure of £78m set their expectations. The cabinet also decided to consult the national executive of the Labour Party and the general council of the TUC at a joint meeting that afternoon – 20 August. MacDonald and Snowden made statements. After a few questions, the delegates from the two bodies left to discuss their positions separately. The Labour Party executive decided to leave matters to the government, but the TUC insisted on another meeting. This meeting did not go well. Citrine and Bevin reported that the TUC would not accept cuts in unemployment pay.

At the following cabinet meeting on 21 August Snowden reported back on the meeting with the TUC the previous evening. He said that it appeared that the TUC 'had no real appreciation of the seriousness of the situation [and] the statements made appeared to be based on a pre-crisis mentality'. The result was that the TUC General Council was 'opposed to any interference with the existing terms and conditions of the Unemployment Insurance Scheme'. MacDonald informed the cabinet that 'in view of the attitude adopted by the [TUC], he had thought it necessary to see the Deputy Governor of the Bank of England' who had insisted that 'particularly from the point of view of the foreign interests concerned ... very substantial economies should be effected on Unemployment Insurance'. The Deputy Governor had 'reported the views of a distinguished and very friendly foreign financier on the vital need of ... securing budgetary equilibrium.' The cabinet minutes went on to record the fateful decision that while there was little support for a reduction of five per cent in unemployment benefit, owing to its comparatively small financial effect, the cabinet were 'almost equally divided on the question whether there should be a reduction of ten per cent or no reduction of benefit at all.' Alternative avenues to solving the crisis all seemed to be closed off, either in reality or in perception. Snowden 'expressed the strongest possible objection to the Government being committed in any way to the principle of a Revenue Tariff.' MacDonald replied, without unequivocally ruling out the option, that 'no decision of any kind had been reached on the subject of a Revenue Tariff.' [6]

The following day, August 22, MacDonald started the first cabinet meeting of the day at 09.30 with the 'most emphatic' assurance that 'there was no ground whatever for the suggestion that the present crisis was in any respect due to a conspiracy on the part of the Banks, all of which were most anxious to render assistance to the Government.' He did also point out though that 'foreign lenders regarded ... heavy financial burdens on industry ... as impairing the security of their loans'. He also emphasised that the savings without the cut in unemployment benefits were 'wholly unsatisfactory' to the opposition leaders, who would seek to recall Parliament with the least possible delay to defeat the cabinet's proposals. Snowden reiterated the constraints on the cabinet by insisting that 'any attempt ... to camouflage the true position would be at once detected', and that it was of 'paramount importance that the Budget should be balanced in an honest fashion, and not by recourse to borrowing.' He cautioned that it was 'a delusion' to imagine that transferring part of the burden from central government to local authorities would be a solution. He also warned that the effect of departing from the gold standard would be the reduction in 'the living standard of the workmen by 50%'. The cabinet also 'agreed to take note that ... His Majesty would be returning to London immediately'.[7] Under the most intense pressure, the cabinet adjourned at 12.10, but agreed to meet again at 14.30. In the meantime MacDonald and Snowden consulted the opposition leaders to establish their potential support in the event that the cabinet agreed to the ten per cent cut.

At the second cabinet meeting on Saturday 22 August, at 14.30, little progress was made. MacDonald reported back on the tentative and provisional support of the opposition leaders to the hypothetical acceptance by the cabinet of the ten per cent cut. MacDonald had arranged for the Deputy Governor of the Bank of England to come to Downing Street at 15.00 to give his views, but cautioned that the Deputy Governor would probably wish to consult the US Federal Reserve Bank before committing himself and it in turn might wish to seek further views. The cabinet meeting broke up with no decision made, but resolved to meet again on the following day, Sunday 23 August 1931 at 19.00 to make a definite decision on the ten per cent cut, by which time the views of the bankers would be known.[8]

In view of the rigid attitudes of the press, the opposition, the banks and Snowden's warnings, MacDonald had by this point probably determined unshakably (and MacDonald could be very unshakable) that the ten per cent cut in unemployment benefits was the only solution which was just to the unemployed in view of the level of deflation and which was the minimum acceptable to the banks and the opposition. He probably determined that his course of action had to be to put maximum pressure on the cabinet to accept the ten per cent cut and that failing their acceptance, this, as a minimum or worse, would be implemented by a government of another political composition. MacDonald was probably wedded more to this, the only policy which he considered viable, than to his loyalty to the unemployed, to the banks, to his colleagues or even to the Labour Party. He had shown similar dogged adherence, at personal cost, to his opposition to the First World War. He had felt vindicated then, as his policies had been largely those adopted by the Labour Party's Memorandum on War Aims in 1917 and his political career had revived, taking him back from the margins to the very centre.

The crunch cabinet meeting took place on the Sunday evening, with time running out before the financial markets opened on Monday morning. The meeting started at 19.00, but was adjourned from 19.45 to 21.10, while the reply from New York was awaited. Although, tentative, the American response was positive enough for MacDonald to be able to claim that it appeared that all obstacles outside the cabinet had been removed and that the only remaining issue was whether the cabinet would accept the ten per cent cut in unemployment benefits, which he described as the 'extreme limit to which he was prepared to go.' It was now time for the cabinet to make their decision and MacDonald made it clear that if there were 'any important resignations, the Government as a whole must resign.' MacDonald also emphasised that if support for the proposal was not forthcoming from the Labour cabinet, 'it was unthinkable that the Government could remain in Office and prevent some other Administration' taking over. Bearing in mind that MacDonald knew that he could count on Snowden's support, the most 'important resignation' which MacDonald had to be concerned about was that of Henderson. A majority in cabinet, including support from Henderson could have been sufficient to swing the Labour movement, albeit very reluctantly, behind the decision. All twenty-one members of the cabinet were present. Each member gave their opinion. It became clear that, although there was a narrow majority in favour of acceptance, the majority, crucially, did not include Henderson.[9]

The cabinet minutes do not specify how each minister voted, but the actions of most of the cabinet have been established, although some doubts remain. MacDonald and Snowden, the authors of the policy, naturally supported it, as did at least three of the peers in the cabinet – Amulree, Sankey and Passfield, joined by the members who were less close to the grass roots Labour movement – Shaw, Thomas, Morrison and Benn. (Nine definites in total.) Those voting against the ten per cent cut included Henderson, Graham, Alexander, Greenwood, Johnston, Adamson, Lansbury, Clynes and Addison.[10] (Nine definites in total.) Those whose votes are in doubt were Bondfield, Lees-Smith and Parmoor – but for certain two of them must have voted for the cuts.

Although he had attended all the cabinet meetings, Benn did not play a central role in the 1931 crisis. His motivation was to keep the Labour government in power by finding an acceptable compromise to deal with the economic situation, which did not violate his core beliefs as a free-trading ethical liberal internationalist with a social conscience. This gave him some room to manoeuvre, but also placed some boundaries. He did not want to see tariffs imposed. He was prepared to see some reduction in the cash value of unemployment benefits, but not a real terms cut. The overall Labour stance on tariffs was similar to the Liberal position. Both parties were opposed, but in both cases the strength of the opposition varied across the membership. Within the Liberals, many would have died in a metaphorical ditch to preserve free trade. Within the Labour Party Snowden would similarly have sacrificed himself, but few others would have joined him. From 1930 onwards MacDonald had begun to shift his position towards protection (as had Keynes), while Buxton and Addison were in favour of agricultural tariffs.

The failure of the cabinet to agree inevitably spelled the end of the second Labour government. This was serious enough for the Labour Party, but a bigger problem was caused by MacDonald's acceptance of the King's proposal that he lead a replacement National Government, which few Labour members were willing to join. Benn was not one of them.

Subsequent analyses of the events hardly mention Benn's role. For example, the book *Britain's second Labour government, 1929-31: a reappraisal*, has one reference only to Benn in a work of over 200 pages and this was in relation to his role as Secretary of State for India.[11] The most excoriating account of the events, that of MacNeill Weir, does not even mention Benn once.[12] Macneill Weir was MacDonald's parliamentary private secretary from 1924 to 1931. In his book, *The Tragedy of Ramsay MacDonald*, he claimed that MacDonald had been intriguing to become head of a National Government for some time. Weir was convinced that there could be 'no doubt that the historian of the future … will inevitably come to the conclusion that the setting up of the 'National' Government by MacDonald was the greatest disaster that has befallen this country, and indeed the world, since the [First World] War. It is comparable … with the setting up of the Nazi regime in Germany.'[13]

With hindsight, Weir's rhetoric is clearly overblown – most 'historians of the future' do not come to his conclusion. But what of Weir's charge that MacDonald had been intriguing to form a national government? MacDonald had indeed, as had many others, mentioned the possibility of a national government at several stages, including as far back as September 1930.[14] On 9 November 1930, MacDonald had speculated in his diary about the formation of a national government, in which he would have served as foreign secretary, or resigned. He did the same again on 1 March 1931, going as far as saying that a national government was 'attractive'. Speculating who would join, he came to the conclusion 'Not the Labour Party'. He hinted too at the possibility of his abandoning Labour and considered the consequences: 'If I leave it, or split it, what remains?' This musing should probably be considered in conjunction with his long-held belief that 'the life of a party is finite'.[15] MacDonald was a politician in a terrible bind, probably feeling that he would be damned whatever he did. It is not surprising that there were times when he felt that the premiership would be easier without his party. Premiers Thatcher, Major, Blair and Cameron probably all had moments when they felt that they could do the job much better if only it were not for their party holding them back and absorbing their energies. The concept of a national government had been aired in the press and discussed by Labour colleagues.[16] It was shared in some Conservative circles. On 3 July 1930, former Conservative cabinet minister, the Earl of Crawford, had written to Irwin: 'It is persistently rumoured that nothing would give [MacDonald] greater pleasure than translation to some high post in. ... a Conservative Ministry.'[17] Industrialists had been persistently lobbying for a national government since late 1930. While the possibility seems to have been in MacDonald's head for some time, he certainly did not have a monopoly on the idea and it was not a secret.

If MacDonald was intriguing to form a national government, was he actually contemplating anything more disloyal or disruptive than Lloyd George's coalition of 1918 to 1922? Lloyd George's reputation is certainly mixed, but he is not universally damned for forming the coalition and he still has many admirers among Liberal Democrats. However, MacDonald's actions have left an enduring aversion to coalitions within the Labour Party and his reputation is poor, almost to the extent of unmentionability, in Labour circles. When historian Professor Kenneth Morgan, a Labour peer since 2000, mentioned MacDonald's name in the House of Lords, he was greeted with a hiss from some of his own party.

Even if it had been MacDonald's plan to engineer a national government out of the 1931 crisis, he was not really in a position to do so.[18] The opposition leaders did not require his presence in government. The Conservatives and Liberals combined could have commanded a parliamentary majority. However, once the option of MacDonald's leading a national government was suggested at the meeting with the King, MacDonald took the opportunity as the best means of ensuring that his policy of the ten per cent cut was implemented, as indeed it was. In this context the King's comment that MacDonald would act as the 'trustee for the poor' makes sense at face value.[19] The opposition leaders were more than willing to accept MacDonald as a human shield, to protect them from potential fallout from the unpopular policies.

In many ways, Weir's accusations are directed at the wrong target, or at least at the wrong point in time. The real damage was done before the National Government came into being, by the cabinet's failure to agree on policy. This was the crucial failure. Of course, MacDonald, as prime minister, bore much of the responsibility for this. The whole episode exposed the economic weakness of the Labour government, which had allowed Snowden to dominate his colleagues. Virtually none felt equipped with enough economic expertise to challenge him. Passfield, one of the best thinkers in the cabinet, later commented 'I have never felt able to deal properly with economic theory'.[20] British socialism was based more on an ethical, than an economic, doctrine. Fervent adherents to the Labour Party could therefore be well steeped in the social implications of their policies, but in relative ignorance of the economic obstacles to fulfilling their ambitions. The uncomfortable truth for those voting against the ten per cent cut though was that they must have known that it, or something more severe, would be implemented by a different government. They avoided doing it themselves, but did not stop it happening. It is possible, but not easy for some, to feel sympathy with all of the figures faced with the decision on cuts in 1931. They had the almost impossible task of reconciling the interests of the country's finances, of the Labour Party and of the unemployed. Each had their own priority.

MacDonald probably believed that the opposition leaders and bankers would accept nothing less than the ten per cent cut and that the TUC and cabinet would accept nothing more, albeit very reluctantly. He felt that the key to getting the TUC to accept the deal was for a significant majority of the cabinet, including Henderson, to accept it. MacDonald may have been convinced that he could call Henderson's bluff, when he asked for the resignations of those opposed, with the warning that any 'significant resignations' would mean the resignation of the whole cabinet. MacDonald may have thought that, faced with the ultimatum, most, if not all, the cabinet would accept the cut. MacDonald probably also realised that he had to be prepared to carry through any actions which he threatened. Once MacDonald's bluff over the cabinet resignations had failed, the thing that he most wanted to hold on to was not the cabinet, nor his own position, but the policy of the ten per cent cut, believing that if this was not implemented a lesser cut would have meant economic disaster for the country and that if the decision was placed in the hands of the opposition, a deeper cut might have been implemented which would have gone against MacDonald's whole reason for being in politics – to safeguard the struggling.

Once the bluff had failed, MacDonald had no definite plan. He was no longer in control of events. He now had little or nothing to lose. His control of the cabinet was lost. The Labour Party had rejected his policy. His premiership was almost certainly finished. No-one can know what was in MacDonald's mind in 1931, but his previous behaviour could act as a guide. He had relinquished the party leadership in 1914 after the outbreak of war, saying the chairmanship was impossible and how glad he was to 'get out of harness'. During the war, Henderson had shown that he was willing to compromise and swallow his pride, whereas MacDonald had shown that he would sacrifice himself for the preservation of his views. His track record was not one of clinging to office against all odds. In 1924 he had seemed relieved to end the first Labour government after less than ten months in office. MacDonald may also have felt, as did John Major after the Exchange Rate Mechanism debacle on Black Wednesday 1992, a sense of responsibility to stay and sort out the mess which had been created by his party's policy failure.

Most attention afterwards focused on the actions of MacDonald and Henderson, but in many ways Snowden honestly, but wrongly, led the cabinet into a trap. Leaving the Gold Standard, introducing tariffs, increasing borrowing and transferring some funding of unemployment benefits from central to local government were not totally impractical elements of a solution. Snowden's blunt approach did not endear him to his colleagues, so although he had the reputation as the most economically-literate member of the cabinet, he swayed few hearts.

Benn's decisions flowed fairly naturally from his beliefs, rather than from personal loyalties. In many ways he was in a more comfortable position than many of the cabinet. He was not torn by ancient and visceral loyalty to the trades unions, nor to MacDonald. It would probably have made little difference to the outcome of the crisis, or to his future career, if Benn had voted against the ten per cent cut. He had plenty to regret over what had happened to the Labour government, but little to feel personally embarrassed, or proud, about. Benn hated coalitions, so he was not willing to join the National Government, nor was he invited to. MacDonald telephoned Benn at home on the morning the National Government was formed, saying 'I'm not going to ask you to join the National Government, because I don't think it's your job. It's the job of you and a few people like you to pull the Party straight again'.[21] Benn's relationship with MacDonald remained cordial. He later felt that MacDonald had ruined the Labour Party, but he did not feel hatred towards him.

Only Snowden, Thomas, Sankey and Amulree from the Labour cabinet followed MacDonald into the National Government. They were expelled from the Labour Party. Some others, such as Morrison, had been tempted to join, although he later tried to deny it. The National Government was headed by MacDonald, now labelled as National Labour, but numerically it was dominated by Conservatives, and was to become more so. The Liberals were represented in the cabinet by Reading at the Foreign Office and Samuel at the Home Office. Lloyd George was put out of action, by his own prostate. He had to undergo an operation which removed him from the Liberal Party leadership, stopped his efforts to prevent a general election and ended any viable threat of Benn's worst nightmare: his taking over the Labour Party. There had been rumours of Lloyd George's wanting to join the Labour Party in an attempt to seize the leadership.

Although later events and historical investigations have shed more light, there is much still to be understood about the 1931 crisis. For some ghoulish reason, Liberal historians are attracted to probing every aspect of the disastrous split in their party between Asquith and Lloyd George, even though it nearly killed the party. Labour historians, on the other hand, tend to be more reticent to prod the entrails of 1931. Partly it is because Ramsay MacDonald serves as a convenient scapegoat. The early histories were written in the heat of the moment, or at least before the Attlee government was formed. Between 1931 and 1935 the prospects for the Labour Party did indeed look bleak and MacDonald appeared to be mainly to blame. But after 1935 the economy was recovering and in the election that year Labour recaptured a hundred seats. By 1945 the damage to the party was repaired, and more. There are a large number of Labour histories which stop at 1929, not 1931. One of those is a PhD thesis "The Labour Party and Political Change in Scotland 1918-29", by a certain Gordon Brown. If anyone needed to know the lessons from 1931, Gordon Brown would be that person, as he was prime minister during the most comparable set of events to 1931 – the financial crash of 2008.

In both cases the origin of the crises was in the financial system, outside of the UK. In both cases the practices of the banks and financial institutions had ranged from imprudent to irresponsible. In both cases the financial institutions sought (with some success both times) to nationalise their mistakes – to preserve their wealth at the cost of a call on all members of society, whether rich or poor. In both cases governments felt compelled to appease the bankers at the cost of higher taxes and reduced benefits for the population at large. At the time of the 1931 crisis there was discussion of a 'bankers' ramp' but later the analysis crystallised into finding a scapegoat among the political figures, with the relatively unprotected MacDonald bearing most of the finger pointing. MacDonald was generally respectful of bankers, but not of industrialists, having deplored the 'incapacity of so many of the leading businessmen'.[22] The mutual disrespect remains. Politicians are held in low regard by the public and by business, but the appearances of leading industrialists before parliamentary select committees has done little to place them any higher in public esteem. In 2008 to 2010, as in 1931, the press played a significant part in putting pressure on the politicians urgently to provide a solution to a problem, which was not of their making and had been brewing for years, if not decades. The lessons from 1931, which did not seem to have been heeded by 2010, were not really about politicians' behaviour towards each other, but about politicians' ability to stand up to pressure from the banks and the press. The Bank of England was not entirely helpful in either case. Sir Mervyn King warned politicians that the government which implemented the austerity measures after the 2008 crisis could be 'out of power for a generation', no doubt with his understanding of 1931 in his mind. This, from a governor who had failed to warn of the impending disaster, was not a helpful interjection. During coalition negotiations in 2010, Vince Cable from the Liberal Democrats met with Alistair Darling from the Labour Party. Darling asked Cable 'how on earth he could agree with the Tory policy on cutting the deficit when he had been so outspoken in this opposition to it?' He said that they had been heavily influenced by what the Governor of the Bank of England had been saying, which had put the frighteners on his party. They had been led to believe that the situation was far worse than they had thought.[23]

The ghosts from 1931 still haunted the Labour Party. Gordon Brown kept telling Darling that he did not want to be labelled 'another Philip Snowden'.[24] The impact of the 1931 crisis still resonates – and not just within the Labour Party. In 2010, after a banking crash, a rise in the government deficit and against the background of the mounting financial crisis in Greece, the British general election produced an inconclusive result, as in 1929. The behaviour of all the parties in the coalition negotiations which followed the 2010 election bore an imprint from 1931. The Labour Party's reticence to agree a deal with the Liberal Democrats reflected the desperate desire to avoid a party split and to stand aloof from a coalition. No-one in the Labour Party today would want to be labelled as a latter-day Ramsay MacDonald. Well aware of the old Liberal Party's tendency to split, the Liberal Democrats were driven by a desire to ensure that their whole parliamentary party had been consulted on the final deal with the Conservatives. Finally, David Cameron, also well-versed in political history, knew that the Conservatives had managed to engineer a major share of power from 1931 to 1945 by working with other parties. Cameron was much less wary of the MacDonald tag, seeing that his potential position at the centre of a coalition would be more comfortable than his position on the left of a minority Conservative government. The Conservatives and the Liberal Democrats had every incentive to enter a coalition and Labour had every reason to feel an aversion. The ghost of Ramsay MacDonald stalked the 2010 coalition negotiations, even if no-one dared to mention that they had felt his presence.

No politicians in 1931 or 2008 seem to have acted illegally or even immorally, whereas the same cannot be said for some bankers and journalists. Compared to the failures of the banks, the press and the credit ratings agencies, politics worked. Individual politicians and political parties may have suffered, but in both cases the worst effects of the crises were mitigated. MacDonald's reputation has since undergone a slow and slight revival, and Gordon Brown's will probably do the same.

One of the values of a political dynasty is the collective learning and passing on of lessons. The Benn family managed to have a ringside seat in successive financial crises. Tony was in the cabinet during the 1976 IMF crisis, where he circulated the minutes of the 1931 cabinet meetings, and Hilary was in Gordon Brown's cabinet during the 2008 to 2010 crisis.

Benn's time in the Labour Party had certainly been a rollercoaster. At the beginning of 1928 he was out of Parliament. By the following year he was back in the House of Commons and in the Labour cabinet. Two years later, with another general election scheduled for Tuesday 27 October 1931, Captain Benn's political career seemed to be heading for the rocks again.

Chapter Seven

Round the World with a Kettle 1931–39

Benn had inevitably neglected his constituency because of his very heavy workload as a cabinet minister during the 1929 to 1931 parliament. Grumblings were aired in the local press about the urgent need for Benn to come to Aberdeen to explain the political situation to his constituents.[1] Events and political re-alignments had moved so fast that most voters were confused or angry. One report declared that Benn's 'record of service was the subject of considerable criticism'.[2] His re-adoption as Labour candidate for Aberdeen North was not a foregone conclusion. Suggestions appeared in the local paper that Benn should fight the neighbouring Conservative-held seat of Aberdeen South and relinquish the Labour candidacy of Aberdeen North to local councillor Fraser Macintosh. He had been the only other potential candidate considered when the ILP had originally endorsed Benn in 1928.[3] Aberdeen South appeared to be a hopeless prospect for Labour in the conditions of 1931. The Conservatives had won over sixty per cent of the vote in a straight fight with Labour at the last election. Benn described the suggestion as 'mischievous'. It was, but the mischief was coming from his own side.

A selection committee meeting was set up for Sunday 11 October 1931 to settle the nominations. In a letter to Margaret, actually written during the selection meeting, Benn complained that 'some semi-communists have been trying to make mischief ... I haven't eased the situation by playing up to the left first because I won't and secondly because I don't think it is necessary'.[4] Despite the local opposition and bad feeling, Benn was re-adopted, but only by the far-from-overwhelming margin of thirty-five to twenty-one votes.[5] Writing again to Margaret after the decision was made, Benn reported that 'the reds tried it on ... but were defeated. Let them go and support the communist'.[6] In the event, nearly 4,000 voters did support the Communist candidate at the poll. Benn's strategy of not appeasing the left was proven to be valid, although it was not enough to save him. Far more voters defected from Labour to the Conservatives, than to the Communists, and Benn was defeated by a margin of over 14,000 votes. The victor was the Conservative candidate, John Burnett.

The criticism by their own former chancellor, Philip Snowden, of the Labour MPs who did not support the National Government for being 'the men who ran away' from the national economic crisis had resonated with the public.[7] Added to this, the splits within the local Labour ranks in Aberdeen, Benn's long absences from the constituency because of his India work and the energetic campaigning by the local Conservative candidate all did for Benn.

General election 27 October 1931 Aberdeen North:

J.G. Burnett	Conservative	22,931
W.W. Benn	Labour	8,753
H. Crawfurd	Communist	3,980
	Conservative majority	14,178 (39.8 per cent)

Benn lost over half his previous vote, both in terms of numbers and as a percentage share. Nationally, the 1931 election was a disaster for the Labour Party, and one which appeared potentially terminal at the time. Of the 1929 to 1931 Labour cabinet who did not follow MacDonald into the National Government, only Lansbury retained his seat. The party fell from 288 seats to just fifty-two – a steeper decline than the Liberals had suffered in 1924. The Labour tally fell back behind the Liberals' total (seventy-two) for the first time since 1922, with the only possible comfort for Labour being that the Liberals were once again split, although it was not clear at the time that the Liberal rift was to be enduring. The Liberals fought the 1931 election in three factions – Lloyd George's family group who completely opposed the National Government, Samuel's followers who temporarily supported the National Government but with reservations over the threats to free trade and Simon's supporters who also supported the National Government, but without the reservations about tariffs. The boundaries between the Samuelites and Simonites were not entirely clear at first and several of the Liberal MPs swapped back or forth during 1931. It was as though the

Liberal iceberg had cracked, but only later did the current of events drive the sections apart, so that eventually the gaps became unbridgeable. The election saw the emergence and disappearance of Mosley's New Party. Given the problems of their opponents, the inevitable winners were the Conservatives who came out of the election with 473 seats. Burnett, the victor in Aberdeen North, was to become the only Conservative MP for the seat in the whole of its history since 1885.

After the 1931 election the surviving Labour MPs sat on the opposition benches in the uneasy company of Lloyd George's family group of Liberals – David, daughter Megan, son Gwilym and Goronwy Owen.[8] Samuel's Liberals initially sat on the government benches, but they left the National Government in 1932, although remaining on the government side of the Commons. They eventually crossed the floor to the opposition benches in 1933 over the issue of tariffs.

Benn turned his back on Aberdeen North after his 1931 defeat and his decision was reported in the local press on 14 January 1932.[9] Benn's resignation letter politely glossed over the real reasons for his abandoning the seat, simply saying that he had been 'thinking over for some time the question of whether or not he should accept the honour of allowing his name to go forward to the selection conference. He had felt from the beginning however, the handicap of living at so great a distance from the constituency … It was with very great regret', therefore, that he had come to the conclusion not to allow his name to be proposed. Benn could, of course, have set up home in the constituency had he wanted to. Even without moving, the distance was not an overwhelming obstacle. He had been willing to go as far as Leith and was later prepared to consider other Scottish seats as far north as Dundee. He was therefore willing to go nearly 500 miles from London to Dundee, so another sixty-six to Aberdeen did not seem insurmountable. In reality he was uncertain that he would receive the Labour nomination. Alternatively, he worried that he might have only received it with lukewarm support and persistent internal opposition. He also had severe doubts whether the seat would be reclaimable for Labour, anyway. By October 1932 it looked as though Benn had made the right decision. A replacement candidate, Henry Hetherington, had been adopted by Labour for North Aberdeen. That year the Independent Labour Party split away from the Labour Party and decided to nominate Fraser Macintosh as their own candidate, in opposition to Hetherington.[10] Further to divide left-leaning voters, there was also the prospect of a Communist contender too. For the next three years Benn was to be without a constituency to nurse, although he had certainly not given up on the idea of returning to Parliament.

Much of the comment on Benn's performance as Secretary of State for India was rather patronising, often referring to him as 'Little Benn' and a 'lightweight'. This was not entirely to Benn's disadvantage though, as much of his work was as a facilitator and, with the exception of Lloyd George, he did not arouse much hostility, even among his political opponents. As the first round table conference got underway, Lloyd George had gone around complaining of a 'Great Betrayal'. Although as the editor of the *Times* commented, 'who has betrayed what is not quite clear', but it seemed fairly likely that Benn was somewhere implicated in the 'Betrayal'.[11] His pleasant manner, industrious attention to detail and lack of self-importance helped Benn to smooth over many potentially difficult situations. Benn's manner was also criticised in some circles for being 'fluffy' and 'sentimental'. These were charges which Benn might well have accepted. He was soft-hearted, easily moved to tears and quite sentimental about others (although this did not extend to himself or to animals). Again, this was seen in some quarters as something of a weakness, but it was one which could disarm his opponents. His experience as a whip helped him to play the party politics game, resulting in the telling verdict on Churchill's behaviour over India from the Conservative chief whip, who wished that he could stir Churchill up 'to hit the Socialists half as hard as he hits his friends'.[12] The issue of India had also helped to drive a wedge between Lloyd George and Simon, who had effectively left the Liberal Party in June 1931. Ironically, in the long run, the events of 1931 did more damage to the Liberals than to the Labour Party and Benn's prising at the cleavage between Lloyd George and Simon had played a part in this.

Benn's tenure as Secretary of State for India was a small, but fairly smooth, step along a tortuous road. He continued a process of reform, adding impetus and removing obstacles. Whilst it was too brief and inconclusive to count as a major success, it certainly was not a failure. In terms of duration and contribution to a positive long-term outcome from a delicate situation,

Benn's tenure could be compared with Mo Mowlam's and Peter Mandelson's roles in the Northern Ireland peace process.

Even though he was no longer Secretary of State for India, and at the end, no longer even an MP, Benn continued to attend the second Indian roundtable conference, which ran from September to December 1931, as one of the Labour delegates. Samuel Hoare succeeded Benn as Secretary of State for India and remained in post until June 1935, by which time, with much difficulty especially from his own party, he had negotiated the 1935 Government of India Act. The act became law in August 1935, after Hoare had been promoted to Foreign Secretary in the National Government. The 1935 act abolished diarchy, devolved more powers to India and increased the number of Indians eligible to vote from seven to thirty-five million. The act continued the policy direction which Benn had pursued, but was regarded in India as too timid and in some UK Conservative circles as dangerously radical.

Having served as Secretary of State for India without actually visiting the country, Benn was now keen to travel. He was multi-modal traveller and keen on trying as many new forms of transport as he could. He was already a horse-rider (although he did not like animals), a pilot (who had rather a lot of crashes), a car driver (but not a very good one), a sailor (although brought up in the East End of London), a balloonist (who fell asleep in the basket), a cyclist (in successful pursuit of a bride) and a sleigh-rider (on honeymoon). Benn resolved to use his enforced absence from Parliament to travel and to improve his language skills, in the hope of finding a role in the pursuit of world peace. He decided that German would be his focus: his French and Italian were already fluent. With Margaret, Benn set off for Germany in the summer of 1932. Ageing and ailing President von Hindenburg was still precariously in office, resisting Hitler's claims to the Chancellorship, after the Nazi Party made gains in the federal elections of the spring and summer of 1932.

The two students, with a combined age of ninety, set off for the university town of Marburg, north of Frankfurt. Margaret was studying as a non-examination external student of King's College, London. Their reading material, which included Margaret's theological books in Hebrew, drew some disapproving reactions from the German border guards on entry to the increasingly anti-Semitic country. Benn's tutor was to be Frau von Pritzlewitz, who accommodated and taught students in her home. Future Labour cabinet minister, Anthony Greenwood, son of Benn's former cabinet colleague, Arthur, was among the other scholars. Temporarily free of parliamentary and parental responsibilities, the Benns enjoyed their break. But in the background were the sound of the Nazi anthem, the sight of the Hitler Youth parades and a pervading feeling of economic depression. Back at home, trusted nurse Olive Winch took over responsibility for Michael, Tony, David and the house.

January 1933 saw the Benns off on another overseas adventure – to the United States. This was to be a working visit: Benn was to undertake a lecture tour to fund the trip. Benn valued the experience of travelling, but was not keen to spend his own money on something which he did not regard as a necessity. Their first stop was New York, where Margaret eventually tracked down a long-lost uncle. She also travelled extensively alone by Greyhound bus, often sleeping on board and observing the impact of the Great Depression. She watched as some passengers offered the driver jewellery instead of cash for their tickets. She explored as far afield as Florida and there she heard the radio broadcast of Roosevelt's inauguration – a turning point in the country's recovery.

In the summer of 1933, as a culmination of a patient, but determined, seven year charm offensive, Benn was able to make a nostalgic purchase: he became the proud owner of the house which his father had built at Stansgate, but sold thirty years previously. The property had been much improved. The merchant banker, who had bought it from Benn's parents, had built a cottage in the garden and had planted an orchard of apple and pear trees. His successor, the grumpy merchant seaman, Captain Grey, had added more land. His plan was to graze cows and use the milk to set up a chocolate factory. With its exposure to the weather coming off the open water, the original timbers of the house had begun to deteriorate. Captain Grey had strengthened the walls with steel and had finished the outside with pebbledash. Inside, he had put hessian and wallpaper on the bare wooden walls and the thatched roof had been replaced with tiles. Another 'improvement' had been the demolition of much of the remains of an ancient abbey, which had still occupied part of the grounds. Careless of its historical value, Grey had used the masonry to repair the road. Evidence of the abbey survives in the form of one wall standing and various bits of masonry in the driveway.

Captain Grey suddenly died of a stroke, aged only in his mid-fifties. He had had a reputation for ordering people away from his property and had been very unfriendly when the Benn family had first returned to rent the property next door in 1926, even refusing to allow access for the family's groceries to be delivered.[13] At one stage he had even wanted to stop the Benns renting the adjacent house. Mrs Grey was less formidable, and would even be quite friendly when her husband was not around, so the Benns had cultivated their relationship with her. The Benns offered Mrs Grey support and practical help in the wake of her domineering husband's death. They negotiated a longer extension to their rental agreement with her. Then Mrs Grey died, also only in her fifties, and her children decided to sell the house. Knowing how much it meant to Benn, Ernest lent his brother £1,500 to buy the whole property.

Keen not to waste money, Benn had a payphone installed in the house – the variety with button 'A' to proceed with the call and button 'B' to get your money back. There was little scope for the family to economise on food. They took no interest in fine dining; eating was more of a necessity than a pleasure. Benn would often be late for meals, believing that his work was a higher priority than eating.[14] The family's frugality extended to their car. The family had the same Morris Oxford for twenty-six years, from 1928 to 1954, when it was eventually replaced – by another Morris Oxford, which is still at Stansgate, although some way short of being in working order.[15] The Morris Oxford was the basis for the Hindustan Ambassador, a familiar sight on India's roads. It amused the family that somewhere in India there could be an almost exact replica of their car and their house.

Stansgate was the one place where Benn would relax. Margaret adapted to Benn's fluctuating moods, enjoying his buoyant periods and keeping out of the way and concentrating on her own work when he was 'on active service' as he called it – drowning out his feelings of depression with hyperactivity. When Benn was totally absorbed in his missions, Margaret used to say to the children that their father's existence was vital to her happiness, but that his presence was not.[16]

The first lecture tour having been successful, another was arranged for 1934. The Benns' second US trip took in Detroit, including a visit to Henry Ford and his car factory. They then crossed to the west coast, where Benn decided that it would be 'sensible' to keep travelling in the same direction and return home via Japan, China and the Soviet Union.[17] Cocooned in the US ship, *President Hoover*, the Benns had been surrounded by American culture until they reached Japan. The country immediately struck them as isolated and isolationist, although they did notice a Japanese drawing of Santa Claus visiting a Shinto shrine.[18] Japanese society was rigid. Men were regarded as more important than women and soldiers more highly respected than businessmen. The Japanese of the early 1930s still regarded war as a 'glorious thing'. The Soviet Union was seen as their big, monolithic threat, but Japan had recently invaded the Chinese region of Manchuria, although the Japanese did not recognise China as an entity.

The Benns arrived in China by ship, sailing up the Whangpoo (Huangpu) River among the junks and sampans. At Nanjing, then the capital, they separated for about a fortnight. Benn went up the Yangtze River to see the nationalist leader, General Chiang Kai-shek, who was engaged in civil war with the Communists. He was at that time commanding more troops on active service than any other leader in the world.[19] Meanwhile, Margaret made her way alone to Peking. She was the only European aboard the train. The divergence was a precaution against kidnap. The *Daily Mail* had recently paid a ransom to secure the release of another female adventurer and Benn realised that the paper was unlikely to pay out a second time, especially for a political opponent. As Benn indelicately put it 'I'm not involving the family in a lot of unnecessary expense.' The plan worked and the couple were reunited after only one minor misfortune incurred by Benn, described by a fellow traveller as a 'broken bottom'. Benn's train to Peking had been so full that he had had to travel in the luggage rack and on climbing out he had ripped his trousers. The only unnecessary expense was thus a tailoring bill, rather than a ransom payment. To such an inquisitive couple, the trip to China would not have been complete without a visit to an opium den. The opportunity arose when the Benns arrived at Harbin, in Japanese-occupied Manchuria. Opium dens had been encouraged by the Japanese as a means of debauching and debilitating the Chinese. The

Benns found and explored a suitable establishment, although they did head for the 'first class' section.

The Benns then set off to cross Siberia by rail. They passed trains loaded with the wings of bombers, military vehicles and troops, heading east to protect the Soviet Union from possible Japanese attack. They visited the Molotov motor factory at Gorky,[20] designed by Henry Ford. In this Communist plant, a cut-out Stalin implored the Russian workers to achieve greater productivity and those who worked fastest qualified for higher pay and a separate canteen. Ironically, their American colleagues, in their capitalist plant, qualified for the highest wages by complying with the requirements of Ford's Sociological Department, which had used investigators to check on employees' private lives including their bank accounts and domestic cleanliness.[21]

On their return home, David greeted his parents, saying 'I remember you, Mummy and Daddy – do you remember me?'[22] The Benns jointly published an account of their adventures, entitled *The Beckoning Horizon*, dedicated to 'Our patient friends, Michael, Anthony and David'.[23] The first illustration shows the Benns with their luggage, which appears to have amounted to one suitcase, an oversize picnic basket, a handbag, a coat and a kettle.

Having seen the nationalistic and anti-Semitic forces at work in Germany, the militaristic and anti-Communist forces driving Japan, China torn by civil war and America bowed under the weight of depression, Benn could not be optimistic about prospects for the future. A visit to a fortune-teller in Japan had not offered any reassurance. The translation amounted to 'It is not good'. Their departure from Japan had been accompanied by an earthquake.

Whilst war was postponed, personal misfortune was to dog the Benns in 1935. Michael had had scarlet fever; then Tony had to have an appendix operation. In August the family were looking forward to a new arrival, but Margaret gave birth at Stansgate to a stillborn baby boy. He was named Jeremy. The doctor took his body away in a white metal container and arranged for him to be buried. (Ten years later the family managed to trace his burial place and Benn managed to get an exhumation order and had Jeremy re-buried near Stansgate.[24]) The same evening David became dangerously ill with tuberculosis and at first the family thought that he was going to die. It took him four years to recover and he was ten by the time he could stand again. Much of his recuperation was spent with nurse Olive at Bexhill. While he was bedridden, he used the opportunity to learn Russian, which eventually contributed to a successful career with the BBC World Service.

The travels had nurtured Benn's ultimate ambition to be Foreign Secretary. However, with the Labour Party still in disarray after the 1931 debacle and Benn without a seat in Parliament, the prospect was very remote. Benn was to suffer several disappointments before he was to gain another nomination. In August 1934 he made it to a shortlist of four potential candidates for the two-member constituency of Dundee. The idea of another Scottish seat certainly did not deter him and Benn felt that Dundee would have been 'very satisfactory'.[25] However, Dundee was not to be: Benn came third out of the four nominees.[26] Despite the previous disappointments, on 7 May 1935 he was adopted as the prospective Labour candidate for Dudley in the West Midlands.[27] His predecessor as Labour candidate, a solicitor named Hadgkiss, had fought the seat in 1931 but had retired as the prospective candidate for the next general election. Benn was to have six months to establish himself in the constituency – longer than he had had at Leith or Aberdeen.

Dudley, regarded as the centre of the Black Country, was a heavily industrialised town with major employment in steel, leather, limestone and coal mining. All Benn's previous constituencies (St. George's, Leith and Aberdeen) had been significant ports. Dudley just had a canal. The mining activities literally undermined the canal, which had subsided on several occasions. Dudley was a marginal constituency, alternating between Liberal and Conservative MPs between 1832 and 1921, and from then, between Labour and Conservative. The most recent Labour MP had been Oliver Baldwin, son of Conservative premier, Stanley. He held the seat from 1929 to his defeat in 1931 by the Conservative, the appropriately named Dudley Joel, by a margin of 3,904 votes (13.8 per cent). Joel was a wealthy racehorse stable owner. He was standing again in 1935.

Local press comment did not offer Benn much encouragement. 'If the Socialists really want – as they certainly need – Mr Wedgwood Benn back in the House of Commons – they should have found him a better prospect than [Dudley]. During the last three and a half years they have selected for

by-elections in safe seats respectable trade union officials who are useless
in the House when the party is in sore need of skilled and experienced
Parliamentarians like Mr Benn. But he is not a trade unionist, and, in spite
of his record, is regarded with suspicion by those who are.'[28] Benn's natural
inclination for individual freedom and his affinity for the underdog partly
explains why he did not form close links with the trades unions. He co-
existed alongside fervent supporters of the union movement, but to Benn
the trades unions were now strong enough to fight their own corner and he
was not motivated to add to, or to diminish, their power. In his view, they
were neither under, nor over, dogs.

On 12 June 1935 Lloyd George, then still an MP, but aloof from the
Liberal Party, launched a supposedly non-party Council of Action for Peace
and Reconstruction, inspired by the New Deal in America. The Council
sent a questionnaire to all candidates in the 1935 election and on the basis
of their response decided which candidates to endorse – mainly Liberal
or Labour candidates opposing the National Government. Benn filled his
in, but added reservations that the scheme should go further. The Council
of Action, however, decided to support Dudley Joel, who became one of
the very few Conservative candidates to receive the blessing of the Council
and the local Liberals, who were not to contesting the seat, decided instead
to offer their support to him.[29] 1935 was the only one of Benn's election
campaigns where he felt that trickery had been used against him.[30]

1935 general election Dudley:

D.J.B. Joel	Conservative	13,958
W.W. Benn	Labour	11,509
	Conservative majority	2,449 (9.6 per cent)

Benn's result represented a small improvement on his Labour predecessor's
performance in 1931, in terms of reducing the Conservative majority and
share of the vote, but it was still a bitter defeat for Benn.

However, had Benn stayed at Aberdeen North, he might well have won, as
that seat returned to Labour in 1935. In 1935 the Conservative John Burnett
was defending his majority of over 14,000. No Communist stood this time,
but the ILP did indeed put up Fraser Macintosh as their own candidate.

Aside from the Conservatives' 39.8 per cent majority and the competition from the ILP, the Labour Party was still also beset with internal difficulties. Henry Hetherington had been the prospective Labour candidate, following Benn's resignation in 1932. However, in late September 1935 Hetherington had been dropped, amid much local bitterness over his treatment.[31] The local Labour Party had not had a ready replacement and looked to the national party, which parachuted in George Garro-Jones. Born in Wales, Garro-Jones had represented a London seat, Hackney South, as a Liberal in Parliament from 1924 to 1929, when he stood down, shortly afterwards following Benn's example in joining the Labour Party. His task seemed daunting. Being selected at such short notice and not being local, Garro-Jones was subjected to ILP taunts that he had 'never seen Aberdeen until the election'.[32] However, against the odds, he reclaimed Aberdeen North for Labour in 1935:

1935 general election Aberdeen North:

G.M. Garro-Jones	Labour	16,952
J.G. Burnett	Conservative	13,990
A.F. Macintosh	ILP	3,871
	Labour majority	2,962 (8.5 per cent)

Five of Benn's cabinet colleagues who had lost their seats in 1931, returned for the same seats in 1935.[33] At the 1935 election the Labour Party received its highest share of vote up to that point (37.9 per cent), but did not regain its best position in terms of seats, winning only 154, but this was a big step on the road to recovery from the disaster of 1931, when the party only won fifty-two. Joel went on to sit as the Conservative MP for Dudley until he was killed in action at sea in 1941. Benn did not stand again at Dudley.

At the end of November 1936 the Benns set off on another lecture tour, this time to central Europe and the Balkans. They were away during the abdication of King Edward VIII. In Vienna they attended a dinner given by Franz von Papen, the German Ambassador to Austria, the purpose of which was to demonstrate the shared cultural roots of Austria and Germany.

In 1937 Benn was thrown a political lifeline, being selected as the Labour candidate for a by-election at Manchester Gorton. To achieve the nomination, he had to defeat a challenge from, among others, his old friend, Christopher Addison. Addison's parliamentary career had been interrupted like Benn's. He had been out of Parliament between 1922 and 1929, when he had been re-elected for Labour at Swindon. He lost his seat in the Labour debacle of 1931, as had Benn. However, Addison had managed to win back Swindon in a by-election in October 1934, only to lose it again at the general election a year later. When Benn was chosen to be the candidate, Addison had shaken his hand and wished him luck. Benn looked into his eyes and felt that Addison sincerely meant it. The defeated Addison did not have to wait long though to be offered an alternative route back into Parliament. He was ennobled as a Labour peer, Baron Addison, on 22 May 1937.

Gorton was a safe Labour seat, having returned a Labour MP at every election since 1906, with the exception of the Labour disaster in 1931. Joseph Compton had held the seat for Labour since 1923, apart from the 1931 to 1935 period. He had won the seat back in 1935 with a majority of 4,206 (11.8 per cent). On 18 January 1937, at the age of only fifty-five, Compton had died. The 59-year-old Benn was selected to stand as his replacement. Benn was much more at home in Gorton than he had been at Dudley, Aberdeen or even Leith. He was able to capitalise on his local connections in the by-election campaign, being able to claim (accurately) that 'his grandfather, father and mother were all Hyde people'. They did indeed all live there for a part of their lives (in fact both his grandfathers did), although his father had actually moved away to London as a baby.

In the 1930s (and even for another four decades or so) voters did not particularly expect that their MP would live in the constituency, although this has increasingly become a requirement. Ramsay MacDonald represented constituencies in England, Scotland and Wales. Churchill moved between North West England, Scotland and Essex. Benn's transfer to his fourth seat was not as remarkable then as it would seem today. Apart from his first constituency at Tower Hamlets, St. George, where Benn had long-standing connections, he had had little time to establish himself in any of his other seats before facing election and could claim little local connection.

The tone of his election address was, as was Benn himself, rather self-effacing. It started with the question 'Who is this Benn?' For a former cabinet minister, this was rather on the modest side, but, of course, the 1931 debacle which terminated his post was still a delicate and misunderstood subject. However, there was no hiding the pride which Benn wanted to display in his family – all of whom appeared in photographs. Michael, Tony ('Anthony' on the caption) and David, smartly dressed, smiled confidently from their picture in descending order of height. It was customary at the time for married male candidates (as most were) to include an election message from their wives, directed to female voters. The Benns compromised slightly on this ritual segregation. Benn's statement was signed off to the 'Ladies and Gentlemen' in the electorate. Margaret added her own statement, addressed to her 'Dear Friends', but commenting first on the role which women would play in the poll.[34] Diana Spearman, wife of Benn's only opponent, the Conservative Alex. Spearman, took the traditional approach and addressed her remarks 'to the women electors of Gorton'.[35] Diana Spearman had stood as the unsuccessful Conservative candidate in the Labour stronghold of South Poplar in 1935, in which election her husband had been unrewarded by the electorate of Mansfield.

Neither candidate in this working class constituency saw fit to mention that he was the son of a baronet, although both were. Alexander Cadwallader Mainwaring Spearman stood as Alex. Spearman, the full-stop shyly hinting that there might have been something more to his name. Spearman did not follow Benn's example and include a 'Who is this Spearman?' section to his address. The answer would have been that he was a Repton-educated stockbroker and descendant of the Baring banking family. He probably correctly surmised that this background would not have endeared him to the Gorton electorate.

Benn's programme included support for the League of Nations, nationalisation of the arms industry, free school meals and increasing the school leaving age to sixteen; at that time it was fourteen and only eventually reached sixteen in 1972. As is fairly typical for by-elections, the contest had a measure of intrigue and dirty tricks. The Conservatives' literature asked the question (although without actually employing a question mark):

'Are you going to back up the National Government's policy of NO INTERFERENCE IN SPAIN ... or are you going to back up a Party which would again bring the Country TO THE VERGE OF

DISASTER AND BANKRUPTCY AS IN 1931, and would also in the interests of the RED GOVERNMENT IN SPAIN allow our Country to drift into War'.

Labour's retort was to deny that there 'was a word of truth' in the Conservatives' claims and to remind voters of the Zinoviev Letter scare from 1924. 'Don't be misled by LAST HOUR SCARES. For Real Peace Vote for Benn.'[36]

The issues of rearmament and the threat of war were something of a double-edged sword in the Gorton by-election. Whilst most of the electors were desperate to avoid another armed conflict, the threat of a war was actually good for business, as the area had significant involvement in arms manufacturing. Spearman had found out, whether by his own initiative or being fed the information is not clear, that the Armstrong-Whitworth works at Openshaw within the constituency was to re-open, creating up to 1,000 jobs in arms manufacturing. In a Freudian slip, the *Evening Chronicle* reported that 'Mr. Speakman' [sic] had announced the re-opening.[37] This was news to many, including Benn, who probably did not derive much pleasure from the front page of the *Manchester Evening News* either, which reported Spearman's statement alongside a photograph of Lloyd George and an item declaring how refreshed the former prime minister was after his holiday in Jamaica.[38] However, none of the last hour scares seems to have affected the result. Nor did the fact that Benn was struck down with a recurrence of his malaria during the campaign. He won.

By-election 18 February 1937 Manchester Gorton:

W.W. Benn	Labour	17,849
A.C.M. Spearman	Conservative	13,091
	Labour majority	4,758 (15.4 per cent)

Benn's victory represented a slight increase in the Labour majority, compared to 1935. He was now back in the House of Commons, after an absence of five and a quarter years and representing his fourth constituency. After the by-election, Benn managed to establish cordial relations with the director of the Armstrong-Whitworth works. He was invited to come and see some of his electors at work, manufacturing automatic guns – a type of product with which he was familiar, as a trained machine-gun operator in the First World War.

Alex. Spearman did eventually win a seat at Scarborough and Whitby in 1941, which he held until 1966, by which time he was married to his second wife – another Diana. The first Diana was again unsuccessful in Hull Central in 1945.

Benn was the last of the 1931 cabinet to make a return to the Commons. Only three members of the cabinet had kept their seats in 1931. Ramsay MacDonald had held his seat at Seaham in 1931, then lost it in 1935, but returned for the Combined Scottish Universities in 1936. Jim Thomas had kept his seat in 1931 and 1935 as a member of the National Government, but had been forced to resign over a budget leak in 1936. George Lansbury had kept his seat in 1931 and 1935 and had taken over the role of Labour Party leader from 1932 to 1935. So, by the time of Benn's return in 1937, only Lansbury from among his former cabinet colleagues had been continually in the Commons since 1931. Three others had been defeated in 1931, but had returned at by-elections during that Parliament. Arthur Henderson had returned to the Commons at a by-election in 1933 – his fourth comeback at a by-election and his fifth different seat. Arthur Greenwood returned at a by-election in 1932. Christopher Addison had lost his seat in 1931, but regained it in 1934. Five members of the cabinet who had lost their seats in 1931 regained them at the 1935 general election – Albert Alexander, Bertie Lees-Smith, Herbert Morrison, Tom Johnston and John Clynes. Tom Shaw did not return to the Commons after his defeat in 1931. William Adamson, defeated in 1931, was beaten by a Communist on his attempt to return in 1935 and died in 1936. William Graham was defeated in 1931 and died in 1932 at the age of only forty-four. Margaret Bondfield was defeated in 1931 and again in 1935. She was never to return to the Commons. Snowden retired from the Commons at the 1931 election and went to the Lords.

By the time Benn returned to the House, Attlee was just over one year into his leadership of the Labour Party. He was to be Benn's party leader for nearly another nineteen years – longer even than Asquith had been. These two leaders dominated Benn's career. The other six party leaders whom he served only amounted to sixteen years between them. While Benn idolised, and was in awe of, Asquith, with Attlee (nearly six years his junior) his relationship was respectful, friendly, loyal and businesslike. Less than nine months after Benn's return to the Commons, Ramsay MacDonald died. He had been losing his ability to communicate effectively, speaking in long, rambling sentences with little real content. His detractors mocked him for this. However, although his speech was affected, his handwriting stayed clear and the content of his diary remained lucid until the end of his life, possibly suggesting that he had been suffering from fluent aphasia, as the result of a stroke.

Despite not having a powerful trade union following, nor a long track record in the Labour Party, Benn was a popular figure within the parliamentary party, as demonstrated by his success in the executive elections. In the 1937-38 election he came seventh and was easily elected to the 12-person executive. In the 1938-39 election, he improved his position, coming fifth.[39] The following year, 1939-40, Benn came second, with only Alexander ahead of him.[40] However, Benn's political position was not to everyone's liking. After failing to enlist Benn's support for his policy of co-operation with the Communists, Stafford Cripps presented Benn with a pink tulip. 'That's your colour, my dear – pale pink!'[41]

Despite his new parliamentary responsibilities, during December 1937 and January 1938 Benn went on another lecture tour including Palestine and Egypt and in the summer of 1938 Benn took Michael and Tony for their first trip abroad, on a day trip to Boulogne, just before Tony started at Westminster School.

Since the 1920s the Labour Party's policy on international relations had been firmly rooted in support for the League of Nations, as an alternative to re-armament. At the East Fulham by-election in October 1933 Labour had won a seat from the Conservatives in what was widely interpreted on all sides at the time as a demonstration that voters were opposed to re-armament. It was true that the Labour candidate was opposed to re-armament and the Conservative in favour. The reality was that the young, personable and eloquent Labour candidate, John Wilmot, had beaten an older and unpopular Conservative landlord, William Waldron. Housing had featured strongly in the campaign, but re-armament had not. National opinions were extrapolated from the views of the sixty per cent of the East Fulham

electorate who had turned out to vote. Whether the views of a well-off
suburban constituency, which might have felt particularly vulnerable to air
raids, would have accorded with those of, say, an impoverished ship-building
town in Scotland is by no means guaranteed. But, nonetheless, the lesson
was drawn that re-armament was a vote-loser. Baldwin made this claim in the
Commons years later – and even inaccurately quoted the margin of defeat.
However, by April 1936 the Conservative Chancellor of the Exchequer in
the National Government, Neville Chamberlain, had increased the budget
for the armed forces. With this and the deteriorating international situation
as the background, the Labour Party initially maintained its stance, but by
the following year the party was calling for re-armament and opposing the
National Government's policy of appeasement. With hindsight, the Labour
Party had belatedly arrived at the appropriate policy.

In 1936 Benn had been the only member of the Labour Party Advisory
Committee on Defence Services who was not an MP. The committee's
deliberations during that year were quite prescient. The minutes of the
meeting on 26 February 1936 identified that there were 'three potential
aggressors – Italy, Japan and Germany and the case of all three being united
must be envisaged'. The committee also recognised the need for a single
Ministry of Defence, represented in cabinet by one minister, with ministers
for each of the three services below cabinet level reporting to the Minister
of Defence. Inertia, vested interests, lack of public pressure and confusion
between strategy and administration were identified as the key reasons why
there was political opposition within the other parties to the unification
of the defence portfolio.[42] Benn was therefore involved in shaping Labour
Party defence strategy even before his return to the Commons.

Defence was only one of Benn's interests. He demonstrated his old free-
trade credentials in several debates, including a February 1938 debate on
tariffs on carrots. Benn mocked the arguments for further trade protection,
saying: 'I have heard many discussions on Free Trade and tariffs, but never
have I heard a speech on the subject like that to which we have just listened
from the Parliamentary Secretary to the Board of Trade. His case was that the
sun shines more strongly elsewhere than it shines at times in this country, and
it is not fair, and we must have protection against that.'[43] Benn later took up
the cause over celluloid dolls and rattles: 'An industry comes along and asks

for a tariff. For what purpose? In order to make more profits at the expense of the consumer.'[44] Benn was always willing to exert his principles to the limits of their application and down to the to the to the smallest detail – carrots, dolls and rattles were not the greatest political issues of the day, but Benn was prepared to invest his time and effort on these unfashionable causes.

After the resignation of Anthony Eden in February 1938, Benn intervened in the discussion on the appointment of Lord Halifax (formerly Irwin) as the new foreign secretary. Benn was well able to estimate Halifax's credentials for the post, having worked so closely with him on India. His personal estimation of Halifax was higher than his opinion of his policies, so he limited himself to saying: 'this debate has nothing to do with the policy of the Prime Minister and that it has nothing to do with the qualifications of Lord Halifax. If we were now estimating Lord Halifax's qualities as a statesman, I should be as well able to do that as any Member of the House.'[45] But Attlee was rather less tactful, pointing out that 'it would be very difficult for [the prime minister] to find somebody who was qualified by experience and ability to hold the position and was at the same time a supporter of his policy. Between those who had held the office already and had not been a conspicuous success, and those who were thought not likely to be successful, the choice was somewhat narrow.'

Benn energetically opposed Halifax's policy of appeasement. He made several interventions in the Munich Debate in October 1938. One was the single word 'monstrous' in response to Samuel Hoare's criticism of the Czech president for not acting more quickly. Another was to interject into Hoare's claim that the Germans intended to behave in a 'fair and reasonable manner' by reminding him that the Germans had invoked martial law in Czechoslovakia. Benn could not accept his claim that 'we have substituted for an unlimited and uncontrolled military invasion a limited and controlled cession of territory'.[46] On the second day of the debate Benn gave equally short shrift to Burgin, claiming it was 'nonsense' when Burgin said that 'The Czechoslovak Government had realised that the State was breaking up from within'.[47] At the end of the Munich Debate on 6 October Benn, in the company of other Labour members, together with Lloyd George, Sinclair and other Liberals, voted against the government, although the government carried the day with 313 to 150.

In April 1939 The Military Training Bill was introduced as Britain's first measure of peacetime conscription, against the background of the deteriorating international situation. The following month Benn proposed that all those registered for military training should be granted the vote, even if they were under the age of twenty-one.[48] The Military Training Bill conscripted men aged twenty or twenty-one for six months' compulsory military training, after which they were to be transferred to the military reserve. Benn spoke in support of an amendment (defeated in the ensuing vote), criticising the government's mishandling of foreign affairs: 'We have not exactly ... been very matey with Moscow ... We think it is because, behind the Prime Minister, sit men who are determined that we shall not be friends with the Soviet Union ... The French ... are thinking of conscription in their sense of the word – a massed rising of millions of men under arms ... To offer them this bill is either deceiving them, or else ... it is the beginning of something else.'[49]

In the event, there was only one cohort of men conscripted on 3 June 1939. The advent of war superseded this limited scheme with full conscription. This was indeed the beginning of 'something else'.

Chapter Eight

Flying Viscount 1939–46

T he initial period of the Second World War is often described as the 'phoney war' and indeed that was how it started for the Benn family. Within minutes of the announcement of war, the air raid sirens sounded in Westminster. Margaret rushed over to meet Benn at the House of Commons and they went down to an air raid shelter. In typical fearless fashion, Benn had to go upstairs to where he thought the action would be. Margaret stayed in the shelter and heard a terrific noise from above. It was a false alarm. What she had thought was a bomb turned out to be the sound of furniture being moved.

MPs were issued with evacuation instructions from London to a secret 'New Destination'. A clue was contained in the fact that a train was to be available at Paddington, pointing to a destination west or north-west of London. Members were told to bring one suitcase and to carry 'a substantial food ration for the journey', suggesting that the destination was some way at least beyond, say, Reading. A trunk could also be sent on separately.[1] It later emerged that Stratford-upon-Avon had been selected before the war as the destination for the MPs. Tony's school was evacuated to various locations in Sussex, Devon and Herefordshire. David, still in poor health but recovering, was being educated at home for the first part of the war. Michael, who was waiting to go up to Cambridge, joined the RAF Volunteer Reserve in readiness for pilot training. Stansgate was requisitioned by the army. The family left some laundry with a neighbour there in 1939 and they eventually collected it back in 1945. Until the tide of war curtailed it, Benn continued his lecturing work for the British Council. He visited Central Europe in February and March 1940, but his later visits were cancelled. He had been booked to speak in Copenhagen two days before the German invasion of Denmark in April.[2]

Churchill succeeded Chamberlain as prime minister in May 1940, after the Norway Debate, in which Benn voted, along with the Labour Party, most Liberals and some Conservatives, against the government, resulting in Chamberlain's resignation from the premiership. Churchill was able to form a genuine all-party coalition, which Chamberlain's 'National Government' had ceased to be. Churchill kept Chamberlain in his war cabinet as Lord President of the Council, but it was really a sinecure. From the Labour Party he brought in Attlee and Greenwood. Churchill respected Benn's military service and personally liked him. He was also rather taken with Margaret, once having offered the flattering, but impersonal, comment to a fellow dinner guest about her: 'Did you ever see anything more charming?'[3] However, their past policy disagreements, especially over India, made it very unlikely that Churchill would include Benn in his coalition government, although some members of the family did think it was a possibility.[4] Benn did not receive office in the coalition. Instead, he was offered the chair of the British Council by Lord Halifax.[5] Benn drafted a reply, declining with faint gratitude, this 'attractive invitation'.

Benn had a more active role in mind for himself. Without consulting Margaret, because he knew that she would disagree, Benn re-joined the RAF. At home he was evasive about his plans, but asked Margaret to meet him at St. James's station the following lunchtime. She was very suspicious, as she had seen Benn ironing a pair of trousers, something she had never witnessed before. When Margaret arrived at the station, she was greeted by the incongruous sight of her 63-year old husband in the uniform of a pilot officer (the lowest commissioned RAF rank and two rungs down from his rank as an army captain in the First World War), but with three rows of medal ribbons from his 1914-1918 service. Despite the mismatch between his age, rank and decorations, culturally Benn fitted well into the mould of an RAF officer, much better than he had ever done as a younger cavalry officer.

With the addition of Benn, fifteen members of the House of Commons were serving in the RAF.[6] Benn was posted to an office job as an intelligence officer, which used his intellectual talents, but which did not satisfy his hunger for action. Initially, his role was to brief senior RAF personnel on current events. This satisfied Benn's passion for collecting newspapers, dissecting and digesting the stories and distilling them into an early morning briefing. Benn slept in his office, so that he could be ready for an early start. Margaret took over Benn's constituency work, occasionally assisted by Michael. So after five years out of Parliament, Benn had captured Gorton in 1937, but three years later had to delegate his duties so that he could concentrate on his RAF role.

In October 1940, the Benns' home at Grosvenor Road caught fire during an air raid. The blaze was actually caused by an electrical fault in Benn's study – part of an 'improvement' scheme which had involved Michael's practicing his re-wiring skills at his father's behest, in order to save money.[7] The house was uninhabitable and, with Stansgate requisitioned, Margaret was temporarily homeless. She stayed in a public shelter beside Lambeth Bridge while she cleared out the house, salvaging and sending to storage all that was worth saving from amongst their belongings. The smashed windows had to be boarded up. There was no electricity, so Margaret worked by the light of a miner's lamp strapped to her head. She then went to live at Blunt House in Oxted, Surrey, which had earlier been owned by Benn's brother, but was by then a girls' school. David came to join her there, while she earned her keep by teaching theology.[8] The family therefore spent much of the year apart, but did manage to gather for Christmas in Oxford.

1941 saw many twists and turns in Benn's career. The government initially wanted him to go to South America, then this was changed and Brendan Bracken, Minister of Information, offered Benn the post of Propaganda Co-ordinator, Ministry of Information in the Middle East, based in Egypt. However, on 16 May 1941 Attlee suggested that Benn take a peerage to augment the Labour Party's strength in the House of Lords. The peerage would be a working appointment, not an honour. There were few surviving and active Labour members in the House of Lords. Benn's old friend and former Liberal colleague, Christopher Addison, ennobled in 1937, was Labour leader in the Lords, but he had few resources to call upon.[9] Of those who served in the first and second Labour governments, Haldane had died in 1928, Muir-Mackenzie in 1930, Russell in 1931, Chelmsford in 1933 and Parmoor died in 1941. Lord Thomson had been killed in the R101 airship disaster. Arnold had left the Labour Party in 1938 and Ponsonby in 1940. Other survivors from the first two Labour governments had followed MacDonald out of the Labour Party and sat as National Labour peers – De La Warr, Sankey and Amulree. Snowden had initially followed MacDonald after being ennobled in 1931, but had gone his separate way before his death in 1937. Not even all the surviving and loyal Labour peers were available for party duties. Lord Marley was unable to be involved in party politics as he was deputy speaker of the House of Lords. Lord Passfield (formerly Sidney Webb) was 81 and in poor health. Lord Olivier was 82 and retired. Addison's predecessor as leader, Lord Snell, had resigned on health grounds in 1940, but was still active in the Lords at the age of 76. Former Liberal, and later Labour, MP, Noel Buxton, had been ennobled and hyphenated in 1930 to become Lord Noel-Buxton. Joseph Kenworthy had inherited a peerage in 1934 and sat on the Labour benches as Lord Strabolgi. He served as Labour whip from 1938. Also among the Labour lords was 2nd Lord Faringdon, who started his address to the Lords with 'My dears' instead of 'My Lords'.[10] They had been joined by the former Liberal and later Labour MP, Harry Nathan, on his ennoblement as Lord Nathan in 1940. The 34-year-old Earl of Listowel took up duties as Labour whip in 1941, but there were few potential recipients of any lashing which he might have been inclined to deliver. Their numbers were slightly augmented by further creations during the war, including Lord Winster (formerly the Liberal and later Labour MP, Reginald Fletcher) and Lord Latham (leader of the London County Council) in 1942 and Lord Westwood (formerly trade unionist William Westwood) in 1944. By contrast with Labour's fewer than twenty peers, there were still over sixty peers taking the Liberal whip at the end of the war, even though the Liberal Party was reduced to only eighteen MPs, compared to the Labour Party's 166.[11] The decision for Benn to join the small noble Labour group was not entirely straightforward. Churchill said that it would be absurd for Benn to be raised to the House of Lords to boost the strength of the Labour Party, only for him to be posted to Egypt. So, Benn would have to relinquish the job in Egypt. He would also have to give up his hard-won seat in the Commons, only four years after his return and, with it, his MP's salary. It would entail a by-election at Gorton. Benn would also bind his successors to a seat in the Lords, with, at that stage, no means of escape. This last objection was easily dispelled when Benn consulted Michael, as his oldest son and therefore the heir to the peerage. Michael intended to go into the Anglican church after the war, and so a seat in the Lords would not have conflicted with his chosen career. In fact it would have given him a platform for promoting his views and put him alongside the twenty-six most senior Anglican bishops, who also had seats in the Lords. Benn did not consult Tony or David. Margaret was happy for Benn to take the peerage, as she thought that it could prolong his parliamentary career, without the need to stand in further elections – exhausting and risky affairs, as they knew only too well. The idea of working alongside Addison was an added attraction. The by-election would be fought under the terms of the party truce, so at least no Conservative or Liberal candidate would stand against Benn's Labour successor. However, many wartime by-elections were fiercely contested, particularly those which took place in Conservative-held seats. This provided an opportunity for independents, such as Tom Driberg, William Brown and Denis Kendall to win, respectively, the Maldon, Rugby and Grantham by-elections (all in 1942) and later Common Wealth to win a total of three seats – Eddisbury in 1943, Skipton in 1944 and Chelmsford in 1945.[12]

The balance of considerations seemed to fall fairly decisively on the side of Benn's acceptance of the peerage. As a former cabinet minister, Benn was entitled to a viscountcy (a rung higher than a baron) and he was attracted to the idea of the title Viscount Stansgate, after the location of their much loved holiday retreat. After a delay, partly due to some indiscreet remarks by Josiah Wedgwood in America, who was also to be ennobled, Benn's viscountcy was confirmed on 17 December 1941, announced to the press on 22 December and became effective from 12 January 1942.[13] Benn was introduced to the Lords by Viscount Cecil (son of former prime minister Salisbury and friend of the Benns whom they had visited during their honeymoon) and Viscount Trenchard (Marshal of the RAF).[14]

Three days before Benn's elevation, it was also announced that he was to be appointed Director of Public Relations at the Air Ministry, responsible for all forms of news, publicity and propaganda for the RAF. Holders of this post have traditionally held the rank of air commodore and Benn was given this rank on an acting basis on taking up the role.[15] As he was only an acting air commodore, Benn was to be paid at the rate of his substantive rank, which was at that stage squadron leader (three ranks lower).[16] He was then promoted to the substantive rank of group captain (only one rank lower than air commodore) on 29 December 1942.[17] The rank of air commodore, and that was how he was addressed, put him among the most senior officers to serve in the House of Commons. Enoch Powell, Frank Medlicott and Jack Profumo reached brigadier, the army equivalent of air commodore. A few MPs had held even higher rank, including Admiral of the Fleet Roger Keyes and Major-Generals Seely and Spears.

Benn was pleased to find that instructions had been issued in 1940 that public relations officers would be allowed to undertake 'flying duties both on training flights and on operational flights, including those over enemy territory, with a view to providing eye-witness accounts of operations'.[18] He certainly did not mind witnessing operations, or, preferably, participating in them – and this he did.

So, Benn, the East End boy, was now officially the Right Honourable Air Commodore First Viscount Stansgate, PC, DSO, DFC. In November 1942 Tony was accepted into the RAF and he took up a posting on 24 July 1943, so father and two eldest sons were all in the RAF at the same time.

The by-election in Gorton caused by Benn's elevation turned out to be an uneventful affair. The only candidate for the poll on 11 March 1942 was William Oldfield, the Labour Party agent for the constituency. Oldfield went on easily to hold Gorton in the 1945 Labour landslide and sat until his retirement in 1955 and the seat has remained in Labour hands ever since. Had Benn not accepted the peerage, he would almost certainly have been able to remain in the Commons until he chose to retire. The difference entailed by a refusal of the peerage would not have affected Benn himself, as much as it came to affect Tony and the whole legal basis of hereditary peerages.

In 1943 Benn led an Empire parliamentary delegation to Ottawa, Washington and Bermuda and this formed the topic of his maiden speech in the House of Lords on 28 October 1943. His exposition of the lessons from the trip was eloquent, but he could not resist adding a little spice to his first address to the Lords: 'Our manner of speech is an offence to the Americans. They think it muffled and tepid, and that it shows a pretentious reserve. That is what they mean when they call us "stuffed shirts." ... I regret to say that the very existence of this House was mentioned as one of the obstacles to Anglo-American understanding ... I was going to say, though I hardly dare do so in a maiden speech, that that is a resolution which has often attracted my favourable notice!' Benn's risqué reference in his maiden speech to the potential abolition of the House of Lords (a subject which he had previously put forward in the Commons) was a foretaste of his future rather maverick approach to political convention. Lord Marchwood, who had accompanied Benn on the mission, indulgently replied that Benn 'always had the happy faculty of being able to tell a most interesting tale in the most witty fashion ... He is a man full of determination.' Viscount Cranborne followed in appreciation of Benn's first offering to the Lords, commenting on his 'brilliant and charming maiden speech', adding that he had 'been wondering when he was going to break his long silence here.'[19]

The Benns found themselves a new temporary London base at Dolphin Square, home to many MPs over the decades. Benn had been ill, suffering 'as usual' from bronchitis when he received a phone call from Archie Sinclair, offering him a new job. Sinclair, still a firm friend of Benn's despite their diverging political positions, had been Secretary of State for Air since Churchill formed his coalition in May 1940. He rang Benn to offer him the post of Vice-President of the Allied Control Commission in Italy. The Commission was established on 10 November 1943 to reconstitute a free Italian government as the allies drove north to liberate the country. The aim was to train equal numbers of British and American officers to take over territory from which the Germans had recently been driven. As vice-president of the Allied Control Commission, Benn had a wide range of responsibilities, ranging from immediate life and death issues to cultural considerations. Reporting to him were sub-commissioners responsible for the interior; health; legal; public safety; property control; education; monuments; fine arts and archives.

Benn had served in Italy during the First World War from 1917 to 1918 and was very keen to accept the opportunity to go back. The circumstances were, of course, rather different. In the First World War, Italy had been an allied force from the time of the country's entry into the conflict in 1915. Benn's post had been supporting the Italians on their border with Austria-Hungary. In the Second World War Italy had again not joined the conflict until a year after the war had started, but this time the UK and Italy were on opposing sides. However, by 1943, the situation in Italy was very complex and rapidly changing. In July 1943 the allies invaded Sicily and begun the attack on the 'soft underbelly' of the Axis. German forces in Italy had been driven northwards, Mussolini had been dismissed and King Victor Emmanuel III had taken command of the Italian military. On 3 September 1943 a secret armistice was signed between Italy and the allies. Italian military forces became split three ways. In the south, forces loyal to the king joined the Allies as co-belligerents. In the north however, some Italians continued to fight alongside the Germans while others gave up arms and were rounded up by the Germans as military internees. Italy was, therefore, effectively in a state of civil war and simultaneously occupied by allied and German forces. The situation was further complicated by the antipathy of the Sicilians, in particular, to the king, and even to Italy. Even before the war, Italy had been industrially weak and short of essential raw materials. The Italian army was generally poorly-equipped and the air force relied mainly on the Fiat CR.42 Falco, a manoeuvrable, but outdated, two-wing, single-seat fighter.[20] By 1943 the situation in Italy was politically, militarily and industrially chaotic and life for most Italians was precarious, with the threat of starvation and disease.

For the fearless Benn, who loved Italy, spoke Italian and who thrived on gathering and interpreting detailed information about complex foreign affairs, the Italian posting was too tempting to resist. Benn had certainly not lost his appetite for flying and recorded that 'after a hearty breakfast ... and a little engine failure' his plane reached Algiers, where he was met and briefed by Harold Macmillan, the resident minister liaising between the allies.[21] Benn then flew on to Bari in southern Italy, to meet Lord Rennell, who described his operation on the ground as 'a dog's dinner', which 'would never work'. Benn's opaque explanation of the role of the Allied Control Commission was that it was 'to provide a stepping stone between the army and AMGOT [Allied Military Government of Occupied Territories] and the re-establishment of local rule'. In terms of strategy, Benn was forced to admit that 'there was nothing an individual like me could do to sway the great forces involved even if I had wished to do so, or knew what I wanted'. Benn then visited Brindisi, where the king had established his government, to meet with American and Italian representatives. Benn had not lost his attraction to a bit of bombing, which had developed during the First World War. His reminiscence was that the meeting 'was brightened' by the fact that it was held opposite the quay where a munitions vessel was anchored. This 'gave a little kick to our proceedings' because of 'a certain amount of bombing'.

Benn described the essence of his work as being to 'feed the hungry and bury the dead'.[22] He came across a stark example of the need to feed the hungry when he visited a prison at Cagliari in Sardinia, where not only the inmates, but the guards too, were nearly starving and calling out, begging for food. One of Benn's key tasks was to organise the clear up of Naples, including the prevention of typhus, which involved the spraying of DDT powder down the necks of the local population. Those sprayed received a certificate. Many of the certificates then went on sale on the black market. Benn mainly concentrated his energy on practical solutions, where he could achieve results. However, out of intellectual curiosity, and to fulfil expectations, he also involved himself in travelling, liaison, investigation and many, many meetings. He liaised with Italians (including the resistance movement in German-occupied northern Italy), Americans and Russians. He travelled to Sicily and around much of southern Italy, frequently stopping overnight at police stations.

During his time in Italy, Benn's health was not good and he spent part of the time in hospital, where his visitors included General Patton. Portentously, Benn's illness meant that he missed the 1944 New Year celebrations; 1944 was not to be a good year for the family. The worst event, which had devastating personal consequences and eventually national political significance, was the death of Michael, on 23 June 1944 at the age of 22. At the outbreak of war on 3 September 1939, Michael was two days short of his eighteenth birthday and waiting to go up to Cambridge. He had immediately applied to join the RAF Volunteer Reserve. He became a night-fighter pilot, flying Beaufighters and later Mosquito fighter-bombers, serving in North Africa, before being posted back to England. He took part in the low-level attack on Amiens prison to liberate inmates, particularly from the French resistance, held by the Germans. The risky daytime attack was partially successful. The planes flew as low as fifty feet above the target. The raid was timed to coincide with the guards' lunch break. Their quarters were hit and the perimeter wall was breached. Around 100 prisoners also died in the attack, but over 250 escaped, although 182 of them were recaptured. In 1943 Michael had been decorated with the DFC, as had his father. He had reached the rank of flight lieutenant, the RAF equivalent of his father's rank of captain at the end of the First World War. Michael was thoughtful and religious. Influenced particularly by his mother, his ambition after the war had been to be ordained as a clergyman. He had had no objection to his father's acceptance of the peerage, saying 'I can make a disturbance in the Lords and Anthony can make a disturbance in the Commons!' Politically, Michael's views were probably the furthest to the left of all his family. He was sympathetic to the policies of Common Wealth.

Late at night on 22 June 1944 Michael set off for what should have been his last operation, before taking up a post as ADC to the air marshal commanding the Far East. He took off in his fully-armed Mosquito to find that the air speed indicator was not working. Crucial for all stages of flight, a malfunctioning airspeed indicator presents a serious threat of stalling or overshooting a runway. (As recently as 2009 all 228 people on board Air France flight AF447 from Brazil to France were killed in an accident at sea resulting from a faulty airspeed indicator.) Another aircraft volunteered to fly alongside Michael to indicate his airspeed, so that he could land back at RAF Thorney Island. Michael managed to bring the aircraft down onto the runway, but he overshot. The plane hit the sea wall and ended up in the water. His navigator was uninjured, but Michael had broken his neck. The navigator held Michael up in the water for half an hour until help arrived. Michael was conscious at first and still able to talk when he reached St. Richard's Hospital in Chichester, but soon after that he lost consciousness, never to regain it. His mother was able to reach the hospital twenty minutes before he died. David was still at school preparing for his Oxford University entrance exam. Tony was with the RAF in Bulaweyo, Southern Rhodesia (Zimbabwe). His father was in Italy and did not arrive back until after Michael's funeral and was then struck down with another bout of malaria. In a sad coincidence, the son of Lieutenant Tandura, Benn's co-conspirator in the First World War parachute mission, was also killed in the same month as Michael.

Although quite sentimental in private, Benn was usually stoic in public. He managed to deal with loss and trauma quite effectively. He had been relatively unaffected by the horrors of the battlefield in the First World

War. His coping mechanisms were to draw strength and comfort from his family and to busy himself with work, to minimise the time available for morbid introspection. The effect of Michael's death on his father however, was profound and lasting. He was not only grief-stricken, but felt guilty that he had 'landed' Tony 'in it' because Tony was now to be heir to the unwanted peerage and this could disrupt his planned career in the House of Commons.

Benn resigned from the Allied Control Commission; his resignation was announced in the *Times* on 15 August 1944. He had himself transferred back to the RAF, where he tried to take Michael's place. Ostensibly, his new role was to give lectures at RAF stations, but as always, careless of regulations and his own safety, he trained as an air gunner. One of his trainers reported him to be a 'very keen and industrious gunner ... diligent to the extreme' and that with further training he would be 'an asset to any crew'.[23] Although officially grounded, he took part in some operational flights. As these were in contravention of orders, the records are rather patchy. However, there are references to his participating as 'air gunner in the rear turret' of a Halifax bomber, as 'air crew' on an Atlantic patrol in a Short Sunderland flying boat, a flight in an 'armed' Fortress bomber to Malta, as 'extra crew' delivering a Liberator bomber to Iceland and references to flights in the 'second pilot's seat' in a Catalina flying boat.[24] Further confirmation of his activities came with a mention in despatches, recorded in the *London Gazette* on 1 January 1945. Benn must have felt at home in this new role; he had trained as a machine gunner in the First World War and one of the two companies which manufactured the rear gun turrets for bombers was Boulton and Paul – the same company which had built the pre-fabricated sections of Stansgate.

One of the first MPs to be killed in the Second World War was 56-year-old Sir Arnold Wilson, serving as an RAF rear-gunner. In total twenty-four MPs died in the Second World War, exactly the same number as died in the First. Again, the vast majority were Conservatives. Among those killed was Dudley Joel, Benn's victorious opponent in Dudley in 1935.

The rollercoaster pattern of Benn's parliamentary activity continued. After being out of Parliament from 1931 to 1937, once he was back in the Commons, he was a very active member until 1939, when he intervened in 210 debates, mainly on the international situation. However, due to the demands of his wartime duties, Benn went from being one of the most vocal parliamentarians, to one of the most silent. In 1940 he only took part in seven debates, in 1941 only two (on eggs and post offices) and in 1942 (the year of his transfer from the Commons to the Lords) none at all. Benn's maiden speech in the Lords on 28 October 1943 was his only parliamentary intervention that year. The following year he made no interventions at all. His relinquishing his constituency to go to the Lords in 1942 was intended to boost Labour's resources in the upper chamber. In the event his other duties meant that he played almost no role at all until the end of the war. Benn applied for release from the RAF to return to parliamentary duties as soon as war ended. His retirement from RAF (at the age of sixty-eight) was announced in the *Times* on 16 July 1945. He ended the war with substantive rank of group captain and the acting rank of air commodore.[25] This 'retirement' was in fact just a prelude to another bout of demanding work, although this time centred on parliamentary and departmental duties.

The 1945 election gave the Labour Party its first ever overall majority in the House of Commons. However, the pattern of party support differed quite significantly from later elections. In 1945 the Labour Party won seats in all parts of the UK and it would have been possible to travel from London to Liverpool without leaving a Labour-held constituency. In contrast, the 1997 election delivered a greater numerical victory for the Labour Party, but the success was geographically more concentrated. In 1997 the traveller would only have reached St. Albans before reaching the limit of Labour-held territory. Conversely, in 1945 the Conservatives won twenty-seven seats in Scotland, but by 1997 the party was completely wiped off the political map north of the border. In 1945 the Liberals only held twelve seats, of which seven were in Wales.

Attlee appointed Benn to his cabinet as Secretary of State for Air, the post which Sinclair had held during the war. A flat came with the job. Attlee's 1945 cabinet mainly comprised proven ministers who had served in the wartime coalition – Jowitt, Morrison, Greenwood, Dalton, Bevin, Chuter Ede, Hall, Alexander, Wilkinson, Westwood, Williams and Cripps. Other cabinet members had held party or parliamentary office during the war. Addison had been Labour leader in the Lords, Pethwick-Lawrence had been leader of the opposition in the Commons and Shinwell had been chairman of the Labour

Party, having previously turned down Churchill's offer of ministerial office. Benn and Lawson were the only reincarnations from earlier administrations who had not held office during the war, but who had previous ministerial experience. The new cabinet was therefore an experienced team. There were only two cabinet ministers – Bevan and Isaacs – who had not previously held office. Benn's parliamentary experience, dating back to 1906, went back further than that of any of his cabinet colleagues; Addison's dating back to 1910 was next. In addition to his departmental responsibilities, Benn sat on the cabinet committees responsible for Defence, India and Burma, Palestine, Allied Supplies and the Far East. He also occasionally attended the Colonial Affairs committee, but delegated his place on the Civil Aviation committee to his under secretary.

The contrast between the formation of the 1929 and 1945 Labour cabinets was stark. MacDonald had been a glamorous and eloquent, but sensitive and prickly, showman specialising in foreign affairs. Attlee was arguably the most self-effacing prime minister ever – confident in himself, businesslike and totally careless of image. He had been in charge of domestic affairs in Churchill's wartime administration. Attlee had a large parliamentary majority; MacDonald had none. Attlee had a full schedule of radical reform proposals; MacDonald had had limited aims. MacDonald had limited resources to call on; Attlee had a team of ministers, tried and tested, but tired. Economics was the weakest area for MacDonald's government. Attlee's was stronger, but arguably still lacking compared to its significant strengths in other areas.

The Benns were invited to spend the first weekend of the new government at Chequers with the Attlees. The Benns were allocated the suite which Churchill had only recently vacated, complete with a king-sized bed with a Churchill-sized dip in the middle. Margaret had not met Violet Attlee before, but the pair soon developed a rapport and decided to take French lessons together. Both women had husbands who had connections with the East End and whose older brothers had helped to finance their careers.

After the First World War public sentiment had been for a return to pre-war conditions and tranquillity. After the Second World War sentiment was almost the exact opposite – a desire for a brave new world and to sweep away the past. In its first year, the Attlee government, with Benn in the cabinet, introduced many significant and long-lasting reforms, including the 1945 Family Allowances Act – the first law to provide child benefit and, in 1946, the Bank of England Act to nationalise the Bank, the Coal Industry Nationalisation Act, the New Towns Act, the Health Service Act; the National Insurance Act and the United Nations Act allowing the crown to implement United Nations Security Council resolutions without the official approval of Parliament. Benn's term of office started on 3 August 1945. Three days later the first atomic bomb ever to be used in war was dropped on Hiroshima. Three days after that followed the last occasion on which an atomic bomb was used in war – the bombing of Nagasaki. On 15 August Japan surrendered.

As Secretary of State for Air, Benn was in charge of the Air Ministry, which ran the RAF. The Ministry had been in existence from 1918, when the RAF was formed. This was, therefore, the second time that the Ministry had had to deal with demobilisation at the end of a world war. The Secretary of State for Air was one of three service ministers, the others being the First Lord of the Admiralty, responsible for the navy (A.V. Alexander in 1945) and the Secretary of State for War, responsible for the army (J. Lawson in 1945). All three were cabinet-level posts. Since 1940 they had all reported to the Minister of Defence – a post which had been held by Churchill during his premiership and which was taken on by Attlee in 1945. The structure was evolving and would eventually lead to the separation of the Defence portfolio from the premiership and for only the Minister of Defence to be in the cabinet. It was not until 1964 that the administration of the three services was combined to form the Ministry of Defence, headed by the Secretary of State for Defence. A.V. Alexander was in his third term as First Lord of the Admiralty – a post which he had previously held in the 1929 to 1931 cabinet and again in Churchill's wartime coalition. Jack Lawson was in the cabinet for the first time, as Secretary of State for War. He was a miner, who had seen military service as a driver in the Royal Artillery in the First World War and, rare amongst Labour MPs, had held his seat continuously since 1919. He had held junior ministerial posts in MacDonald's governments. All three were hard-working, popular and down-to-earth ministers. Of the three, Alexander was the most experienced in his post, but Benn had held the most senior rank in the services.

In 1929 Benn had taken on the India portfolio with no notice, no preparation and most of his knowledge of the issues had come from his regular scouring of the *Times*. In 1945 Benn had just finished active service in the RAF, an organisation of which he had been part on the day of its formation in 1918. He was chosen by Attlee as a calm, efficient, safe pair of hands, acceptable to the RAF hierarchy. Benn knew, personally or by reputation, virtually every senior officer in the service, he had visited vast numbers of bases and was familiar with every type of aircraft. The RAF was faced with a major transformation from wartime to peacetime operations. The sheer scale of the force – 1.1 million personnel (around thirty times the scale of the modern RAF) – needed radical pruning, while at the same time operations needed to be continued in Europe, the Middle East and the Far East. Prisoners of war had to be repatriated and food, clothing and medical supplies had to be delivered to meet urgent needs. During the war, the priority had been to produce aircraft as quickly as possible. The return of peace meant that choices had to be made over the direction of research and development. The two looming issues were the move to a new generation of jet aircraft and the development of a British atomic bomb.

The government recognised that a period of assessment and reflection on the lessons from the war was necessary before making strategic changes to the organisation of the armed services. Nevertheless, there were almost immediate calls for the integration of the three services, with some calling for complete amalgamation, while others argued for the three services to remain separate but with an independent combined general staff to be established to make strategic decisions. Benn had been involved in Labour Party discussions as far back as 1936 about the need for defence co-ordination and was in agreement with the integration of the political leadership of the services into one defence minister (separate from the prime minister) in cabinet. In the meantime, part of his role was to defend the temporary status quo, while final decisions were made and while the scale of immediate tasks meant any reorganisation would have been too disruptive to implement. The deliberate delay in reorganisation was characterised in some parts of the press as 'the brass hats' having won the argument to keep the three services entirely separate. However, as with many other areas of policy, the Attlee Government was not afraid to make changes and their plans were presented in the Defence White Paper of 1946.[26] The principle was that whilst defence needed co-ordination at the top political level to avoid competition for scarce resources, 'it should be the men responsible in the Service departments for carrying out the approved policy who are brought together in the central machine to formulate it'.

Aside from the parliamentary, strategic and administrative sides of Benn's job, the role gave him contact with the new types of aircraft being brought into service by the RAF. During Benn's tenure the first RAF flights took place for a range of new aircraft. At the small end of the scale were the *De Havilland Chipmunk* and *Percival Prentice* trainers and the *Westland Sioux* helicopter. In the mid-range there was the *de Havilland Devon* for short-haul transport and communication. At the large end there were the *Handley Page Marathon* and *Hastings* transport planes, the latter being the largest plane yet flown by the RAF. During the war the Brabazon Committee had taken decisions on the development of new civil aircraft to be spun off from the advances in technology during the war. The committee had identified six types of aircraft to be developed, of which only two were to come to be regarded as a commercial success – one of which was the *Viceroy*, although its name was later changed to the *Viscount*.

Fatal accidents were around a fortnightly occurrence in the RAF during Benn's tenure. The actual number of accidents had increased, but this was mainly the result of the increased mileage being covered. In October 1945, the total number of passenger miles flown was four times the total for January that year. There were protests and refusals to take up assigned duties among some RAF personnel who felt aggrieved at the pace of demobilisation, which was inevitably slower in the RAF than the army, as the air force had to provide the means of repatriation for many of the army personnel.

Having been an eager supporter of women's suffrage before the First World War, as had Margaret and her mother (but not her father), Benn was delighted to find that his post at the Air Ministry offered him the opportunity to generate some trouble in the cause of women's advancement in the air force. Benn had ultimate responsibility for the appointment of chaplains to the RAF. Most were Anglicans and the Church of England did not allow women priests. However, some chaplains represented other denominations, including the Free Churches, and they had fully trained and ordained women ministers. Benn, urged on by Margaret, was determined to appoint one of them, Reverend Elsie Chamberlain, as an RAF chaplain, well realising the backlash he was likely to receive. Margaret had first met Elsie Chamberlain when she had been studying at King's College, London in the early 1930s and Elsie had since gone on to be a Congregational minister. Despite considerable internal opposition, Benn made the appointment. It drew from Canterbury what became known in the Benn family as the 'Archbishop's stinker': 'I cannot but deeply regret that you have not heeded my warnings ... What steps are to be taken to secure that all Church of England personnel are strictly warned that under no conditions must they intentionally or by inadvertence attend Services at which she administers the Sacraments?'[27]

Benn had won the first round, but the Church of England still had other leverage over the situation. Elsie Chamberlain was engaged to an Anglican curate, John Garrington. The Bishop of London warned Garrington that, if they married, he would be denied his own parish. The Bishop suggested that if they went ahead 'he can go and be a butcher's boy'. Benn was having none of this bullying, on top of the sexism which he had fought to overcome. So, he went straight to the Lord Chancellor, William Jowitt, who had church livings in his gift, and Jowitt arranged for Garrington to be given his own parish. The furore did not end there. When Benn found out that Elsie Chamberlain's appointment had been recorded in the Air Force Annual as that of a 'welfare worker', he ordered the entire print run to be pulped and reprinted.[28]

In April 1946, Bevin, apparently without consulting Attlee beforehand, asked Benn to undertake a mission to agree a new Anglo-Egyptian treaty. A previous treaty had been agreed between the two countries in 1936, when Egypt had been under threat from Mussolini's imperialist expansion. That treaty had entitled the UK to keep forces in Egypt to protect the Suez Canal. During the Second Word War, the UK had enjoyed the use of facilities far in excess of those envisaged in the 1936 treaty and still maintained air bases for long-range attack, a large military headquarters, over 200,000 troops and 100,000 prisoners of war, including a large number of personnel in the centre of Cairo and Alexandria, which were becoming a particular irritant to the Egyptian public. As Benn pointed out to the cabinet, 'We could not pretend that the existing Treaty entitled us to all the facilities we now enjoyed and we could not expect to obtain recognition of them' in the negotiations for the new treaty. Presciently, Benn warned the cabinet that the alternative to a treaty on the lines proposed would be 'an Egypt united in hostility to us'.[29] Benn spent a considerable amount of time in Egypt, but the negotiations dragged on inconclusively.

Benn was not alone in missing many cabinet meetings during his involvement in the Egyptian negotiations. At times cabinet meetings attracted the attendance of only around half the eligible ministers, as so many were involved in overseas negotiations. One week, Bevin and Alexander were in Paris, Benn was in Egypt, Cripps was in Switzerland, Morrison was in Ireland, Isaacs was in Canada and Williams was in Denmark, while Lawson was ill and Dalton was about to depart for the US. At the beginning of October 1946, Benn was in Egypt when he received an urgent telephone call from Attlee, asking him to come home at once by any sort of aircraft. He was met at the airport and taken straight to see Attlee in Downing Street. Benn recalled: 'Attlee hummed and hawed. He wanted me to resign to clear the ground for his new defence scheme. I told him he needn't have made such a fuss'. Benn and Attlee wrote out an exchange of letters, settling Benn's departure from the cabinet.[30] Benn wrote: 'In view of the new organisation of the Defence Ministries, I am putting my resignation in your hands. May I say that I have greatly appreciated the opportunity of working under your premiership and am grateful for the many kindnesses shown to me by you and my colleagues.'

Attlee, known for his economy with words, actually wrote a slightly longer reply which was equally genuine, but also businesslike, including the comments: 'I appreciate very much the excellent work you have done at the Air Ministry. You held office during a most difficult period when you were faced with the problems of demobilization and the transition from war to peace. You surmounted them successfully … It has always been such a pleasure to work with you.'[31] Benn's later, more succinct but not at all bitter, summary of the event was 'Clem sacked me'.[32] However, Benn was asked to continue with the Egyptian negotiations, which limped on, but failed to reach an agreement and were eventually abandoned.

Benn's departure from the cabinet was part of a major defence reorganisation, which followed the outline which had been set out by the

Labour Party Advisory Committee on Defence Services as far back as 1936 and on which Benn had sat. All three service ministers left their jobs, which were later filled by ministers outside the cabinet. Benn (aged 69) and Lawson (aged 64) left the government, while Alexander (slightly younger, at 61) remained as Minister without Portfolio, pending the creation of the new cabinet post of Minister of Defence, which he was designated to fill. There was a hiatus of two and a half months while new legislation had to be passed to establish the new Ministry of Defence, before Alexander was appointed to head the new department. Benn was the last Secretary of State for Air to sit in the cabinet.

Attlee had made a good choice in appointing Benn to the air ministry. Benn was a competent and industrious administrator, reassuring and acceptable to the RAF at a time of significant change, in sympathy with the government's policy thrust of integrating the political control of the armed services, but due to his age and temperament, expendable at short notice and without fuss. Benn harboured no grudges from his removal from office. In both cases after his departure from the cabinet he made himself available to complete aspects of work in progress – the second Indian roundtable conference in 1931 and the Egyptian treaty negotiation in 1946.

Benn was free to contemplate his next move – he could have made the journey from Westminster to Southminster (the nearest station to Stansgate) and put his feet up at his ancestral home.

Chapter Nine

The Noble Lord Shall Be No Longer Heard 1946–60

G iven Benn's workaholic temperament, his 'retirement' from the cabinet inevitably meant that he looked for more work. At the age of 69, he did not anticipate another recall to government – he had already received one more than he had realistically expected. Benn's major unfulfilled ambition was to have served as foreign secretary. He accepted that he had come within one rung of achieving his ambition, but that that was as close as he was going to get. His membership of the House of Lords gave him a permanent toe-hold in Parliament, without the need to stand for election. It meant that he could remain in touch with his old friends and colleagues and cause enough trouble to get into the national press from time to time. But, this was not enough to satisfy his hunger for something useful to do – preferably something with an international dimension. Margaret was also keen to travel, as long as they could travel together.

An opportunity presented itself for Benn to take up a role with a grand-sounding job title in an international organisation with idealistic ambitions and luxurious working conditions – the role of President of the Inter-Parliamentary Union. Founded in 1889, the IPU is the oldest multi-lateral political organisation in the world. It is headquartered in Geneva. The organisation's aim is to promote international peace and understanding by organising links between parliamentarians of different countries, many of whom are former senior ministers. Benn was certainly tempted by the role, but had doubts about the organisation's effectiveness. However, the IPU had played an influential role in the creation of the United Nations and in promoting the role of women in politics – both issues close to Benn's heart. The organisation was to become important in maintaining relations across the Iron Curtain during the Cold War and in helping to re-establish effective democracies in the wake of conflicts. The multi-lingual, internationalist

Benn was well-suited to the role, which he accepted in 1947 and which was to be a major focus of his life for the next decade. The IPU roll of office-holders records Benn, his name appearing as 'Mr. Viscount Stansgate', as the president with the longest tenure of office in the 125 year history of the organisation, except for that of his immediate predecessor, who served for thirteen years.

The IPU gave the Benns many opportunities to escape from rationed and chilly Britain; the winter of 1947 was exceptionally cold and coal was among many essentials which were still rationed. In order to fulfil his role, Benn had to stay in palaces, top hotels and castles. The work took him, amongst many other destinations, to: Baku, Bombay and Berlin; Nice, New York and Nanking; Paris, Peking and Phnom Penh; Karachi, Khartoum and Kunming. As always, Benn kept a job book, which started with overall objectives for the year. It illustrated the high ambitions of his and Margaret's work: for Benn the focus of 1947 was the 'IPU' and the 'Lords', while for Margaret it was 'God'.[1]

1947 was to see the fruition of one of Benn's earlier struggles – the passage of the Indian Independence Act, which Attlee later described as the greatest achievement of the Labour government. In the Lords debate on 26 February 1947, he used his experience to caution the Lords to keep their focus on India, rather than on party politics, as had happened seventeen years previously: 'It was a real battle, cut and thrust and parry, attack and counter-attack … A good time was had by all. [We] started to lay the foundations [of the] Act of 1935. But the Conference was hamstrung by the debate in your Lordships' House and by people directing more attention to the sins of the Government than to the treatment of a sick patient.'[2] On 18 July 1947 the Indian Independence Act received royal assent. India and Pakistan became two new independent dominions. It was the completion of the process on which Benn had worked so hard between 1929 and 1931. The hugely significant achievement, however, was marred by death and violence as groups from the minority religions fled between the new states and by the unresolved issue of the status of Jammu and Kashmir.

On a much smaller scale, Benn was appointed to a privy council committee of inquiry into conditions on the Channel Island of Alderney, the northernmost of the islands. The Channel Islands were the only part of the British Commonwealth to have been occupied by the German army during the Second World War. The 1,442 population of Alderney had been evacuated, except for seven islanders, who had refused to leave. When the Germans arrived it was to all intents and purposes deserted. The Germans ran Alderney as a heavily fortified military base and prison camp. They had a garrison of 3,000 and a workforce of 4,000. Many buildings and field boundaries were destroyed and concrete fortifications constructed. Alderney's records of land ownership and other government records were lost. Following the liberation of Alderney on 16 May 1945, the pre-war population was slow to return. The task of post-war reconstruction and regeneration was difficult, as Alderney was no longer an attractive place to live and by the end of 1946 less than half of the pre-war population had returned. In July 1947 in the absence of tangible progress, the committee of the privy council was appointed to enquire into the state of Alderney, particularly its government, its relationship with the neighbouring islands, its financial position, its system of land tenure and its economic prospects. Benn went with Home Secretary Chuter Ede and Conservative MP Osbert Peake to Alderney in September 1947.[3] The committee recommended that Guernsey should take over responsibility for Alderney's most important public services. The States of Guernsey would assume financial, legislative and administrative responsibility for Alderney's airport, health, social and educational services, police and immigration, main roads, drains and water supply. Despite some local opposition, the States of Alderney agreed to the loss of sovereignty in return for the prospect of rehabilitation of the island.[4]

From the late 1940s onwards, Benn drifted towards an increasingly independent line, from the point of view of both party politics and what others considered to be mainstream issues. However, a consistent theme of Benn's was always to support the underdog. He preferred to take on the causes of the weak and the forgotten. Benn was always on the lookout for an underdog to champion, a cause in pursuit of which he seemed to leave no dog unturned. In this vein in 1949 Benn involved himself in a moral skirmish against an unlikely opponent, the John Lewis Partnership.

The worlds of politics and shopping overlap surprisingly little. There are, however, two retail operations with unusual characteristics, which are often cited as models by politicians. One has a very clear political affiliation, the other is generally regarded as politically neutral.

The Co-operative Group is a retail and wholesale business which is owned by its members, who receive a share of its profits as a dividend. It spawned a political arm and some MPs, including A. V. Alexander, were elected under the Co-operative Party banner. The political wing of the movement eventually merged with the Labour Party and Alexander, ennobled as Lord Alexander, became Benn's boss as Leader of the Labour Party in the House of Lords in 1955. The party name lives on with MPs, such as Ed Balls, being elected as Labour and Co-operative Members of Parliament. However, issues with the Co-operative Bank and the labyrinthine structure of the business have damaged its reputation.

The other retailer which has intermittently attracted attention from politicians for a variety of reasons is the John Lewis Partnership, and it was against this unlikely target that Benn chose to take up arms. In recent years the Partnership has had praise lavished on it by politicians, although its practise of contracting out cleaning services to companies which pay low wages and provide no profit share has come in for some criticism.[5]

In 1949 Benn chose to make a principled objection to the proposed introduction by the John Lewis Partnership of a political test for its partners, which would have effectively excluded Communists from working for the business. This was, of course, the beginning of the Cold War, but it was before the era of McCarthyism in the US.

The John Lewis business became a partnership, distributing most of its profits to its workers, under the inspiration of the emotional, combative and outspoken John Spedan Lewis (son of the founder), whose actions demonstrated a mixture of autocracy and altruism. Spedan's politics were obscure (perhaps even to himself). He had turned down an offer to stand as a Liberal candidate in 1910.[6] He repeatedly refused to be drawn on his politics,[7] even though some of his partners wrote to the house magazine, the *Gazette*, that it was a revolutionary socialist design.[8] However, Spedan Lewis did not draw all of his politically-minded partners from Labour circles. He also engaged the services of Colin Thornton-Kemsley, a Scottish National Liberal (to all intents and purposes by this time, Conservative) MP from 1939 to 1964. Thornton-Kemsley, the Partnership's Director of Public Relations, proposed a motion that all current and potential future partners be required to sign a declaration that they were neither members of the Communist Party, nor in sympathy with its doctrines. As a concession, Thornton-Kemsley was prepared, if the Communist bar was imposed, to extend the restriction to Fascists. This could be considered to be a lop-sided arrangement, as at that stage the Communist Party of Great Britain actually had two MPs, while the British Union of Fascists had been driven out of existence in 1940, only to be replaced by its rather anaemic successor, the Union Movement, founded by Mosley after his release from wartime internment. Benn felt that if someone was acceptable as a Member of Parliament, they ought to be acceptable to serve in a John Lewis shop.[9] Benn raised the matter in the Lords on 10 May 1949.[10] The Partnership's response was to emphasise the democratic nature of the business, which worked through a network of local bodies elected by secret ballot among the partners, who enjoyed unfettered free speech, including through a weekly newspaper, to which they could even contribute anonymously. In the event though, the political test was dropped.[11] But John Lewis lost a customer: Margaret closed her account. The episode illustrated that in a democracy, either industrial or political, the views of an influential elite can steer the attention, even if not necessarily the opinions, of voters towards a particular issue, with which they might otherwise have contentedly lived (whether it be Communists, immigrants, religious minorities or the European Union).

Benn pursued his quest against anti-Communist agitation again the following year, when Lord Vansittart, the former diplomat, claimed that the Church of England and the Civil Service had been infiltrated by Communists. Benn proposed a motion of censure against Vansittart, but received no support whatsoever in the House of Lords.[12] Another unpopular case which Benn also took up was the expulsion of Paul Garland from the Scouts for being a Communist.[13] Again, Benn had virtually no support in the Lords. He was to be a consistent opponent of McCarthysim as well as the damage that unfounded and unnecessary witch hunts did to people's careers and reputations.

In October 1950 the Lords moved back into their own chamber, when the Commons restoration was complete. After the bombing, the Commons had sat in the Lords' chamber from June 1941 to October 1950. So, up to this point Benn had sat in the Lords' chamber as an MP, but never as a lord.

On 30 November, in another building block of the political dynasty, Tony Benn was elected as Labour MP for Bristol South East in a by-election caused by the resignation on health grounds of the former chancellor, Stafford Cripps. When Benn had accepted the peerage in 1941, Michael had volunteered that he would have been happy to succeed, so that he could cause a fuss in the Lords, while Tony could cause a fuss in the Commons. Of course, this was never to be. But at least for the time being, Tony was in the Commons, and his father was in the Lords. After Michael's death, his father had tried to take his place in the RAF by volunteering for some of the most dangerous missions as a rear-gunner. The same motivation probably stirred him into action in the Lords. Once free of political office after 1946, Benn was able to operate as something of a loose canon, albeit with his sights set in particular directions. He set out to make a fuss and there was relatively little that anyone could do, or would want to do to stop him. He had no party position to lose, no financial incentive to toe the party line. He could not be expelled from the House of Lords. Peers could at that stage only be temporarily excluded if bankrupt or imprisoned, otherwise, an act of parliament was required to remove them. Two peers had been expelled in this way in 1917 for supporting the King's enemies, but that had been the last time. If anything, Benn would have been glad to have had a way out of the Lords. The threat of withdrawal of the party whip was hardly enough to make Benn quaver. As with John Major's withdrawal of the whip from the Maastricht rebels, the party tends to suffer more than the whipless. Benn was indulgently left to plough his own furrow. Invitations to meetings of the Labour peers became fewer and further between.[14] Since the causes he chose were altruistic and morally-grounded, it would have looked unethical for his party to try and discourage him. Among a rather limited field, Benn was probably the most liberal and the most socialist member of the House of Lords after the war. He had moved gradually to the left, but never lost his liberal instincts.

1951 was a watershed year for Benn's life in the House of Lords. In October 1951 Churchill finally won his first election, after two failed attempts, and the Conservatives returned to government, so Benn became an opposition back-bencher in the House and was therefore even more free to pursue his own agenda. 1951 was also a watershed personally; Benn was about to have another change of name. He and Margaret became grandparents and his grandchildren called him Tappa and Margaret was renamed Didi. Benn had four grandchildren, Stephen (born in 1951), Hilary (1953), Melissa (1957) and Joshua (1958) all born to Tony and his wife, Caroline. David and his wife, June, later also had two children, Piers and Frances, but they were born after their grandfather had died.

On 11 December 1951 Addison died. He had served as Labour leader in the House of Lords from 1940 and as Leader of the House of Lords during the Labour governments. He had effectively been Benn's boss since his ennoblement. However, the pair were friends, colleagues and equals. Addison was not inclined to contemplate disciplining Benn when he went off on one of his excursions to find lost or neglected causes to raise in the House. Benn paid fulsome tribute to Addison in the House. Their career paths had been remarkably similar, serving together as Liberal MPs before the First World War and as members of Ramsay MacDonald's second Labour cabinet, meeting again as prospective candidates for the Labour nomination for Gorton in 1937 and eventually ending up together in the Lords as Labour peers for nearly a decade.

Unlike Benn, Addison was eventually reconciled with Lloyd George, and in 1937 was even offered the opportunity to be a trustee of the Lloyd George Fund. Addison declined this offer from Lloyd George, which could have created a strange conflict of interest: Lloyd George was still a Liberal MP and Addison was a Labour peer. Had he accepted, Addison would have had an influence over the spending of part of the budget of a rival political party.

Addison was eight years Benn's senior and had died at the age of eighty-two. Not for the first time, Benn managed to gain the emotional support of the House, while simultaneously attacking its very existence, as he reminisced about his collaboration with Addison: 'Our friendship was much strengthened by the growing disapproval of the Liberals whom we were trying to reform. They were glorious days. There were Liberals and Tories. The Liberals hated the Tories and the Tories hated the Liberals; both were sure they were right. In particular, Lord Addison and I joined in denouncing your Lordships' House as a Citadel of Reaction – which indeed it was, and still is ... Do your Lordships remember the day, a year or two ago, when His

Majesty came down to open Parliament in full feudal splendour? There he was with his Robe and Crown. There was the Lord Chancellor, on bended knee. There was the Sword of State, as it might have been in the time of Richard the First. There was the Cap of Maintenance, carried by a High Officer of State. But look again at the picture: the Sword of State is held high by a Socialist doctor. The Cap of Maintenance is carried by a Welsh miner. The Speech from the Throne is a Socialist manifesto. The whole structure of society is being transformed, yet the facade of Parliamentary institutions is unaltered'.[15]

The period from 1951 to 1955 was one of the most uneventful in the history of the House of Lords. In fact 1954 was probably the most uneventful year in British politics during the whole century. The contrast with the uncertain and volatile politics of the inter-war years was stark. There was no great constitutional clash and two dominant parties with no great ideological gulf between them. The House of Lords was entirely male, entirely hereditary, almost entirely white (Baron Sinha was the only ethnic minority peer), mainly wealthy, mainly elderly and mainly Conservative. After the 1945 election many more Labour peers had been created and the party gained the adherence of a few other succeeding hereditaries, including 3rd Baron Holden (former Liberal, then National Labour supporter), Oliver Baldwin on his succession to his father's Earldom and the 6th Earl of Lucan – son of a Conservative and father of the disappearing murder suspect.[16]

The powers of the House of Lords had been severely limited by the Parliament Act of 1911 and further curtailed by the Act of 1949, which prevented the Lords from overturning finance bills and limited their influence on all other legislation to a maximum delay of one year for any legislation passed in two successive sessions in the Commons. In addition, the Salisbury convention had already determined that policies put forward in a winning party's manifesto would not be subject to challenge in the Lords. Aside from the restrictions on the Lords' power, a Conservative-dominated Lords was not likely to try and disrupt a Conservative government's legislative programme. Even the opposition peers were relatively well disposed towards much of the new government's programme, as Churchill left in place most of the key reforms of the Attlee Government – the NHS, National Parks, National Insurance and decolonisation. Churchill's government even had a benign attitude towards the trades unions, to the extent that the Minister of Labour, Walter Monckton, became known as the 'oil can' for his willingness to lubricate relations between the government and the unions with cash. This was the height of the era which has come to be known as the 'consensus'.

The personnel in the Lords also lacked some of the key figures who would typically be expected to inhabit the upper chamber. The last prime minister to sit in the Lords had been Salisbury in 1902. The chamber was also lacking the usual sprinkling of ennobled former prime ministers – Asquith, Bonar Law, MacDonald, Baldwin, Lloyd George and Chamberlain were all dead. Churchill stayed in the Commons after he resigned the premiership and never came to the Lords (an example which has since been followed by Heath, Major and Blair). Attlee did not arrive in the Lords until late 1955, after eventually relinquishing his twenty-year party leadership. Few other former party leaders who had not made it to the premiership sat in the Lords. The only Conservative leader not to have become prime minister, Austen Chamberlain, was dead. All the former Labour leaders Hardie, Henderson, Barnes, Adamson, Lansbury and Clynes were also dead. The Liberals had two – Samuel who had been Liberal Party leader from 1931 until he lost his seat in 1935, and Benn's friend and predecessor as Secretary of State for Air Archie Sinclair, who had followed Samuel, both in terms of leading the Liberal Party and in losing his seat. After his defeat in 1945, Sinclair had tried unsuccessfully to return to the Commons, but eventually gave up the struggle and was ennobled in 1952. However, that year he suffered a stroke and this curtailed his active involvement in the Lords.

The party balance in the Lords was very heavily weighted towards the Conservatives. The Liberals were in decline from their sixty-three peers in 1945, through deaths and defections, such as those of Lords Milverton and Rennell. The Labour Party was growing, but from its very low base of only sixteen peers in 1945. Benn was not really in awe of any of the personnel in the upper house. He was closest to Addison, he liked Alexander and he was friendly with Sinclair, but he had scant regard for many of the other peers, especially those whose titles originated during the time of the Lloyd George sale of honours regime.

The Conservatives retained power after a relatively uneventful general election in 1955, called by Eden on taking over from Churchill. However,

1956 did see the political temperature significantly raised. In a debate on the abolition of the death penalty, Benn complained in the Lords that: 'We in this House notoriously have very little to do – a couple of hours three days a week – but when it comes to this, which is the most important criminal and constitutional question for a long time, the House is being, I consider, indecently forced into an abbreviation of debate.'[17] Benn was among the minority of ninety-five (most Labour, Liberal and some Conservative peers as well as a majority of the bishops) in favour of abolition, who were defeated by the 238 (mainly Conservative) lords who voted against. The following year though the Homicide Act reduced the categories of crime punishable by death and in 1965 a private member's bill was passed to suspend capital punishment. Four years later the suspension became permanent.

The main event which stirred up British politics in 1956 though was the Suez Crisis, an event in which Benn indirectly played a role. Only in 1954 had the 1936 Anglo-Egyptian treaty finally been replaced by the Suez Canal Base Agreement, which allowed for a gradual evacuation of the British-occupied facilities by June 1956, by which time a lot more irritating of the Egyptians had taken place, including the withdrawal of the offer of funding for the construction of the Aswan Dam. Within weeks of the departure date of the British troops, President Nasser announced the nationalisation of the Suez Canal, which led to the Suez Crisis and the downfall of Anthony Eden's premiership. Benn intervened over eighty times in the Lords' debates during the Suez Crisis, including on 2 August 1956, one week after Nasser had nationalised the canal, saying: 'We are all very angry about this affair … Colonel Nasser has behaved in an unconscionable way. If you read back a little in the *Times* … you come to the time when Colonel Nasser was the "blue-eyed boy" when we offered him the money … as a matter of fact I talked to him for about an hour at Christmastime on this point … He said: "You and the Americans offer us money, but there are so many conditions … but when the Russians make an offer, they say simply, 'There is the money'. I said to him, "Are you not aware that it may be very dangerous to have a vast horde of Russian technicians here? You may get Communists amongst them, for I am afraid there are Communists even in engineering." He said "I do not know anything about the Russians. I want the money. I understand I can have both.'" Benn warned the government: 'do not attempt to use Israel as a pawn in the game in fighting the Arabs. That would be a fatal mistake.'[18] Eden made the mistake, but it only became fatal for his career when he lied about it in the House of Commons. Had Benn's 1946 attempt at a new Anglo-Egyptian treaty been successful, the conditions which led to the Suez Crisis might well have been avoided. Benn therefore inadvertently played a part in Eden's downfall, although few would argue that Eden was not the author of his own hubristic political demise. In 1957 Eden was replaced by Macmillan as premier, without an election.

That year – 1957, the year in which Benn reached his eightieth birthday – he relinquished his presidency of the IPU. He was not forced to give it up because of old age or illness. In fact, despite his 'usual bronchitis' and the malaria bouts from which he had intermittently suffered since the First World War, Benn's health remained quite robust. His respiratory problems were presumably not helped by his pipe-smoking, but part of the illness was probably connected with the London smog, before the advent of the Clean Air Act in 1956. At least the pipe was likely to be less harmful than cigarettes which were then smoked by two-thirds of men in the UK. More as an economy – rather than a health measure, Benn rationed his pipe smoking. He did not over-eat, as he had little interest in fine dining and was usually too busy to linger over meals. As a teetotaller, his health had been preserved from the ravages of alcohol which affected so many politicians, including Asquith, Masterman, Clement Davies and John Smith. Benn was a tea drinker – but not to quite the extent of his son Tony, who was calculated to have drunk 29,000 gallons over the course of his life. The timing of Benn's tea drinking may not have helped his overall well-being though, given that a good night's sleep seems to correlate with good health. Benn used to take a thermos of tea to bed with him. He found that if he woke up in the night (typically at about 03.00), his mind was usually clear and he could have a productive thinking session, prolonged by the tea. As most people have found out though, this is not an ideal way to get back to sleep. As with most other aspects of his life, Benn kept detailed records of his health. In amongst mentions of 'bad nights', 'coughs' and 'tight chest' are more prosaic entries such as 'left nostril closed' and 'slight vomiting' [an unusual ailment, as for most people it tends to be more of an all-or-nothing occurrence], but there were other more positive entries, even past the age of eighty, such as 'very well' and 'all night party at the Savoy did no harm'.[19]

In the pre-DNA testing days, responding in the Lords to the statement by Lord Woolton that 'whereas maternity was a matter of fact, paternity was a matter of opinion', Benn managed to raise a laugh with his observation that this was a 'dangerous remark to make in an hereditary chamber'.[20] However, even in those days, paternity was not to be lightly disregarded. Tony was desperate to find a way not to inherit his father's viscountcy, so that he could keep his seat in the Commons after his father's death. Father and son explored several possible avenues to achieve this. Their first attempt, in 1954, was a petition for the introduction of the Wedgwood Benn (Renunciation) Bill, which would have meant that the viscountcy would have skipped a generation and been inherited by Tony's eldest son Stephen, on the death of his grandfather. Stephen was at that stage three years old and not really in a position to decide on the precise nature of his future career and on the benefits, or otherwise, of inheriting a peerage. An explanatory note with the draft of the bill recalled that the viscountcy had originally been created not as a political honour or reward, but 'as a special measure of state policy ... to strengthen the Labour Party in the upper house, where its representation [was] disproportionate at a time when a coalition government of three parties [was] charged with the direction of affairs' during the war.[21]

A revised version of the bill was proposed in February 1955, which addressed the imposition of the title on Stephen while he was a minor, who might later wish to renounce the title himself. The new version proposed that the title should go into abeyance on Benn's death and remain in abeyance until Tony's death, when it would be restored to his heir.[22] Tony addressed the Personal Bills Committee of the House of Lords for an hour and a half, pointing out that until the seventeenth century it had been quite common for peerages to be surrendered. But it was to no avail. The committee decided that the objects of the bill were not 'proper to be enacted by a personal bill'.[23] Taking this view on board, the bill was reworded into a form which made it more general and Benn presented it to the House of Lords on 26 April 1955. However, the Wedgwood Benn (Renunciation) Bill was finally defeated in the Lords by fifty-two votes to twenty-four, despite the Benns having managed to get a letter of recommendation from Winston Churchill, stating that he was 'strongly in favour of sons having the right to renounce irrevocably the peerages they inherit from their fathers'.[24] Although the Benn family failed to get the succession laws changed, 1958 did see some noticeable changes, particularly the introduction of life peerages and the arrival of the first female peers. But the 1958 Life Peerages Act still did not allow for the renunciation of peerages.

In many ways there was at least as much divergence within the Labour Party as there was between the leadership of the two main parties. In opposition, and especially after Attlee's retirement from the leadership, the Labour Party became increasingly divided between the supporters of Bevan and those of Gaitskell. In 1958 George Garro-Jones, since ennobled as Lord Trefgarne, defected back from Labour to the Liberals. Garro-Jones had followed Benn out of the Liberal Party to Labour in 1929. He had then recaptured Benn's former seat of Aberdeen North for Labour in 1935 and sat for the ten years until the next election in 1945, when he stood down, moving to the Lords two years later. There had been signs of a limited recovery for the Liberals, particularly in by-election performance, since the end of 1954. Jo Grimond took over the Liberal leadership from Clement Davies in 1956 and the tide of defections from the Liberal Party started to reverse. Benn was not enticed back down this path. His age, his relative freedom of action within the Labour Party in the Lords and Tony's position as a Labour MP, all prevented him actively considering following suit, but Grimond's leadership presented a moment of temptation for some into the Liberal Party, which had not existed for decades and Garro-Jones made the return journey.

Benn enjoyed quite a few verbal jousting matches with the Conservative, Lord Hailsham in the House of Lords. They shared some character traits – both being clever and witty, with an impish outspokenness and a physical bravery, although Hailsham was rather more acerbic and waspish. In a debate on outer space in the House of Lords in June 1959 Benn drew Hailsham on whether the government admitted 'the sovereignty of the moon and stars?' Hailsham, entering into the spirit of the question responded: 'I never thought the moon was sovereign, or, indeed, that the stars were sovereign; and I think it is extremely doubtful whether any sovereignty exists over them at international law.' But Benn, not only keen to preserve the independence of individual people, but also of heavenly bodies, persisted, asking about: 'their own sovereignty over themselves?' Hailsham was finally drawn to make the observation, which taken out of context would have led some to question his grip on reality: 'My Lords, I do not recognise the moon and stars as being sentient creatures which could have sovereignty over themselves.'[25]

On 12 May 1960 Benn became involved in another verbal altercation in the Lords, which was at the same time both rather farcical and very serious. The topic of discussion was indeed serious, namely the disappearance of two US aircraft over Russian territory. The loss of the aircraft was an established fact, but the reasons for their incursions into Russian territory and their actual fate was not established. The US claimed that they were 'photographing clouds' and might have strayed 'accidentally'. The Russians claimed to have shot them down. Benn, knowing that the government would not enter into a discussion of intelligence matters, submitted a private notice question – a device for members to request that a government minister appear at short notice to answer a question which is of great public importance. Benn asked: 'Two American planes have been destroyed in what is now really enemy territory. The Government are asked what is their policy in this matter, and they give the reply which has always been given in these matters – namely, that they cannot deal with this private inquiry business at all. That we understand. But there is a vast difference between sending a man to try to collect information in a country and sending an aeroplane, which might be armed, over the other person's country.' Hailsham responded rather predictably that: 'As I am sure the noble Viscount is well aware, it has long been the accepted practice of successive Governments from both sides of the House that matters relating to intelligence are not discussed in public.' Benn persisted, but Hailsham was determined to close down the debate with the rarely used device of moving the motion: 'I beg to move that the noble Viscount be no longer heard.' Benn was willing to accept the view of the House, but wanted to check whether his own party leader, Alexander, agreed to the gagging: 'I am not clear whether my noble Leader is supporting the Motion that I be shut up or not.'[26] Hailsham's motion was carried and Benn was 'shut up', without Alexander having to make clear whether he supported the gag. However, Benn had managed to air his point even if he did not, as he undoubtedly expected, did not get a reply.

Six months later, Benn was finally no longer to be heard. On 16 November 1960 he suffered a heart attack while he was sitting on the Lords' benches, waiting to speak. An ambulance was called to take him to Westminster Hospital. Tony was called and he and Lord Amulree helped Benn into the ambulance. The following morning, which was the Benns' fortieth wedding anniversary, he seemed better. In a reassuringly characteristic frame of mind, he insisted that he needed his job list for the day and that he should be allowed home. Tony, David and Margaret all sat with Benn at the hospital during the day, but in the evening his condition worsened. The medical staff ushered the family from the room, and at 19.40 the doctor came to tell them that Benn had died. His family could at least comfort themselves with the knowledge that Benn had lived to the age of eighty-three and had died, still working, surrounded by his loved ones, after the briefest of illnesses, but with some forewarning.

However, having inherited the peerage which immediately disqualified him from being an MP, Tony had not only lost his father, he had also lost his job and his salary.

Chapter Ten

Renunciation and Resurrection 1960–

N ine years after Benn had paid tribute to his friend and colleague Addison, Hailsham, as leader of the House of Lords, led the tributes for Benn. Six months earlier, without malice, he had tried to stop Benn speaking in the Lords and now his plea that the 'noble lord be no longer heard' was to be permanently fulfilled. Hailsham considered that Benn was one of the Lords' 'most remarkable and colourful figures [who] never became pompous or dull; and ... never became old ... I doubt whether Lord Stansgate ever paused to consider how much affection he aroused even among those – and they were probably the majority – who did not agree either with his views or with some of the ways he had of expressing them ... He was brave ... physically and morally ... He could be called mischievous, but he was never mean; he could be aggressive, but never spiteful or malicious; and he was always honest. There may have been something quixotic about his character, but ... he was always ... a shining example of integrity [even though] the causes which he espoused often aroused little sympathy.'

Lord Amulree declared that Benn 'was one of the real Radicals left in the country ... With his complete courage, complete sincerity and that wonderful wish to help whatever people or countries he knew about and felt were being oppressed ... no matter what was the feeling, he rushed to their assistance immediately [with] an enormous amount of friendliness and charm, and with a great wit, gaiety and amusement.' Attlee reminisced: 'I remember coming to the House in 1922, and already he had had sixteen years' Parliamentary experience ... What always struck me about "Wedgie" was that, although he was now well on in years, he still had the heart of a boy. He had an extraordinary zest for life ... He was a great character ... I think that he himself would have liked to die in harness – the happy warrior'.[1]

The *Times'* obituary described Benn as 'vivid', 'endearing', 'provocative' and 'witty'. 'His sharp brown eyes could pierce to the heart of any sham: they could blaze with righteous fury and twinkle with fun.'[2] Benn's entry in the *Oxford Dictionary of National Biography* captures Benn as others saw him: 'His persistence might cause temporary annoyance [but his] patent sincerity, his complete freedom from malice, and his natural modesty of manner, made many admirers. While his perpetual effervescence, buoyancy, and wit conveyed an impression of the gay cavalier, 'Wedgy Benn' was really the happy warrior, a man of profound ethical conviction, with a great love for his fellow human beings.'[3] This was a fair assessment of the public Benn, but it was somewhat selective, missing out the privately often stressed, workaholic and sometimes depressed behind-the-scenes side to his character. There was no doubt that Benn had very many admirers, even among those with whom he disagreed. The description of Benn as a Cavalier might sound at odds with his appearance and demeanour but once, when Margaret had described herself as a passionate Cromwellian, she was surprised that Benn said he would have been a Cavalier. He had of course risked his life in the war fighting for 'King and Country', rather than for 'Parliament and Country'. Benn's loyalties had a clear order of priority, tested in public and in extremity. First came his loyalty to his country, for which he voluntarily risked his life in both world wars. Second came his wife and children, whom he valued intensely and guarded fiercely, but whom he was to leave behind of his own volition to fight in the Second World War. Third was his loyalty to Asquith, well ahead of his adherence to any other political leader. Fourth was his loyalty to radical politics in the interests of the deprived within society. Fifth was his loyalty to the Labour Party, which came ahead of his loyalty to the Liberal Party, as he left the latter for the former. Geographically, Benn's greatest loyalty was to England, rather than Scotland. He favoured the East End of London, the location of his first constituency (and his birthplace) over the other three constituencies which he represented. However, it was to be Essex from where he chose the title of his peerage – the East End to Essex being a well-worn upwardly-mobile migration route.

There are objective and impersonal measures of success for a political career, but to form a view on one individual's career, we need to understand their motivations and goals, to see if they achieved them. Some politicians' working lives undoubtedly fit the definition of a career, seeing in advance a series of steps leading to a defined goal within a specified timescale. Michael

Heseltine laid out a path to the premiership. By most people's standards he had a very successful career, but according to his own plan, he failed – (only) reaching the position of deputy prime minister. Gordon Brown set his heart on the premiership, but probably does not look back entirely with satisfaction on the culmination of his political career. Rosebery set out to become prime minister, to own a Derby-winning racehorse and to marry an heiress. He achieved all three – in fact he over-achieved on the racehorse front, but according to many observers he was a rather bitter man and certainly not a successful prime minister. Nigel Lawson went into politics to become Chancellor of the Exchequer, so by his measure he was successful. Some would agree, others would not. Paddy Ashdown's career in some ways resembles Benn's, with a mixture of military service and politics and yet Ashdown declared that he could not see how he came to follow the path which he did. Understanding his choices and motivations, perhaps reveals something too about Benn's career.

We can discern some of Benn's enduring motives. In common with Gladstone, Benn needed to have a clear conscience and to use his life to the maximum. Both men documented their lives and were prepared to endure self-inflicted pain to that end – Gladstone resorting to self-flagellation and Benn to resigning his seat, without prospect of a return to Parliament. Benn was also clearly motivated by being close to the action, even at the cost of potentially fatal consequences.

Benn's electoral record was strong. He fought thirteen elections and won eleven. His near-eighty-five per cent success rate compares favourably with the average of 61 per cent achieved by the 707 people who sat as a Liberal MP at some point between 1910 and 2010.[4] All eight of Benn's candidatures as a Liberal were successful, but only three of his five attempts for Labour were. He served a total of just over twenty-one years as a Liberal MP and slightly more than eight years as a Labour MP, making a total of over twenty-nine years' service in the Commons. He then served nearly nineteen years in the Lords, amounting to a total of forty-eight years in Parliament – a substantial contribution, but not a record. Winston Churchill served nearly sixty-four years in the House of Commons and Lloyd George nearly fifty-five. Lord Carrington exceeded seventy years in the House of Lords. Tony went on to serve forty-seven years in the Commons.

Benn's parliamentary service:

	years	months	days
Tower Hamlets St George 12 January 1906–14 December 1918	12	11	2
Leith 14 December 1918–15 February 1927	8	2	1
Total as a Liberal MP	21	1	3
Gap between resignation as Liberal and re-election for Labour	1	6	1
Aberdeen North 16 August 1928–27 October 1931	3	2	11
Gap between loss of Aberdeen and re-election at Gorton	5	3	22
Manchester Gorton 18 February 1937–12 January 1942	4	10	25
Total as a Labour MP	8	1	5
Total in House of Commons	29	2	8
House of Lords 12 January 1942–17 November 1960	18	10	5
Total in Parliament	48	0	13
Secretary of State for India 7 June 1929–24 August 1931	2	2	17
Secretary of State for Air 3 August 1945–4 October 1946	1	2	1
Service in cabinet	3	4	18

Benn represented four different constituencies (two in England and two in Scotland) for two different parties, so he could not devote his attention to the people of just one place. Representing four geographically distinct constituencies would today be virtually out of the question, as local connections feature strongly in candidate selection. Among his contemporaries, Benn was still very unusual in representing four different seats. Only Arthur Henderson exceeded this, sitting for five (Barnard Castle, Widnes, Newcastle East, Burnley and Clay Cross). MacDonald and Churchill equalled Benn's record of four.[5] Within society the Liberals of the early twentieth century and the Labour MPs of the mid-century represented generally a working class electorate in the more deprived areas and the welfare of these people was Benn's priority.

Of the fifty-four years of Benn's political career, in and out of Parliament, from his first election in 1906 to his death in 1960, two party leaders dominated the timespan – Asquith for the Liberals (eighteen years) and Attlee for Labour (twenty years). By comparison, in terms of time, all the other leaders – Campbell-Bannerman, Lloyd George, MacDonald, Henderson, Lansbury and Gaitskell were relative bit-part players, accounting for only sixteen years between the six of them. However, Lloyd George and MacDonald loomed much larger in Benn's career than the timespan of their leadership would suggest, while Benn was out of Parliament for almost the whole of Henderson's and Lansbury's terms of party leadership between 1931 and 1935.

Party leaders served by Benn:

Campbell-Bannerman	1906–08	Benn's first election to C-B's retirement
Asquith	1908–26	Asquith's assumption to Asquith's retirement
Lloyd George	1926–27	Lloyd George's assumption to Benn's defection
MacDonald	1927–31	Benn's defection to MacDonald's expulsion
Henderson	1931–32	Henderson's assumption to Henderson's resignation
Lansbury	1932–35	Lansbury's assumption to Lansbury's resignation
Attlee	1935–55	Attlee's assumption to Attlee's retirement
Gaitskell	1955–60	Gaitskell's assumption to Benn's death

Benn enhanced the Labour Party's reputation and performed effectively as a Labour cabinet minister. However, as a natural opposition politician, his major contribution to the Labour Party was the damage he inflicted on his opponents. This turned out to be particularly so with his attacks on the Lloyd George Liberals. He also inflicted collateral damage on some Conservatives.

Churchill's reputation was certainly not enhanced within his own party over his exaggerated opposition to Benn's Indian policies – although this did help to secure Baldwin's leadership. Benn's failure to renegotiate the Anglo-Egyptian treaty in 1946 did little damage to the Labour Party, but indirectly led to the festering problems between the two countries which ultimately ended in the Suez Crisis and Eden's downfall. Above all, Benn's refusal of Lloyd George's offer of the position of joint chief whip in 1916 turned out to be pivotal for the Liberals and for the Labour Party.

Over the decades Benn made thousands of interventions in Parliament, an average of over 200 for each year that he sat in one or other house. He was an extremely active parliamentarian. Like the wartime aviator that he was, Benn's interventions were typically a well-planned attack on an opponent's weakest spot, being single-minded and ruthless, but lasting only as long as was necessary. Benn was naturally better suited to opposition than to government, preferring attack to defence. He usually operated alone, rarely joining in a chorus of approval or disapproval, often finding his own route of attack. He was bold, brave and blunt, using facts as ammunition, but not making personal attacks. He did not speak for the sake of speaking, but to achieve a goal. He did not consider himself to be a natural orator and had once sought advice from a speech therapist called Hulbert, who was recommended to him by Christopher Addison.[6] He did not usually rely on emotion in his arguments. This contrasted with Churchill who, on a good day, could capture hearts as well as minds and draw tears; but on a bad day would make a sentimental and overblown pitch. Benn went for the head, winning people's hearts over the long term through his sincerity and humanity, but not in the course of any one speech. Benn's style was simple, direct, modern and more colloquial than of most parliamentarians', for instance when he was talking about the UK's not having 'matey' relations with Russia.

Benn was typical of Liberal defectors in his timing. The serious exodus of Liberal MPs and former MPs, which lasted from 1918 to 1956, saw 116 depart. Chronologically, Benn was number fifty-eight – exactly in the middle of this exodus. Lloyd George was the Liberal Party leader who suffered the worst rate of outward defections, but Asquith was the next worst, followed by Clement Davies.[7] Benn was unusual, but not alone, in that his departure from the Liberal Party was actuated more by personal distrust of Lloyd

George than by any other factor. It is easy to understand the origins of Tony Benn's insistence that politics should be about 'policies not personalities'.

Benn did not defect from the Liberal Party for personal advantage, quite the reverse. However, with hindsight it is possible to determine whether his defection from the Liberals to Labour enhanced or damaged his career. On average, defections by MPs did turn out to be career-enhancing moves. Defectors were more likely to achieve ministerial office and a peerage than non-defectors. Of the Liberal MPs and former MPs who defected from the party thirty-three per cent achieved ministerial office and thirty-one per cent a peerage, compared to the loyalists for whom the equivalent figures were only fourteen per cent and thirteen per cent.[8]

Was Benn's defection a career-enhancing move? Had Benn remained in the Liberal Party, it is likely that he would have retained his seat at Leith in the 1929 election. His Liberal successor, Ernest Brown, held the seat. In 1931 and 1935 Brown held Leith as a Liberal National. We can be virtually certain that Benn, as a convinced free-trader with an abhorrence of coalitions, would not have joined the Liberal Nationals, but that he would have adhered to Samuel's Liberals. As such, he probably would still have kept his seat in 1931. The Conservatives did not consistently contest Leith. At the 1931 election Samuel's Liberals were supportive (but with reservations especially over the prospect of tariffs) of the National Government, so the Conservatives would have been very unlikely to mount a challenge to a sitting Liberal MP. Even if they had, with the drastic reduction in Labour votes in 1931, a Liberal candidate would have likely been the net beneficiary and would have held the seat.[9] In 1935 the situation would have been more difficult, but not insurmountable. By then Samuel's Liberals had crossed the floor to the opposition benches. Most of the Liberal losses in 1935 were to Labour. The Labour vote nationally recovered from 33.0 percent to 40.3 percent – putting it roughly on a par with their performance in 1922 and 1923. But in both these elections, Benn, as a Liberal, had beaten off the Labour challenge.[10] Benn would almost certainly have seen off a Labour challenger and a Conservative or Liberal National contender was no more likely than in 1931. So, again, even in the more hostile circumstances of 1935, Benn could probably have held Leith as a Liberal. However, in 1945 the Labour landslide would almost certainly have swept aside a sitting Liberal MP at Leith, as indeed it swept away Ernest Brown as a Liberal National.

Only twelve Liberal MPs survived the 1945 election and none of them was in Scotland. With a fair degree of certainty we can say that, had Benn stuck with the Liberals, he could have kept his seat at Leith until 1945, but not beyond. In terms of maintaining a seat in the Commons, Benn's defection was almost certainly not advantageous. His principles cost him income and continuity in Parliament.

Had Benn not resigned his seat at Leith when he left the Liberals in 1927, but had stayed as a Labour MP, which is what most defectors would have done, would he have kept the seat? This is hard to say with certainty. He would have been entitled to stay until the next general election and would have had time to try and sway opinions towards his new party. There would have been no by-election in 1927, had Benn not resigned, so the next contest would have been the 1929 general election. The Labour Party had put up a candidate in Leith at every general election since 1918, and at each successive contest the party's share of the vote had increased from 19.1 per cent in 1918, 23.5 per cent in 1922 and 35.5 per cent in 1923 to 40.4 per cent in 1924. There was clearly a move towards Labour among the electorate. At the 1929 election Labour further increased their share of the vote to 43.5 per cent, but failed to win the seat. Assuming that that election had been a two-way contest (as it actually was in 1929), with Benn as the Labour candidate and a replacement Liberal contender, there is a possibility that Benn could have retained the vote which went to Labour (43.5 per cent) and converted enough of the former Liberal vote to his new cause. He would have had to convert around one in six of the former Liberal voters in order to win the seat. He might have achieved this, but the Labour disaster of 1931 would almost certainly have cost him his seat. Labour only held fifty-two of the party's safest seats and Leith would not have been one of them. We can be certain that Benn could have remained as Labour MP for Leith until 1929 and virtually certain that he would have lost it in 1931. The intervening two years were too close to call.

In reality Benn sat as the Labour MP for Aberdeen North from 1928 to 1931. By resigning his seat at Leith in 1927, at worst, he missed out on one and a half years' service in the Commons between early 1927 and mid-1928. However, at the time he made the decision to resign at Leith, he had no guarantee of any return to the Commons. At the time it was a bold move, although with hindsight there had been rather less at stake than it seemed at the time.

In terms of a cabinet appointment though, the situation was rather different. Had Benn remained a Liberal, he would obviously not have served in the 1929 Labour government. However, four Liberals did serve in the cabinet of the National Government from 1931 – the Marquis of Reading at the Foreign Office, Herbert Samuel at the Home Office, Donald Maclean at Education and Archibald Sinclair at the Scottish Office. In every case their tenure was brief. Maclean died in 1932 and the others left the government later the same year in protest over tariffs. In terms of seniority, Benn would have been regarded as junior to Reading and Samuel (both former cabinet ministers) and also to Maclean (who had served as leader of the opposition), but arguably Benn would have out-ranked Sinclair (an MP only since 1922). As an MP for a Scottish seat, Benn might well have claimed the Scottish Office ahead of Sinclair. Had Benn been appointed to the Scottish Office, he would likely have served just over one year until the Samuelites withdrew from the government in September 1932. After this, the next possible opportunity for ministerial office for a Liberal would have been during the wartime coalition under Churchill. Competition for office came from all parties and no Liberal was a member of the war cabinet. Sinclair served as Secretary of State for Air, but outside the war cabinet. Benn might have been a contender for this post, but Sinclair's prior connections with Churchill from their First World War service might well have given him priority. A few other Liberals were appointed to junior ministerial office. Therefore, it seems likely that Benn's actual term of service in his two Labour cabinets (three years, four months, eighteen days) amounted to more than his likely cabinet tenure had he remained a Liberal. From the point of view of cabinet office, Benn's defection almost certainly was a career-enhancing move, as it tended to be for most defectors.

In terms of a peerage, which was not a particular ambition of Benn's, he could have obtained this either as a Labour member or as a Liberal, but his prospects were probably better under Labour. The newer Labour Party was short of members of the House of Lords in comparison to its strength in the Commons, whereas the declining Liberals had sixty-three peers even when the party was reduced to only twelve MPs in 1945.[11] So, Benn arrived sooner in the House of Lords as a Labour member than he would have been likely to have done as a Liberal and the rank of a viscount was the highest that he would have been likely to have received. Samuel, having lost his seat while party leader in 1935 was appointed a viscount in 1937 and Sinclair in 1952. In terms of a peerage, Benn's defection was probably a career-enhancing move, or at any rate, certainly not a hindrance.

Benn never harboured any ambition for, nor did he have any realistic prospect of, achieving the leadership of the Labour Party. However, could he have achieved the Liberal Party leadership, had he not defected? In 1931 it was Lloyd George's prostate which removed him from the Liberal Party leadership, after Benn had already left the party. Had Benn still be a Liberal MP, he could have been a contender for the vacancies which occurred in 1931, when Samuel took over and again in 1935 after Samuel lost his seat. In 1931 Benn would probably have still been too divisive a figure after his very recent and public disputes with Lloyd George to have been an acceptable successor. The more emollient and experienced Samuel was a stronger contender. However, by 1935, the parliamentary Liberal Party only comprised twenty members. With lesser competition and with the Lloyd George family still aloof from the party machinery, Benn might have been able to mount a successful challenge, had he wished. His main rival would have been Sinclair. The pair would have had similar strengths and weaknesses. Whether Benn would have succeeded is pure speculation. Whether the prize would have been worth winning, is a moot point.

The inevitable question asked about politicians is: 'Was Benn prime ministerial material?' The short answer in Benn's case is 'no', primarily because he never wanted the role. Essentially only those who actually made it to the top have proved that they possessed the right combination of skills, support, ambition and luck – and even then some of them were found wanting. Benn never put himself in the running for the premiership and this alone meant that he was not prime ministerial material. He lacked ruthlessness and competitiveness. He had leadership qualities and was *a* natural leader, but not *the* leader. Within the cabinets in which he served, Benn was generally deferential to the heavyweights – to Snowden and MacDonald in 1929 to 1931 and to Attlee and Bevin in 1945 to 1946. His willingness to accede to Bevin's request to undertake the Egypt mission in 1946 without even consulting

Attlee suggests that Benn saw himself as subordinate to Bevin. In all cabinets there is an unofficial hierarchy, but officially the only post-holder whose boss is in the cabinet is the Chief Secretary to the Treasury, who is subordinate to the Chancellor of the Exchequer. However, Benn was by no means the most junior member of either of his cabinets. He behaved in cabinet as though he felt comfortable as a specialist contributor, but without pretentions to lead it.

The careers of some of those who very nearly made it tell us about some of the less-visible ingredients which are vital to gaining the premiership. Roy Jenkins, by most people's assessment, was prime ministerial material, but, by his own admission, lacked 'deadliness' and ambition. He also failed to cultivate parliamentary followers or trade union backing and was only really interested in taking on the premiership under conditions which suited him, while others, such as Wilson and Callaghan were prepared to gain the premiership whatever the circumstances. Michael Heseltine missed out primarily because he failed to cultivate a few more supporters within his own party; he was not quite clubbable enough. Rab Butler, having missed out on the premiership in 1957, gained a reputation, and arguably the demeanour, of an unlucky man. He fulfilled this destiny when he missed the prize again in 1963. Benn was self-deprecating – a good quality in a friend, but suggestive of a certain reticence and shortfall in self-belief. As a teetotaller, who did not like to spend time or money in bars or restaurants, Benn did lack a certain clubbability, although he did become a member of the Athenaeum Club. Had he sought the highest office, Benn could have deliberately set about rectifying this. He enjoyed political intrigue and he demonstrated, with his plan to repurchase Stansgate, that he could run a patient and effective charm offensive.

At first sight, Benn's political friends amounted to an ill-assorted group – ranging from Sidney and Beatrice Webb, Charles Masterman and Christopher Addison on the left to Reginald McKenna, Murray Sueter and Oswald Mosley on the right. But there is a pattern. They tended to be the radicals and the innovators from across the political spectrum and they were mainly people who did not fit comfortably into the mould of party politics. Although others enjoyed his company, Benn was never keen on socialising, believing that it was a waste of both time and money; so, to a large extent, his friends were a by-product of his work.

Benn's judgment on the major issues was sound and progressive. He was on what history has come to judge as the 'right' side of most of the key divides – Irish home rule, equal votes for women and men, House of Lords reform, appeasement, Munich, Norway, Indian independence and the abolition of the death penalty. Arguably, but not with universal agreement, he was on the right side in the 1931 crisis, being willing to take responsibility for the ten per cent cut in unemployment pay to avoid a bigger cut being imposed by another party grouping, but being unwilling to join any form of coalition. One aspect of Benn's world view was noticeable for its absence – racism, or at least what we would today understand as racism. In the 1920s and 1930s many politicians would make anti-Semitic statements or derogatory comments about people from other countries without any reaction from their audience. Benn was unusual in that he went out of his way to make positive comments about people of different races and religions.

Although below the level of the great issues, Benn was not a keen policy maker, he was a good administrator and a good party manager. Beatrice Webb accurately described him as a politician, not an economist or a philosopher. Benn's morals, intelligence, humour, organisation and absence of enemies placed him well for high office. He had the mental capacity, bravery, resilience and political antennae, but lacked the interest in over-arching policy and the focus on the one key goal. He was prone to be too involved in detail and systems and his slightly puritanical outlook meant that he did not fully comprehend the workings of the minds of people who did not share his moral compass. He was not always able to translate his principles into practical policies.

By general standards of integrity, industry, modesty and determination, Benn was undoubtedly a very good politician – if not always a good party politician. By similar measures, with the addition of loyalty, he was undoubtedly a very good friend and family member, if not always the most relaxing company. Perhaps above all else though, Benn was conspicuously brave – risking his life in two world wars, standing up against Lloyd George and resigning his seat on transferring to the Labour Party. Very few could claim all these attributes. Churchill shared many – but not the modesty. What took Churchill to the very top, which Benn lacked, was self-importance, flexibility and grand strategy.

Among those who did achieve the premiership, Benn had most in common with Campbell-Bannerman from the Liberals and Attlee from the Labour Party. Attlee defied common perceptions but was, in the views of many, the most successful peacetime premier of the twentieth century. Comparing Benn's attributes with Attlee's, there is a gap between their skills, but not a wide gulf. In terms of bravery, humanity, modesty and intelligence the two were well matched. Where Attlee scored more highly was in terms of single-mindedness on clear policy objectives, being a good butcher, ruthlessness and managing a team. Their First World War records provided a clue to their eventual achievements. Captain Benn enjoyed his military service, followed his particular interests in technology and gadgets which led him into the RAF, turning down a chance to return to political office and afterwards wrote about his experiences. Major Attlee did not enjoy his war, but stuck it out in the mainstream of the army until the war was won.

Benn was politically and personally brave. He was a risk-taker and was lucky to have survived to old age. Prime ministers need to be risk-takers, but only up to a point. Thatcher, Eden and Lloyd George were arguably the greatest risk-taker prime ministers of the twentieth century, but their risk-taking turned to recklessness and proved their undoing over the poll tax, Suez and Chanak.

Benn's work output was prolific. He was exhausted, but never overwhelmed, by the volume of work, even on taking up the unfamiliar and sensitive role of Secretary of State for India, which required dealing with a huge workload. Benn's health tended to suffer after periods of great strain, but when he needed the energy, he seemed to find it.

So did Benn fulfil his potential? Very nearly, and closer than most. He was never found wanting and was never over-promoted (although Irwin might have disagreed initially). To be Labour's Foreign Secretary was Benn's highest ambition. Benn never coveted the premiership, which was probably beyond his abilities, but his ambition to be foreign secretary was probably a realistic aim – had time and circumstances gone in his favour. He probably could have performed better than many who held the office and could be imagined in the mould of Robin Cook – short in stature, high in charm, thoughtful and with an ethical dimension to his policy.

Benn served in the governments of Asquith, MacDonald and Attlee and in two cabinets, sixteen years apart – arguably the least and the most successful peacetime cabinets since 1918. In 1929 Benn was a youngish politician on the rise, in 1945 he was an old hand, still active and dynamic, but less hungry for responsibility. Interpolating between his two periods in the cabinet, it seems reasonable to assume that the peak of Benn's political powers, when he had the optimum blend of ambition and experience, would have been in the late 1930s. However, like many other politicians, Benn's probable peak coincided with his party being in opposition. The same would have been true for other Labour figures whose powers were at their greatest during the years of opposition from 1931 to 1940, 1951 to 1964, or 1979 to 1997. For Conservatives, the unfortunately-timed were those whose abilities reached their zenith between 1997 and 2010. Son Tony was luckier than his father in terms of his timing, as was Tony's son Hilary.

The most comparable careers to Benn's would be Christopher Addison's and Archibald Sinclair's – politicians of similar abilities, the former of whom took Benn's route from the Liberals to Labour, while the latter remained with the Liberals. Benn was Benn through and through in private and in public. Sinclair's biographer, Gerard De Groot, tells us much of his private life and how it impacted on his career,[12] but Kenneth Morgan, historian, Labour peer and biographer of Addison (together with his late first wife), declares of his subject that 'the private man is, frankly, not of much historical interest'.[13] The same could not be said of Benn. The private Benn sheds light on the public Benn and vice versa. His family were vitally important to him – in his words 'the most important thing'. Benn's life is of particular interest, because of the Benn family.

Addison and Benn leapfrogged over each other in their respective ascents of the political hierarchy. Benn was first into Parliament (1906 vs January 1910). Addison was first to defect from the Liberals to Labour (1923 vs 1927). Benn was first to be elected as a Labour MP (1928 vs 1929) and first into the Labour cabinet (1929 vs 1930). Addison was first into the Lords (1937 vs 1942), but Benn was first to reach the rank of viscount (1942 vs 1945).

Sinclair took the Liberal path to the House of Lords, but his destination was the same as Benn's. Benn was thirteen years Sinclair's senior, so he had a head start, but their careers both peaked as Secretary of State for Air and they both ended up as viscounts.

	Addison	Benn	Sinclair
Born	1869	1877	1890
Educated	Sheffield/Barts	London Univ	Eton/Sandhurst
Military service	none	captain	major
		air commodore	
First elected	1910 (Jan)	1906	1922
Elected	1st contest	1st contest	1st contest
Success rate in elections	5/9	11/13	6/8
Years in Commons	16	29	23
Highest office held	Min of Health	SoS for Air	SoS for Air
Peerage	viscount	viscount	viscount
Wealth at death	£16,220	£37,889	£39,745
Died	1951 (82)	1960 (83)	1970 (79)

In some respects it is still too early to come to a final verdict on Benn's career, even though he died over half a century ago. He was the second of at least four consecutive generations of the family in Parliament and at least three in the cabinet. Of course this record could be extended. The historiography will change. Different light will be cast on past events. The banking crash of 2008 changed attitudes to capitalism and state ownership. The ensuing recession has been calculated to have been worse than that of the 1930s. Only in retrospect will a full analysis and comparison with the record of former governments be possible.

To become a first-class honours graduate, a decorated wartime pilot, a cabinet minister and to die aged 83 still doing the job you enjoy, is pretty unequivocally a success. However, Benn's role as a link in a political dynasty and the influence he ended up having on the legislation on peerages, means that Benn has a significance beyond his own achievements.

On 17 July 1922 Benn had raised the issue of hereditary peerages in the House of Commons during a debate on the awards being made purely on the basis of public service. His point was that sons and heirs should not be in receipt of honours which had been bestowed because of a public service already rendered by their ancestor.[14] At the time, he had quite a different perspective on the issue, with Lloyd George and his coalition colleagues selling honours. In the 1950s he and Tony had tried to introduce a peerage renunciation bill to free Tony from having to move to the House of Lords on his father's death, but this move had failed. However, after Benn's death Tony did manage to get the law changed, but it was not a quick or easy task.

The day after his father's death Tony received his National Insurance cards from the House of Commons, his membership of the Commons was terminated with immediate effect and his parliamentary salary stopped. He was regarded as a peer, whether he wanted to be or not – in this case, not. The Committee on Privileges decided that, as the law stood, a member of the House of Lords could not sit as an MP. Erskine May, the bible of Parliamentary procedure, stated categorically that 'an English or Scottish Peerage is a disqualification' to being a member of the House of Commons.[15] Tony, supported by Dingle Foot, once a Liberal but by then a fellow Labour MP, tried several lines of defence to avoid the disqualification. Initially Tony argued that whilst he had inherited the opportunity to have a seat in the Lords, he had not taken the necessary steps to receive it. He claimed that succession only occurred on receipt of a writ of summons to the House of Lords, and the writ was only issued on the request of the inheritor. Tony had made no such a request. In the four months it took for his case to be considered, Tony continued to represent the people of Bristol South East. He was given access to offices at the Commons but did not draw an MP's salary. Having failed in his first attempt to shake off his peerage, Tony's next line of defence was that, on 22 November 1960, he executed an 'Instrument of Renunciation'. This was a legal device of dubious validity. Centuries earlier a few impecunious members of the peerage had tried such devices when attempting to disclaim their titles to avoid the financial obligations which then came with the peerage. Again, the Committee on Privileges did not accept the arguments, being satisfied that there was no instrument available to disclaim a peerage. Among the precedents quoted by the Committee was Dodderidge from 1626 which stated that a peerage was 'a personal dignity annexed to the posterity and fixed in the blood'. Tony was determined that the peerage was not to be annexed to his posterity.

However, the committee's findings meant that a by-election had to be called in Bristol South East. Tony was nominated as the Labour candidate for the by-election and his nomination was accepted, even though he was ineligible to sit as an MP if he won. Tony won the by-election with an increased majority, up from 5,827 at the general election to 13,044. However, he was then declared barred from the Commons, by force if necessary. His defeated Conservative by-election opponent, Malcolm St Clair, presented a petition to the electoral court and for the first time since it was established in 1868, the court awarded the seat to the defeated candidate. It also gave a bill for £7,518 costs to Tony. An added irony was that St Clair was also heir to a peerage. While the law had been upheld, the will of the electorate of Bristol South East had clearly been frustrated, and they ended up with St Clair as their MP, who in the by-election had been nearer to losing his deposit than to gaining a majority. Tony refused to give up. His complaints drew an offer from St Clair that he would apply for the Chiltern Hundreds, resigning the seat, if Tony guaranteed not to stand again at a subsequent by-election. Of course, such a guarantee was not forthcoming. Tony then embarked on a lengthy campaign to have the law changed, and on 30 May 1963 the Peerage Act was passed by the House of Commons, paving the way for hereditary peers to renounce their titles and their seats in the House of Lords, enabling them to contest seats in the Commons. Tony became the first peer to renounce his title under the Peerage Act. It became law on 31 July 1963. Tony made his application within twenty minutes of the change in the law. Malcolm St Clair fulfilled his pledge and resigned the Bristol seat, precipitating another by-election, which Tony won.

Three consecutive generations of the Benn family were to go through the courts in pursuit of their political careers, although of the three, Tony's case aroused the most sympathy and carried by far the most significant consequences. At the other extreme, his grandfather's failed attempt to make 352 allegations stick against his victorious 1895 election challenger provoked considerably less sympathy and was justifiably described at the time as a futile and 'squalid dispute'. The combative spirit of the successive generations may have been misguided in the earliest example, but it was put to good use in the last. Tony learned to be careful in his actions. His grandfather had been cavalier with the courts. His father had been careless with his words and paid a financial penalty, but Tony was more cautious with the law and in his actions. It was in his ideas that he gave free reign to thoughts, and that scared some people. This was where his boldness showed.

The opportunity to renounce a peerage was soon taken up by others, especially when a vacancy for the premiership was created by Harold Macmillan's resignation in October 1963. In the end, Macmillan's successor emerged as the Earl of Home, who for four days was prime minister in the House of Lords, before renouncing his peerage and turning himself into Sir Alec Douglas-Home. For twenty days he was prime minister without a seat in either house, before he fought and won a by-election at Kinross and West Perthshire.

Viscount Hailsham had also hoped to be considered for the vacant premiership – there was no leadership election in the Conservative Party in those days. He renounced his peerage, being reincarnated as Quintin Hogg. He then fought and won a by-election at St. Marylebone – a seat which had become vacant when the incumbent had inherited a peerage. It was also the seat that his father had held between 1922 and 1928, when he had been elevated to the peerage. Although Hogg had initially been considered to be a front-runner for the premiership, he lost out to Home during the behind-the-scenes manoeuvring within the Conservative Party.

The legislation governing membership of the House of Lords changed again significantly with the 1999 House of Lords Act, introduced by Tony Blair's government. This legislation removed the automatic right of hereditary peers to sit in the House of Lords. The Lords thus shrank in size and became dominated by life peers. Hereditary peers still had a potential means of remaining in the House of Lords, by standing for election by their own party group for one of ninety-two seats reserved for elected hereditaries. As a result of this legislation, Quintin Hogg's son, Douglas, who was an MP when his father died, did not need to leave the House of Commons or renounce the title. However, three years after he left the Commons, he stood unsuccessfully for election to one of the ninety-two hereditaries' seats in the Lords.

Archibald Sinclair's grandson, John, inherited the Viscountcy of Thurso on his father's death in 1995, but the 1999 act meant that he was able to stand for the Commons without renouncing his title. John, Viscount Thurso, was elected as a Liberal Democrat MP in 2001.

Benn was never wealthy and never poor, partly because all his life he disliked and worried about money. He had two major sources of income during his working life – his 'pension' from Benn Brothers and his (intermittent) parliamentary salary. When Benn entered the Commons, MPs were unpaid. He was first paid for his role as a whip in 1910. Backbench MPs first received a salary from the beginning of 1912, at a rate of £400 per year. This was increased to £600 per year in June 1937, shortly after Benn's return to the Commons. Ministers received higher salaries. Members of the House of Lords did not receive any salary during Benn's service in the upper house. Benn also had intermittent earnings from his lecturing for the British Council, from writing and for his military service, but he had pursued his career out of a sense of duty, commitment and interest, rather than for money. After his death, his estate was valued at £37,889 (worth around £870,000 in 2015 terms). Compared to this, his brother Ernest had died in 1954 leaving £101,414 (worth around £2.3m in 2015 terms), after pursuing his lucrative business career. Political defectors tended to have more financial success than those who did not defect. This was reflected in the fact that on average defectors left an estate worth £42,457, while loyalists on average left £28,919.[16] Benn's estate was between these figures. He was thus fairly typical of parliamentarians of his day in terms of wealth, remarkably unremarkable for someone from a successful political and business dynasty.

Benn was unlucky to have served in Parliament during a time of party disruption, affecting the Liberals from 1916 and Labour after 1931. The unusual chronology of Benn's life meant that he was a very young MP (twenty-eight), an old second lieutenant in the First World War (thirty-seven), an old bridegroom (forty-three), an old first-time father (forty-four), an average age first time cabinet minister (fifty-two), a very old pilot officer in the Second World War (sixty-two) and an old appointee to his final cabinet post (sixty-eight).

Benn lived to a good age (eighty-three) and died on his fortieth wedding anniversary. He was married for the second half of his life. However, Margaret, twenty years her husband's junior, and who survived to the age of ninety-four, lived for twenty-three years before her marriage, but for thirty-one years after being widowed. During their marriage, Benn had absorbed much of Margaret's time and organisational energy, although she gave this willingly. At the same time, he did nurture her intellectually and enabled her to travel and to study. She was widowed when she was sixty-three and from then on she used her new-found freedom to explore her main interest – theology. In 1948 she had attended the inaugural assembly of the World Council of Churches in Amsterdam as an Anglican delegate. However, she had disagreed with Archbishop Fisher, particularly over the ordination of women, and had joined the Congregationalists, whose puritan principle of autonomy for local churches she was keen to defend. In 1972, together with Elsie Chamberlain, Margaret refused to agree to the formation of the United Reformed Church, which came about as a merger of the Congregational Church in England and Wales and the Presbyterian Church of England. Together they led a breakaway group, the Congregational Federation, which comprised around 300 churches (about one fifth of the total), and Margaret became its first president. Margaret was also vice-president of the Council of Christians and Jews and she helped raise funds in Britain for the Hebrew University in Jerusalem. In 1975 the library at Mount Scopus was named after her and in 1982 she was made an honorary fellow of the Hebrew University.[17] While Benn had died before the swinging sixties had got underway, Margaret lived to see John Major in number 10. She died on 21 October 1991. Her family tended to be long-lived and so there was a good genetic inheritance from both sides of the family for Tony, David and in turn for their children. Margaret's father had lived to the age of ninety-two, dying in 1955, just two years after her mother, who had warned her children back in about 1904 that she might 'slip away' at any time.[18] She was then forty, but lived to be nearly eighty-nine.

Benn was one of six children. His younger brother Christopher died in infancy. His brother Oliver was killed in the First World War. The eldest brother Ernest, who inherited the baronetcy from their father, died in 1954. This title was in turn inherited by his eldest son, John Andrews Benn who died in 1984, and from him it passed to Sir James Jonathan Benn, born in 1933, the fourth baronet. Benn's sister (Lilian) Margaret was active in the Women's Land Army in the First World War and produced prize-winning red setters, cakes and delphiniums. She was married to Cecil Eldred Hughes, an expert on oriental rugs and a talented artist whose work was exhibited at the Tate Gallery. They lived at the thirteenth century *Priory* in Orpington.[19]

Cecil died in 1941 and Margaret in 1953. Benn's other sister (Eliza) Irene remained more closely involved with Benn and his family. She was married to Arthur Pain, and after his death secondly to Dr Theodore Craig. Irene outlived all the others, surviving until 1974.

For John Williams Benn, his parliamentary service was arguably only the third most important aspect of his career. He founded the publishing dynasty in 1880, which provided the money for the family to take part in politics. He was then elected to the LCC on its foundation in 1889 and served until he died in 1922. The parliamentary dynasty started in 1895, when John Williams Benn was first elected to Parliament, and has now stretched to four generations and over 120 years, although with several interruptions.[20] Of course, this may turn out to be only be a staging post on a much longer span. A cricketer passing a century still cannot know if it will turn into a double century. A feature of the Benn political dynasty is that it was the successive second sons – William Wedgwood Benn, Tony Benn and Hilary Benn – who took up careers in politics. However, this may change and the female members of the Benn family may well take up the political reins in the coming generations, with Stephen's daughter Emily focussed on a career in the Commons and Melissa's daughters having chosen to study politics at university. The 1945 and 1950 general elections have been the only elections since 1892 (over thirty elections) when a member of the Benn family did not stand. (Even then the family was represented in the Lords and Tony Benn's first victory was in a by-election only nine months after the 1950 general election.) Sir John Benn stood in all elections from 1892 to December 1910. William Wedgwood Benn stood in all those from 1906 to 1935. Tony Benn stood in all from 1951 to 1997 and Hilary Benn has contested all the elections since then.

Both William Wedgwood Benn and Tony Benn can be regarded as being of political significance beyond their roles as practical politicians, where both had a somewhat mixed record. Both displayed honesty, authenticity and fallibility. Their rare willingness to speak out on causes which were unpopular meant that they injected a wider perspective and fuelled debates. The quality which they both brought was judgement and the confidence to follow up on their own judgement. Arguably, this was easier in the days before opinion polls. It is probably easier to put forward a point of view with no knowledge of public opinion, than to promote one which you know to be unpopular. Opinion polls, although valuable tools in many respects, do inhibit the promotion of minority views. This has certainly contributed to the rise of the communicator, at the expense of the conviction politician. Even when they were on the losing side of the debate, they had contributed something.

There can be no doubt that Benn was a significant influence on his son. When Tony Benn died in 2014, George Eaton's obituary in the *New Statesman* included the comments: 'Whether you agreed with him or disagreed with him, everyone knew where he stood and what he stood for. For someone of such strong views, often at odds with his party, he won respect from across the political spectrum. [The] causes he cared about [were] often unfashionable ones. [He] was an incredibly kind man.' Every word of this could have applied equally to his father, William Wedgwood Benn.

On Tony's death in 2014, Stephen succeeded as the third Viscount Stansgate. The peerage lives on. Stansgate, the flat-pack ancestral home, has survived the ravages of time and the 'strong' Essex air. It is now over 100 years old. It remains in the family, together with the slaughterhouse in the garden, which has been joined by four 'Welsh cottages' and six shipping containers of family archives.

Notes

Chapter 1

1. Tony Benn, ed. Ruth Winstone, *Years of Hope: Diaries, Papers and Letters 1940–1962* (Hutchinson, 1994), p2.
2. Benn, draft autobiography, ST/292/2/1, Stansgate Papers.
3. Robert Jenkins, *Tony Benn – A political biography* (Writers and Readers Publishing, 1980), p16.
4. A.G. Gardiner, *John Benn and the Progressive Movement* (Ernest Benn, 1925), pp8–17.
5. Gardiner, *John Benn*, p35.
6. Benn, draft autobiography, ST/292/2/1, Stansgate Papers.
7. Sydney Higgins, *The Benn Inheritance* (Weidenfeld and Nicolson, 1984), p11.
8. Margaret Stansgate, *My Exit Visa* (Hutchinson, 1992), p55.
9. *Exit Visa*, p54.
10. Infant mortality was around 160 per thousand in 1880, before rates began a steep decline around 1900 to the current level of about 4 per thousand according to Alain Bideau et al, (eds.), *Infant and Child Mortality in the Past* (Oxford University Press, 1997), p79.
11. Dr P.G. White, http://www.counselingstlouis.net/effects.html, accessed 5 September 2013.
12. Alan Palmer, *The East End* (John Murray, 1989).
13. Ferncliff Road was previously called Clifton Road. Leases held by the Hackney Archives Department, refs M3297 and M3299, suggest that the name was changed between February 1878 and May 1880.
14. Charles Booth, *Life and Labour of the People* (1889). The maps were produced before her marriage to Sidney Webb and Beatrice was then known as Beatrice Potter.
15. 1881 Census.
16. Marc Brodie, 'Benn, Sir John Williams, first baronet (1850–1922)', *Oxford Dictionary of National Biography*, Oxford University Press, 2004; online edn, Jan 2008 [http://www.oxforddnb.com/view/article/58236, accessed 25 Feb 2014].
17. Rosebery from 1889-90 and 1892, Benn from 1904–5.
18. Gardiner, *John Benn and the Progressive Movement*, p190.
19. *Times*, 2 April 1896, p9, cols. c-d.
20. National Probate Calendar 1858–1966.
21. Sometimes spelt *'Hoppy'* or *'Hoppey'*.
22. http://www.upminster.com/history/places/hoppey-hall.htm, accessed 6 September 2013.
23. Benn, draft autobiography, ST/292/2/1, Stansgate Papers, Parliamentary Archives.
24. Benn, draft autobiography, ST/292/2/3, Stansgate Papers, Parliamentary Archives.
25. Arnold Bennett, *How to live on 24 hours a day* (Doran, New York, 1910).
26. Benn, draft autobiography, ST/292/2/1, Stansgate Papers, Parliamentary Archives.
27. Benn, draft autobiography, ST/292/2/1, Stansgate Papers, Parliamentary Archives.
28. Professor Chris McManus, UCL, quoted in http://www.bbc.co.uk/news/magazine-23988352, accessed 7 September 2013.
29. *Exit Visa*, p51.

30. Benn, draft autobiography, ST/292/2/1, Stansgate Papers, Parliamentary Archives.
31. Benn, draft autobiography, ST/292/2/2, Stansgate Papers, Parliamentary Archives.
32. ST/283/6, Stansgate Papers.
33. Benn, draft autobiography, ST/292/2/2, Stansgate Papers, Parliamentary Archives.
34. Leslie Hale, 'Benn, William Wedgwood, first Viscount Stansgate (1877–1960)', rev. Mark Pottle, *Oxford Dictionary of National Biography*, Oxford University Press, 2004; online edn, Jan 2008 [http://www.oxforddnb.com/view/article/30705, accessed 26 June 2013].
35. *Times*, 21 February 1918, p3, col c.
36. Benn, draft autobiography, ST/292/2/2, Stansgate Papers, Parliamentary Archives.
37. Straus unsuccessfully contested a by-election in the nearby constituency of Tower Hamlets, Mile End in 1905, but went on to be elected for that seat at the following general election.
38. Benn, draft autobiography, ST/292/2/3, Stansgate Papers, Parliamentary Archives.
39. Benn, draft autobiography, ST/292/2/2, Stansgate Papers, Parliamentary Archives.
40. Interview, David and Tony Benn, 4 June 2013.
41. Tony, Benn, *Dare to be a Daniel*, (Arrow, 2005), p65.
42. Among others, Michael Crick in a *Channel 4 News* blog post after Tony Benn's death in 2014 referred to Stansgate as an 'ancestral home'.
43. Osea Island was the location for the films, *Black Island* and *The Woman in Black* and also where Andrew Lloyd Webber later held his televised competition to select a new *Jesus Christ, Superstar.*
44. Joshua Benn, c 1976, notes of an interview with his grandmother, punctuated by a break when she stopped to 'drink some *Complan*'.
45. *Daniel*, p83.
46. According to the transcript of the c1976 interview, the banker was probably called Solly and worked for *Child and Co.*, one of the UK's oldest banks, subsequently taken over by the *Royal Bank of Scotland.*
47. Elizabeth Benn Shinkman, *The most estimable place and time – Recollections of an English childhood before, during, and after World War 1*, (published privately, 1990), p83.

Chapter 2

1. In 2010, Poplar and Limehouse.
2. Under £10 per year unfurnished rent per person, but also a maximum of two voters per lodging.
3. *Inheritance*, p41.
4. Benn, draft autobiography, ST/292/2/3, Stansgate Papers.
5. *Inheritance*, p41.
6. Alun Wyburn-Powell, *Defectors and the Liberal Party 1910 to 2010 – A Study of Inter-party Relations* (Manchester University Press, 2012), p27.
7. Benn, draft autobiography, ST/292/2/3, Stansgate Papers.
8. *HC Deb 28 March 1906 vol 154 cc1362–89.*
9. Benn, draft autobiography, ST/292/2/1, Stansgate Papers.
10. Letter, McKenna to Benn, 31 December 1916, ST/24/3/1, Stansgate Papers.
11. D. M. Cregier, 'McKenna, Reginald (1863–1943)', *Oxford Dictionary of National Biography*, Oxford University Press, 2004; online edn, Jan 2011 [http://www.oxforddnb.com/view/article/34744, accessed 11 Sept 2013].
12. Josh Benn, interview with grandmother, c1976.
13. Martin McLaren was Conservative MP for Bristol North-West from 1959 to 1966 and again from 1970 to October 1974. His tenure as a Bristol MP overlapped with Tony

Benn's. In 1979 McLaren died and Tony attended his funeral, considering that in some kind of surreal way the two of them could have been related. Interview, Tony Benn, 6 July 2012.

14. Sydney Higgins in *The Benn Inheritance,* (p52), refers to the 'sister of a parliamentary colleague' whom he says Benn had contemplated marrying, but that this 'second woman ... first encouraged and then rejected him'. Higgins' book provides no further details or source for this information and no corroboration for this story has come to light in the research for this book.

15. Benn, draft autobiography, ST/292/2/8, Stansgate Papers.

16. The Chamberlains, who had missed the dinner due to Joseph's health, still both remained together in the Commons. Joseph had had a stroke in 1906, but continued to sit as an MP for another eight years, despite serious restrictions to his mobility and difficulty with his speech.

17. Duncan Brack (ed.), *Dictionary of Liberal Biography* (Politico's, 1998), p99.

18. T. G. Otte and Paul Readman (eds.), *By-elections in British Politics, 1832 to 1914* (Boydell), p228.

19. For the whole period from 1868 to 1914, 40 per cent of by-elections were uncontested.

20. These figures relate to North Shropshire (1908) and Liverpool West Derby (1903) respectively, quoted in Otte, *By-elections,* p229.

21. *Times,* 1 March 1910, p12, col. a.

22. *Times,* 13 December 1910, p3, col. d.

23. Otte, *By-elections,* p232.

24. *Times,* 2 December 1910, p3, col. d.

25. *Times,* 13 December 1910, p3, col. d.

26. *Times,* 14 December 1910, p3.

27. *Times,* 21 January 1911, p3, col. f.

28. Benn, draft autobiography, ST/292/2/3, Stansgate Papers.

29. *Times,* 18 February 1911, p3, col. c.

30. *Times,* 21 March 1911, p8, col. f.

31. Benn, draft autobiography, ST/292/2/1, Stansgate Papers.

32. Benn, draft autobiography, ST/292/2/1, Stansgate Papers.

33. Benn, draft autobiography, ST/292/2/3, Stansgate Papers.

Chapter 3

1. Otte, *By-elections,* pp245–6.

2. MacDonald, diary, 23 September 1914, MacDonald Papers, National Archives.

3. Stuart Wilks-Heeg and Andrew Blick, Democratic Audit, http://bit.ly/SyriUK, accessed 12 May 2014.

4. Only France, Cyprus and Greece have a similarly low level of parliamentary powers.

5. Benn, draft autobiography, ST/292/2/1, Stansgate Papers.

6. William Wedgwood Benn, *In the Side Shows,* (General Books, Memphis), p2.

7. *Times,* 14 April 1915, p10, col. e., reported that seven men had been killed and that the vessel had been towed to Queenstown. The cause of the explosion was unknown at that stage.

8. *Side Shows,* p4.

9. James Benn, his great-great-nephew, researched the military career of Oliver Williams Benn (1887–1915).

10. James Benn, quoting evidence from Private Merrick, who in turn reported a statement from Sergeant White about Oliver's being shot through the head.

11. James Benn, quoting evidence from Corporal Noakes.
12. Deryck Abel, 'Benn, Sir Ernest John Pickstone, second baronet (1875–1954)', rev. Marc Brodie, *Oxford Dictionary of National Biography*, Oxford University Press, 2004 [http://www.oxforddnb.com/view/article/30704, accessed 8 July 2013].
13. *Sideshows*, p5.
14. *Sideshows*, p8.
15. *Exit Visa*, p37.
16. Report by Lt Col Sir Mathew Wilson Bt Commanding 1st County of London Yeomanry, 'Middlesex Hussars War Diary (supplementary notes)', http://1914-1918.invisionzone.com/forums/index.php?showtopic=160761&st=25, accessed 1 July 2013.
17. *Sideshows*, p11.
18. *Sideshows*, p12.
19. *Sideshows*, p19.
20. The first successful landing of a plane onto a moving ship took place in August 1917, but the aviator involved was killed on his third attempt.
21. R. D. Layman, (1989). *Before the Aircraft Carrier: The Development of Aviation Vessels, 1859–1922*. (Annapolis, Maryland: Naval Institute Press), p44.
22. E. C. Shepherd, 'Samson, Charles Rumney (1883–1931)', rev. Mark Pottle, *Oxford Dictionary of National Biography*, Oxford University Press, 2004 [http://www.oxforddnb.com/view/article/35927, accessed 10 July 2013].
23. Fifteen sorties together are recorded in Benn's log, ST/287/9, Stansgate Papers.
24. *Sideshows*, p35.
25. Letter Asquith to Venetia Stanley, 17 January 1915, *HH Asquith Letters to Venetia Stanley*, Michael and Eleanor Brock eds. (Oxford University Press, 1982), p384.
26. Letter Asquith to Venetia Stanley, 20 January 1915, *Asquith Letters to Venetia Stanley*, p387.
27. Letter Asquith to Venetia Stanley, 27 January 1915, *Asquith Letters to Venetia Stanley*, p400.
28. Lloyd George to Benn, (corners missing), 8 December 1916, ST/24/1/1, Stansgate Papers, Parliamentary Archives.
29. Benn to McKenna, 8 December 1916, ST/24/1/5, Stansgate Papers.
30. Benn to his father, 9 December 1916, ST/24/1/6, Stansgate Papers.
31. McKenna to Benn, 10 December 1916, ST/24/1/2, Stansgate Papers.
32. Benn to Lloyd George, 10 December 1916, ST/24/1/7, Stansgate Papers.
33. Benn's father to Benn, 11 December 1916, ST/24/1/8, Stansgate Papers.
34. Benn's father to Benn, 16 December 1916, ST/24/1/9, Stansgate Papers.
35. McKenna to Benn, 31 December 1916, ST/24/3/1, Stansgate Papers.
36. Benn, draft autobiography, ST/292/2/3, Stansgate Papers.
37. Letter, Benn to Lloyd George, ST/24/4, Stansgate Papers.
38. *Sideshows*, p37.
39. J. Caruana; Andy Field; Michael Head; *et al.* (December 2012). "Question 33/48: British Seaplane Tender Sunk by Turkish Artillery". *Warship International* (Toledo, Ohio: International Naval Research Organization) 49 (4), pp298–9.
40. Caruana, *Warship International*, p299.
41. *Sideshows*, p50.
42. Peter Kemp, 'Sueter, Sir Murray Frazer (1872–1960)', rev. *Oxford Dictionary of National Biography*, Oxford University Press, 2004 [http://www.oxforddnb.com/view/article/36368, accessed 16 July 2013].
43. *Sideshows*, p49.

44. The subject of Ernest Hemingway's *Farewell to Arms*.
45. *Sideshows*, p60.
46. Benn, draft autobiography, ST/292/2/1, Stansgate Papers.
47. *Sideshows*, p72.
48. *Sideshows*, p68.
49. The only seats with fewer electors were Durham with 2,601, Bury St. Edmunds at 2,740 and Whitehaven with 3,050.
50. It is not entirely clear what Benn meant by the term 'shake-down', but it probably refers to a makeshift bed.
51. List No 5, 'Unknown', F/21/2/28, Lloyd George Papers.
52. Benn, draft autobiography, ST/292/2/1, Stansgate Papers.
53. Benn, draft autobiography, ST/292/2/1, Stansgate Papers.

Chapter 4
1. Otte, *By-elections*, pp288–289.
2. Alistair B. Cooke 'Gladstone's Election for the Leith District of Burghs, July 1886' *The Scottish Historical Review* , Vol. 49, No. 148, Part 2 (Oct., 1970), pp172–194.
3. H. C. G. Matthew, 'Ferguson, Ronald Crauford Munro, Viscount Novar (1860–1934)', *Oxford Dictionary of National Biography*, Oxford University Press, 2004; online edn, May 2009 [http://www.oxforddnb.com/view/article/33110, accessed 24 June 2013].
4. Compared to 467 Liberal candidates in December 1910.
5. The result was Kiley (Lib) 3,025, Ambrose (Lab) 2,522, Cohen (Coalition Con) 2,489 and Raphael (Ind) 614.
6. Joseph Kenworthy, *Sailors, Statesmen – and Others* (Rich & Cowan, 1933), p4.
7. Benn, draft autobiography, ST/292/2/3, Stansgate Papers.
8. The Asquithian gains were Leyton West, Hull Central and Aberdeen & Kincardine Central in 1919, Louth in 1920 and Bodmin in 1922.
9. *HC Deb 21 February 1921 vol 138 cc555–624*.
10. Benn diary, 14 March 1922, ST/66, Stansgate Papers.
11. Memorandum, Guest to Lloyd George, 13/3/19, LG/F/21/3/9, Parliamentary Archives.
12. Gordon Pirie, *Air Empire* (Manchester University Press, 2009), p21.
13. *HC Deb 17 February 1919 vol 112 cc666–87*.
14. *HC Deb 24 July 1919 vol 118 cc1597–706*.
15. Benn, draft autobiography, ST/292/2/6, Stansgate Papers.
16. *Exit Visa*, p2.
17. *Exit Visa*, pp22–3.
18. *Exit Visa*, p8.
19. Roger T. Stearn, 'Benn, Margaret Eadie Wedgwood, Viscountess Stansgate (1897–1991)', *Oxford Dictionary of National Biography*, Oxford University Press, 2004 [http://www.oxforddnb.com/view/article/50714, accessed 26 Aug 2014].
20. Letter, Mother to Margaret 'Peggie', 25 March 1912, ST/290/11, Stansgate Papers.
21. *Exit Visa*, pp43–4.
22. Benn, draft autobiography, ST/292/2/3, Stansgate Papers.
23. Benn, draft autobiography, ST/292/2/3, Stansgate Papers.
24. In *Exit Visa*, p35, Margaret dates their first meeting to John Gulland's wedding in December 1912.
25. *Exit Visa*, p46.
26. *Daniel*, p67.
27. *Exit Visa*, p51.

28. *Exit Visa*, p44.
29. *Exit Visa*, pp20–1.
30. Fragment of letter, no date or addressee, signed 'Love from W', ST/287/9, Stansgate Papers.
31. Biographical notes on Sir John Benn, Ernest Benn, ST/286/3, Stansgate Papers.
32. *Exit Visa*, p16.
33. *Exit Visa*, p58.
34. *Estimable Time*, p93.
35. *Estimable Time*, p85.
36. Benn, draft autobiography, ST/292/2/1, Stansgate Papers.
37. Benn, diary, 3 January 1922. [Pages have apparently fire damaged edges, but otherwise legible.]
38. Benn, diary, 14 February 1922.
39. The Labour Party polled 4,241,383, compared to the combined Liberal total of 4,189,527.
40. Roy Douglas, *History of the Liberal Party, 1895–1970* (Sidgwick and Jackson, 1971), 176n.
41. Wyburn-Powell, *Defectors*, p18.
42. Benn, diary, probably 14 January 1924 [Page damaged].
43. Benn, diary, 16 January 1924.
44. Benn, diary, 27 January 1924.
45. Benn, diary, 14 March 1924.
46. Benn, diary, 11 March 1924.
47. Benn, diary, 13 March 1924.
48. Benn, diary, 19 January 1924.
49. Benn, diary, 10 March 1924.
50. Benn, diary, 15 April 1924, [Marked 'Secret: Please destroy'.]
51. Benn, diary, 14 May 1924.
52. Benn, diary, 7 July 1924.
53. Benn, diary, 2 October 1924.
54. Benn, diary, 29 May 1924.
55. Roy Douglas, *Liberals* (Hambledon & London, 2005), p208.
56. Benn, diary, 8 October 1924.
57. Benn, diary, 2 October 1924.
58. Benn, diary, 12 November 1924.
59. John Whitley had also sat continuously since Benn's first election, but he had been Speaker since 1921.
60. Henry Cowan, Arthur Evans and Albert Bennett.
61. Bertie Lees-Smith, Arthur Ponsonby, Charles Trevelyan, Josiah Wedgwood and Noel Buxton.
62. Abraham England, Thomas Robinson, John Ward and Hugh Edwards.
63. Winston Churchill, Hamar Greenwood and Algernon Moreing. Alun Wyburn-Powell, 'The Constitutionalists and the 1924 Election', *Journal of Liberal History*, Issue 79, Summer 2013, pp6–14.
64. Benn, diary, 2 December 1924.
65. Benn, diary, 7 November 1924.
66. Benn, diary, 10 November 1924.
67. Unnamed press cutting, 3 December 1924, ST/80/1, Stansgate Papers.
68. Letter, Benn to press, 5 December 1924, ST/80/1, Stansgate Papers.

69. Michael Brock and Eleanor Brock, *Letters to Venetia Stanley by HH Asquith*, (Oxford University Press, 1982).
70. The resumption was temporary. From the 1930s the couple lived separate lives, although remaining on friendly terms. Lady Wimborne was later involved with the composer, William Walton.
71. Benn, diary, 13 and 20 November 1924. Benn also discussed the situation with Arthur Murray.
72. Freddie, Henry and Oscar Guest became Conservative MPs. Viscount Wimborne (Ivor) Guest became the first president of the Liberal Nationals.
73. The Radical Group included Thomas Fenby, Joseph Kenworthy, McKenzie Livingstone, Percy Harris, Rhys Hopkin Morris, Frank Briant, Trevelyan Thomson, George Thorne and Horace Crawfurd.
74. Benn, notes on the Radical Group, ST/80/1, Stansgate Papers.
75. Benn, diary, 20 November 1924.
76. *Exit Visa*, p68.
77. *Exit Visa*, p59.
78. *Daniel*, p103.
79. Benn, diary, 26 October 1925.
80. Benn, diary, 25 November 1925.
81. Benn, diary, 2 December 1925.
82. Benn, diary, 26 January 1926.
83. David Marquand, *Ramsay MacDonald* (Cape, 1977) p321.
84. Benn, diary, 25 November 1925.
85. Benn, diary, 3 December 1925.
86. Kenworthy, *Sailors*, pp220-2.
87. *Manchester Guardian*, 25 October 1926, LG/H/234, Lloyd George Papers, Parliamentary Archives.
88. Simon to Lincolnshire, 2 December 1926, quoted in Hart, MW, 'The decline of the Liberal Party in parliament and in the constituencies, 1914-1931', D.Phil. (1982), University of Oxford, p103.
89. Benn, draft autobiography, ST/292/2/1, Stansgate Papers.
90. Draft letter, Benn to Munro, n.d., [probably January 1927], ST/85/1, Stansgate Papers.
91. Benn to Asquith, 4 January 1927, ST/85/3/251, Stansgate Papers.
92. Asquith to Benn, 11 February 1927, ST/85/3/252, Stansgate Papers.

Chapter 5
1. *Inheritance*, p109.
2. 707 people were elected as a Liberal or Liberal Democrat MP between 1910 and 2010. Of these, 116 eventually defected from the party (16%).
3. Scott, diary, 26 December 1925.
4. Of the 116 former Liberals who defected in the century from 1910, forty-six per cent were motivated by prospects, thirty-seven per cent by policies, three per cent by personalities and the remainder had mixed motives.
5. Another twenty-one went to other right-of-centre parties, such as the Liberal Nationals. A further fourteen became independent.
6. Benn, diary, 20 March 1922.
7. The other former Asquithians who defected to the Conservatives were Cyril Entwistle, Courtenay Mansel, Samuel Pattinson, Albert Bennett, Leslie Hore-Belisha and Hilton Young. The last two were initially Asquithians, but transferred their allegiance to the coalition.

8. Letter, Nicholas to McKenna, 29 October 1922, MCKN 9/17, McKenna Papers, Churchill Archives Centre, University of Cambridge.

9. Deryck Abel, 'Benn, Sir Ernest John Pickstone, second baronet (1875–1954)', rev. Marc Brodie, *Oxford Dictionary of National Biography*, Oxford University Press, 2004 [http://www.oxforddnb.com/view/article/30704, accessed 8 July 2013].

10. Interview David Wedgwood Benn, 4 June 2013.

11. *Exit Visa*, p177.

12. *Estimable Time*, p43.

13. Benn, draft autobiography, ST/292/2/1, Stansgate Papers.

14. Benn, diary, 8 March 1922.

15. *Liverpool Evening Express*, 21 November 1923, c.203/29, Addison Papers, Bodleian Library, University of Oxford.

16. Letter, David Wedgwood Benn to author, 11 April 2013.

17. Marquand, *MacDonald*, p283.

18. Benn, draft autobiography, ST/292/2/1, Stansgate Papers.

19. *Exit Visa*, p128.

20. Benn, draft autobiography, ST/292/2/3, Stansgate Papers.

21. Benn, draft autobiography, ST/292/2/1, Stansgate Papers.

22. *Exit Visa*, p119.

23. John Davis, 'Webb, (Martha) Beatrice (1858–1943)', *Oxford Dictionary of National Biography*, Oxford University Press, 2004; online edn, May 2008 [http://www.oxforddnb.com/view/article/36799, accessed 24 Sept 2013].

24. *Exit Visa*, pp123-4.

25. David Howell, 'Lawrence, (Arabella) Susan (1871–1947)', *Oxford Dictionary of National Biography*, Oxford University Press, 2004 [http://www.oxforddnb.com/view/article/34434, accessed 24 Sept 2013].

26. *Exit Visa*, p124.

27. *Daniel*, p71.

28. *Daniel*, p80.

29. Letter, Redfern and Co to Benn, 9 March 1936, ST/285/3, Stansgate Papers.

30. *Aberdeen Press and Journal*, 31 July 1928, p6, col.b.

31. Aberdeen North by-election leaflets, 1928, ST/88, Stansgate Papers.

32. *Aberdeen Press and Journal*, 6 August 1928, p4, col.e.

33. Although he later denied ever having been a Liberal, Malone's 1918 election address described him as the 'Liberal, Radical and Coalition Candidate'. Malone, election address, 1918, Bristol University Information Services, Special Collections.

34. *Walthamstow, Leyton and Chingford Guardian*, 6 August 1920, p5, cols. d-e.

35. Scott, diary, 10 January 1928, Scott Papers.

36. Communist Party of Great Britain website, www.cpgb.org.uk , accessed 6 September 2008.

37. Marquand, *MacDonald*, p 483.

38. British Movietone, http://www.youtube.com/watch?v=dMyv6vFVd5w, accessed 16 December 2013.

39. Benn, diary, 27 January 1925.

40. Letter, Davidson to Irwin, 9 November 1929, quoted in Ball, *Conservative Politics*, p287.

41. Letter, Davidson to Irwin, 27 May 1929, quoted in Ball, *Conservative Politics*, p326.

42. *HC Deb 24 February 1930 vol 235 cc1838–9.*

43. *HC Deb 22 July 1929 vol 230 c879.*

44. *HC Deb 31 January 1930 vol 234 c1373W.*

45. *HC Deb 07 November 1929 vol 231 cc1303–39.*

46. Letter, Crawford to Irwin, 8 November 1929, quoted in Stuart Ball, *Conservative Politics in National and Imperial Crisis* (Ashgate, 2014), p284.
47. Benn's passports, ST/287/10, Stansgate Papers.
48. *HC Deb 26 May 1930 vol 239 cc825–949.*
49. *HC Deb 23 December 1929 vol 233 c1873.*
50. Saklatvala had been the third Indian to sit in the House of Commons, after the Liberal, Dadabhai Naoroji and the Conservative, Sir Mancherjee Bhownaggree.
51. *HC Deb 09 December 1929 vol 233 cc3–4.*
52. *HC Deb 14 April 1930 vol 237 cc2608–9.*
53. *HC Deb 09 July 1930 vol 241 cc454–5W.*
54. *HC Deb 12 May 1930 vol 238 c1453W.*
55. *HC Deb 26 May 1930 vol 239 cc781–2.*
56. Letter, Dawson to Irwin, 28 September 1930, quoted in Ball, *Conservative Politics*, p363.
57. Willingdon took up the post on 18 April 1931.
58. Martin Gilbert, *Winston S. Churchill: The Prophet of Truth: 1922–1939*, (C&T, 1976), p618.
59. *HC Deb 12 March 1931 vol 249 cc1413–541.*
60. Letter, Trevelyan to MacDonald, 6 January 1924, Ramsay MacDonald Papers, RMD/1/14/79, John Rylands University Library, University of Manchester.
61. MacDonald diary, 22 February 1931, National Archives, Kew.
62. Unsent draft letter, MacDonald to Trevelyan, 28 February 1931, RMD/1/14/83, MacDonald Papers, University of Manchester.
63. Letter, Hoare to Irwin, 15 July 1930, quoted in Ball, *Conservative Politics*, p347.

Chapter 6
1. Charles Mowat, 'The Fall of the Labour Government in Great Britain, August 1931', *Huntington Library Quarterly*, vol 7, no 4, August 1944, pp353-386.
2. Quotations taken respectively from *Daily Mail*, 22 August 1931, *Times*, 22 August 1931, *Times*, 24 August 1931, *Daily Mail*, 24 August 1931 and *Times* 21 August 1931, quoted in Mowat, 'Fall'.
3. Cabinet minutes, 19 August 1931, National Archives.
4. Different sources quote slightly different figures, but within the range of £56m to £58.575m.
5. Cabinet minutes, 20 August 1931, National Archives.
6. Cabinet minutes, 21 August 1931, National Archives.
7. Cabinet minutes, 09.30 meeting, 22 August 1931, National Archives.
8. Cabinet minutes, 14.30 meeting, 22 August 1931, National Archives.
9. Mowat, 'Fall', p372 suggests 11 to 10 majority, while Marquand, *MacDonald*, p364, states 11 to 9.
10. *Times*, 25 August 1931 includes all these members and Clynes among those opposing the ten per cent cut, although the *Daily Herald* did not include Clynes.
11. John Shepherd, Jonathan Davis and Chris Wrigley (eds.), *Britain's second Labour government, 1929-31: a reappraisal* (Manchester University Press, 2011).
12. Lauchlan MacNeill Weir, *The Tragedy of Ramsay MacDonald* (Secker & Warburg, 1938).
13. Weir, *Tragedy*, p 565.
14. Letter MacDonald to Buchan, 8 September 1930, quoted in Marquand, *MacDonald*, p575.
15. Marquand, *MacDonald*, p143.
16. For example, J. L. Garvin had discussed the idea in the *Observer* on 25 January and 22 February 1931.

17. Letter, Crawford to Irwin, 3 July 1930, quoted in Ball, *Conservative Politics*, p344. The original text contained the ellipses, as set out here.
18. Snowden, who accompanied MacDonald to the meetings with the opposition leaders, recorded that MacDonald 'gave no hint' of the possibility of a National Government. Philip Snowden, *Autobiography* (Nicholson & Watson, 1934), p952.
19. Mowat, 'Fall', p377.
20. John Davis, 'Webb , (Martha) Beatrice (1858–1943)', *Oxford Dictionary of National Biography*, Oxford University Press, 2004; online edn, May 2008 [http://www.oxforddnb.com/view/article/36799, accessed 22 Aug 2014].
21. *Exit Visa*, p144.
22. Marquand, *MacDonald*, p576.
23. Alistair Darling, *Back from the Brink – 1,000 days at Number 11* (Atlantic, 2011), p304.
24. Darling, *Brink*, pp262–4.

Chapter 7
1. *Aberdeen Press and Journal*, 10 September 1931, p8, col.e and 24 September 1931, p8, col.a.
2. Report of ILP meeting, 5 October 1931, *Aberdeen Press and Journal*, 6 October 1931, p6, col.b.
3. *Aberdeen Press and Journal*, 9 October 1931, p7, col.e.
4. Letter, Benn to Margaret, 11 October 1931, ST/286/4/1, Stansgate Papers.
5. *Aberdeen Press and Journal*, 12 October 1931, p4, col.d.
6. Letter, Benn to Margaret 'My dearest old Sweet + Comfort', 12 October 1931, ST/286/4/1, Stansgate Papers.
7. *Times*, 27 October 1931, p10, col.a.
8. Goronwy Owen's and Gwilym Lloyd George's wives were sisters.
9. *Aberdeen Journal*, 14 January 1932, p8.
10. The ILP had originally proposed Benn to contest the seat in 1928, when Macintosh had been the only other candidate under consideration.
11. Letter, Dawson to Irwin, 25 November 1930, quoted in Ball, *Conservative Politics*, p377.
12. Letter, Lane-Fox to Irwin, 12 March 1931, quoted in Ball, *Conservative Politics*, p413.
13. Josh Benn, interview with grandmother, c1976.
14. Interview, Melissa Benn, 12 August 2014.
15. *Daniel*, p70.
16. *Daniel*, p67.
17. *Exit Visa*, p152.
18. The Rt. Hon. Wedgwood Benn and Margaret Benn, *The Beckoning Horizon*, (Cassell, 1935), p104.
19. *Beckoning Horizon*, p186.
20. Now Nizhny Novgorod.
21. http://www.thehenryford.org/research/englishSchool.aspx, accessed 15 April 2014.
22. *Exit Visa*, p182.
23. *The Beckoning Horizon*, (Cassell, 1935).
24. *Daniel*, p117.
25. Letter, Benn to Margaret 'M.O.D.' [My Old Dear], 9 August 1934, ST/286/4, Stansgate Papers.
26. Aberdeen Press and Journal, 8 November 1934, p8, col.a.
27. *Times*, 8 May 1937, p8, col. f.
28. *Nottingham Evening Post*, 26 April 1935, p6, col.e.
29. *Aberdeen Press and Journal*, 8 November 1935, p5, col.c.

30. *Daniel*, p63.
31. *Times*, 2 November 1935, p8, col. d.
32. W. Hamish Fraser and Clive H. Lee (eds.), *Aberdeen 1800–2000* (Tuckwell, 2000), p215.
33. Alexander, Lees-Smith, Morrison, Johnston and Clynes.
34. Benn, Gorton by-election address, 1937, ST/101, Stansgate Papers.
35. Spearman, Gorton by-election address, 1937, ST/101, Stansgate Papers.
36. Gorton by-election literature, 1937, ST/101, Stansgate Papers.
37. *Evening News*, 17 February 1937, ST/104, Stansgate Papers.
38. *Manchester Evening News*, 17 February 1937, ST/104, Stansgate Papers.
39. ST/103, Stansgate Papers. In 1938–39 Benn received 103 votes, behind Morrison on 119, Alexander on 113, Dalton on 110 and Grenfell on 106. The previous year, Benn had received 97 votes.
40. *Times*, 23 November 1939, p3, col.g.
41. *Exit Visa*, p185.
42. Minutes of meeting, Labour Party Advisory Committee on Defence Services, 12 February 1936, ST/97, Stansgate Papers.
43. *HC Deb 01 February 1938 vol 331 cc191–7.*
44. *HC Deb 14 February 1938 vol 331 cc1609–43.*
45. *HC Deb 28 February 1938 vol 332 cc861–86.*
46. *HC Deb, 3 October 1938 vol 339 cc40–162.*
47. *HC Deb, 4 October 1938 vol 339 cc169–308.*
48. *Times*, 17 May 1939, p7, col. e.
49. *HC Deb, 08 May 1939 vol 347 cc45–167.*

Chapter 8

1. House of Commons Evacuation instructions, ST/105, Stansgate Papers.
2. Benn, draft autobiography, ST/292/2/9, Stansgate Papers.
3. *Exit Visa*, p136.
4. Letter, nephew Peter to Benn, 22 May 1940, ST/286/3, Stansgate Papers.
5. Correspondence Benn and Halifax, ST/106, Stansgate Papers.
6. *HC Deb, 23 May 1940, vol 361 c326W.*
7. *Daniel*, p82.
8. *Exit Visa*, p192.
9. Addison was advanced from baron to viscount in 1945.
10. Francis Wheen, *Tom Driberg: The Soul of Indiscretion* (Fourth Estate, 2001) p258.
11. Alun Wyburn-Powell, *Clement Davies – Liberal Leader*, (Politico's, 2003), p149.
12. Five of these six victors had left-wing inclinations, but the same was not true of Denis Kendall.
13. Benn, chronology notes, ST/292/2/9, Stansgate Papers.
14. *Times*, 22 January 1942, p8, col. b.
15. The only holder of the post between 1940 and 2004 who was not an air commodore was Augustus 'Gus' Walker, who was in the post from 1959 to 1961 with the more senior rank of air vice-marshal.
16. *Times*, 10 January 1942, p2, col.b.
17. *London Gazette*, 12 February 1943, p756 reports Benn's promotion to the war substantive rank of group captain.
18. Air Council letter, 28 November 1940, ST/287/9, Stansgate Papers.
19. *HL Deb 28 October 1943 vol 129 cc447–58.*
20. Fiat CR.42 Falco was a sesquiplane – a two-winged plane, but unlike most biplanes the lower wing was much smaller than the upper.

21. Benn, draft autobiography, ST/292/2/2.
22. Benn, draft autobiography, ST/292/2/2.
23. Benn's RAF service record, entry for 23 March 1945, ST/287/9. Stansgate Papers.
24. RAF training log, entries for 10 March 1945, 26 July 1942, 16 February – 26 March 1943, 9 August 1943, 5 February and 24 March 1945, ST/287/9, Stansgate Papers.
25. *London Gazette*, 1 January 1945, p60 describes Benn as 'acting air commodore' and *Supplement to the London Gazette*, 30 October 1945, p5276 describes his rank on resignation from the RAF on 3 August 1945 as group captain.
26. *Central Organisation for Defence*, Cmd. 6923, October 1946.
27. Letter Archbishop of Canterbury to Benn, 20 March 1946, ST/116/2, Stansgate Papers.
28. *Exit Visa*, pp198-200.
29. Cabinet minutes, 6 June 1946, National Archives.
30. Benn, chronology notes, ST/292/2/9, Stansgate Papers.
31. *Times*, 5 October 1946, p2, col.d.
32. Benn, chronology notes, ST/292/2/8, Stansgate Papers.

Chapter 9
1. ST/287/2, Stansgate Papers.
2. *HL Deb 26 February 1947 vol 145 cc994-1068.*
3. *Times*, 26 September 1947, p2, col.c.
4. http://guernseyroyalcourt.gg/article/1955/States-of-Alderney-Historical-Review, accessed 26 August 2014.
5. Polly Toynbee, *Guardian*, 13 September 2012, accessed on-line at http://www.guardian. co.uk/commentisfree/2012/sep/13/john-lewis-model-ethical-cleaners on 10 June 2013.
6. Bernard Miller, 'Lewis, John Spedan (1885–1963)', rev. Geoffrey Tweedale, *Oxford Dictionary of National Biography*, Oxford University Press, 2004; online edn, May 2005 [http://www.oxforddnb.com/view/article/34515, accessed 10 June 2013].
7. Spedan's brother, Oswald, whom Spedan had bought out from the business by 1928, was a Liberal councillor who defected to the Tories and became Conservative MP for Colchester from 1929 to 1945.
8. Abby Cathcart, 'Directing Democracy – the case of the John Lewis Partnership', PhD thesis, University of Leicester, (2009), p22.
9. Letter, David Wedgwood Benn to author, 11 April 2013.
10. *HL Deb*, 10 May 1949 vol 162 cc424-5.
11. Mike Hughes, *Spies at Work – The Rise and Fall of the Economic League* (1 in 12 Publications, 1995), Chapter 7, http://www.1in12.com/publications/archive/ spiesatworkcontents/spieschapter7.html, accessed 10 June 2013.
12. *Exit Visa*, p224.
13. *Daniel*, p64.
14. *Exit Visa*, p202.
15. *HL Deb 30 January 1952 vol 174 cc949-62.*
16. The 7th Earl disappeared after the murder of his children's nanny in 1974.
17. *HL Deb 09 July 1956 vol 198 cc561-3.*
18. *HL Deb 02 August 1956 vol 199 cc563-95.*
19. ST/292/2/9, Stansgate Papers.
20. *Times*, 1 November 1945, p2, col.a.
21. *Times*, 18 December 1954, p6, col.f.
22. *Times*, 16 February 1955, p5, col.g.
23. *Times*, 19 February 1955, p4, col.f.

24. *Times*, 27 April 1955, p6, cols. a–b.
25. *HL Deb 11 June 1959 vol 216 cc975–7*.
26. *HL Deb 12 May 1960 vol 223 cc735–8*.

Chapter 10
1. *HL Deb 22 November 1960 vol 226 cc728-33*.
2. *Times*, 18 November 1960, p19, col. a.
3. Leslie Hale, 'Benn, William Wedgwood, first Viscount Stansgate (1877–1960)', rev. Mark Pottle, *Oxford Dictionary of National Biography*, Oxford University Press, 2004; online edn, Jan 2008 [http://www.oxforddnb.com/view/article/30705, accessed 14 July 2014].
4. Includes Liberal Democrats, but excludes Liberal Nationals who did not also sit as Liberals at any stage.
5. Churchill sat for Oldham, Manchester North West, Dundee, Epping and Woodford, but the Woodford constituency was created in 1945 by the division of the Epping seat.
6. Benn, draft autobiography, ST/292/2/1, Stansgate Papers.
7. Allowing for the different lengths of time in the leadership and the varying numbers of potential defectors (sitting MPs and living former Liberal MPs) left in the party, Lloyd George's attrition rate was 1.6 per cent per year. Asquith was the next worst with 0.9 per cent. Later leaders generally fared better, with Clement Davies losing 0.6 per cent per year and Samuel 0.5 per cent, equal to Paddy Ashdown's record.
8. Wyburn-Powell, *Defectors*, p18.
9. Virtually no contests pitted Liberal National candidates against Liberals, so a Liberal National challenge would have been extremely unlikely.
10. A Liberal National contender would again have been very unlikely to have entered the contest.
11. David Dutton, 'Lord Rea', *Journal of Liberal Democrat History*, 27, Summer 2000, p18.
12. Gerard De Groot, Liberal Crusader – Life of Sir Archibald Sinclair (Hurst, 1993).
13. Kenneth and Jane Morgan, *Portrait of a Progressive – The Political Career of Christopher, Viscount Addison* (Clarendon, 1980), p5. Kenneth Morgan's name appears before that of his late wife, Jane, who co-wrote the biography, although Lord Morgan has described it as his late wife's book.
14. *HC Deb, 17 July 1922, vol 156 cc1745-862*.
15. Jad Adams, *Tony Benn, A Biography* (Macmillan, 1992), p165.
16. Wyburn-Powell, *Defectors*, p17.
17. Roger T. Stearn, 'Benn, Margaret Eadie Wedgwood , Viscountess Stansgate (1897–1991)', *Oxford Dictionary of National Biography*, Oxford University Press, 2004 [http://www.oxforddnb.com/view/article/50714, accessed 26 Aug 2014].
18. *Exit Visa*, p 14.
19. *Estimable Time*, pp119-122. Betty Benn, born 1907, was the elder daughter and third of five children of Ernest and Gwen Benn. She married American, Paul Shinkman and emigrated to the United States.
20. John Williams Benn was out of the Commons from 1895 to 1904. William Wedgwood Benn was out of the Commons from 1927 to 1928 and again from 1931 to 1937. Tony Benn was debarred from the Commons on his father's death in 1960, but returned in 1963, but was again without a seat between 1983 and 1984.

Chronology of William Wedgwood Benn's Life

1877   Born Ferncliff Road, London – 10 May
1878   Birth of brother, Christopher – 27 November
1879   Death of brother, Christopher – 29 December
1880   Moved to 241 Dalston Lane
       Father, John Williams Benn, launched *Cabinet Maker,* founding business which supported family involvement in politics
       Birth of sister, (Lilian) Margaret
1882   Death of maternal grandmother
       Birth of sister, (Eliza) Irene
1883   Paternal grandfather, Rev. Julius Benn, murdered by his son Rutherford (Benn's uncle)
       Moved to 37 Kyverdale Road, Stoke Newington
1885   Moved to 17 Finsbury Square
1887   Birth of brother, Oliver
1889   Father, John Williams Benn, elected onto newly-formed LCC, where he sat for rest of his life
       School in France with brother, Ernest
1890   Financial problems at *Cabinet Maker*
       Moved from house at 17 Finsbury Square to flat at 50 Finsbury Square
       Death of paternal grandmother – 30 December
1891   Family moved to *Hoppea Hall,* Upminster
       Father rented 203 Cable Street (renamed *Gladstone House*)
1892   Father elected Liberal MP for Tower Hamlets, St. George
1895   Father defeated in general election
1897   Father defeated as Liberal candidate at Deptford in by-election – 15 November
       Age 20, birth of future wife, Margaret – 7 June
1898   Graduated from London University
1899   Father built holiday house at Stansgate
1900   Father defeated as Liberal candidate at Bermondsey in general election – 1 October
1903   Father sold Stansgate
1904   Father elected Liberal MP for Devonport in by-election – 20 June
1906   Father re-elected Liberal MP for Devonport
       Age 28, elected as Liberal MP for Tower Hamlets, St. George
       Maiden speech in Commons – 6 March
       Father knighted
1909   Age 31, marriage proposal to Barbara Jekyll rejected
1910   Re-elected Liberal MP in general election – 15 January
       Father defeated as Liberal candidate for Devonport – January
       Appointed Liberal whip

	Re-elected Liberal MP in by-election following appointment as whip – 1 March
	First flight, in Boxkite biplane at Hendon
	Re-elected Liberal MP in general election – 3 December
	Father defeated as Liberal candidate at Clapham in last Parliamentary contest – December
1911	Daniel Turner Holmes (future father-in-law) elected Liberal MP for Govan in by-election – 22 December
1912	Organised relief for striking dock workers
	Age 35, first meeting with future wife, Margaret (age 15)
1914	Father created baronet
	Age 37 commissioned into Middlesex Yeomanry – October
1915	Fought at Gallipoli
	Death of brother, Oliver, on active service
1916	Refused Lloyd George's offer of post of joint chief whip
1918	Elected Liberal MP for Leith
	Daniel Turner Holmes (future father-in-law) defeated as Liberal candidate for Govan
1919	Published *In the Side Shows*, account of First World War service
1920	Daniel Turner Holmes unsuccessful Liberal candidate in Edinburgh South by-election – 9 April
	Age 43, married Margaret (age 23) – 17 November
	Moved into flat opposite Church House, Westminster
1921	Moved to house at 15 Cowley Street
	Age 44, birth of first son, Michael – 5 September
1922	Father, John Williams Benn, died – 10 April
	Re-elected Liberal MP for Leith at general election
1923	Re-elected Liberal MP for Leith at general election
1924	Re-elected Liberal MP for Leith at general election
1925	Moved to 40 Grosvenor Road (later renamed Millbank) – Beatrice and Sidney Webb at 41
	Birth of second son, Tony – 3 April
1926	Travel to Middle East and Soviet Union with Margaret
	Rented farmhouse next to the Stansgate property which his father had built, but later sold
1927	Defected to Labour Party and resigned seat at Leith
1928	Home at Grosvenor Road flooded – 8 January
	Elected Labour MP for Aberdeen North at by-election – 16 August
	Mother died
	Birth of third son, David – 28 December
1929	Re-elected Labour MP for Aberdeen North
	Age 52, appointed Secretary of State for India in MacDonald's cabinet
1931	Defeated as Labour candidate for Aberdeen North
1932	Declined to stand again at Aberdeen North
	Visit to Germany with Margaret
1933	Lecture tour to US with Margaret
	Bought Stansgate property originally built by his father in 1899, but sold four years later
1934	Shortlisted, but not selected, to be Labour candidate at Dundee
	Trip with Margaret to US, Japan, China and Soviet Union

1935   Publication of *Beckoning Horizon*
        Fourth son, Jeremy, stillborn
        Defeated as Labour candidate for Dudley in general election
1936   Lecture tour of Central Europe and Balkans with Margaret
1937   Elected as Labour MP for Manchester Gorton at by-election – 18 February
        British Council lecture tour of Near East with Margaret – December to January
        1938
1939   Continues British Council lecture tours
1940   British Council lecture tours to Italy, Scandinavia and Netherlands
        Declined Halifax's offer of chair of British Council – 29 May
        Age 63, Enlisted as pilot officer in RAF
        Appointed RAF intelligence officer
        Home at Grosvenor Road damaged by fire during air raid – October
1941   Attlee proposes peerage – 16 May
        Bracken offers Propaganda Co-ordinator, Ministry of Information, Middle East –
        17 Sep
        Churchill vetoes Middle East post, offered Director of Public Relations with Air
        Ministry
        Promoted to acting rank of air commodore
        Viscountcy confirmed – 17 December, to be announced to press on 22 December
1942   Elevated to House of Lords as First Viscount Stansgate – 12 January
1943   Moved to flat in Dolphin Square
        Maiden speech in House of Lords – 28 October
        Vice-President of Allied Control Commission in Italy
1944   First son, Michael, killed in RAF – 23 June (age 22)
        Resigned from Allied Control Commission and returned to RAF
1945   Mentioned in despatches – 1 January
        Applied for release from RAF to return to Parliamentary duties as soon as war
        ended
        Age 68, Appointed to Attlee's cabinet as Secretary of State for Air – 3 August
1946   Sacked from cabinet – 4 October
1947   President of the Inter-Parliamentary Union
1950   Son, Tony, elected Labour MP for Bristol South East at by-election – 30 November
1951   Birth of first grandchild, Stephen.
1953   Birth of second grandchild, Hilary.
1957   Birth of third grandchild, Melissa.
1958   Birth of fourth grandchild, Joshua.
        Lease expires on home at Grosvenor Road (Millbank) and house demolished.
        Moved to North Court, Great Peter Street, Westminster
1960   Age 83, died on 40th wedding anniversary – 17 November
        Son, Tony, forced to leave House of Commons on inheriting viscountcy, causing
        by-election
1961   Son, Tony re-elected to House of Commons at by-election – 4 May, result declared
        void
        Election court installed by-election runner-up, Conservative Malcolm St Clair, as
        MP
1963   Peerage Act enabled hereditary peers to disclaim their titles and seats in the Lords
        Son, Tony renounced viscountcy on day Peerage Act passed – 31 July

	Malcolm St Clair resigned as MP for Bristol South-East
	Son, Tony re-elected to House of Commons at Bristol South-East by-election – 20 August
1966	Son, Tony, appointed to cabinet as Minister of Technology by Harold Wilson
1974	Son, Tony, appointed to cabinet as Secretary of State for Industry by Harold Wilson
1975	Son, Tony appointed to cabinet as Secretary of State for Energy by Harold Wilson
1983	Benn Brothers taken over by Extel
1987	Extel taken over by United Newspapers
1991	Death of widow, Margaret – 21 October (age 94)
1999	Grandson, Hilary, elected as Labour MP for Leeds Central at by-election
2003	Grandson, Hilary, appointed Secretary of State for International Development by Tony Blair
2007	Grandson, Hilary, appointed Secretary of State for Environment, Food and Rural Affairs by Gordon Brown
2014	Death of son, Tony – 14 March (age 88)
	Succession to peerage of Stephen, as third Viscount Stansgate.

Index

DISCOVER MORE ABOUT MILITARY HISTORY

Pen & Sword Books have over 4000 books currently available, our imprints include; Aviation, Naval, Military, Archaeology, Transport, Frontline, Seaforth and the Battleground series, and we cover all periods of history on land, sea and air.

Keep up to date with our new releases by completing and returning the form below (no stamp required if posting in the UK).

Alternatively, if you have access to the internet, please complete your details online via our website at **www.pen-and-sword.co.uk.**

All those subscribing to our mailing list via our website will receive a free e-book, *Mosquito Missions* by Martin W Bowman. Please enter code number ACC1 when subscribing to receive your free e-book.

Mr/Mrs/Ms ....

Address..

....

Postcode............................ Email address...

Website: www.pen-and-sword.co.uk Email: enquiries@pen-and-sword.co.uk
Telephone: 01226 734555 Fax: 01226 734438
Stay in touch: facebook.com/penandswordbooks or follow us on Twitter @penswordbooks

Freepost Plus RTKE-RGRJ-KTTX
Pen & Sword Books Ltd
47 Church Street
BARNSLEY
S70 2AS